OUTSIDE THE WIRE

OUTSIDE THE WIRE

RIDING WITH THE "TRIPLE DEUCE" IN VIETNAM, 1970

JIM ROSS

STACKPOLE
BOOKS

Published by
STACKPOLE BOOKS
5067 Ritter Road
Mechanicsburg, PA 17055
www.stackpolebooks.com

10 9 8 7 6 5 4 3 2 1

Cataloging-in-Publication data is on file with the Library of Congress.

*In memory of
Paul Myers—poet, teacher, dear
friend—who made me promise
to finish it*

TULSA
There are streets that can
Keep me from crying, if I
Walk down them late at night
when the sidewalk clicks.
It's better then, without
The rattle of pool tables.

If you're the lady who lives
Over the Indian Bar and who sells
Pot holders on the corner,
Wave when I walk by because . . .
The light in your window
holds my world together.

—PAUL MYERS

CONTENTS

PREFACE

I t took twenty-seven years to get this done. It began in the 1980s with a
need to externalize it all, but at the time, I had neither the writing skills
to sustain the effort nor the lung capacity to draw a breath deep
enough to fully explore the depths. After an initial hard charge with dismal
results, I parked it in a drawer, where it was destined thereafter to serve
terms of one to three years at a time. When it beckoned, I would blow off
the dust and renew the attack. Inevitably, another chapter or two would
earn a trip to the drawer. I grew to regard the stack of typed pages with the
eye of an adversary, as if it were a petulant demon I had to face when fresh
out of excuses to keep it confined. This pattern was repeated throughout
the 1990s. By then, I knew it had to be finished, that it would never let me
rest otherwise, but setting a deadline wasn't something I could enforce.
Eventually, I reached the most painful part of the story, and its parole was
revoked once again, this time for five years.

Along the way, I got involved with coworker, fellow veteran, and writer
Paul Myers. He ushered me into a writers group for veterans and quickly
became a steady source of inspiration. We collaborated on two books about

the Oklahoma City bombing and over time developed a treasured friendship. Paul died from lung cancer in 1999, leaving a void that remains unfilled, not only in my life but in the lives of all who knew him. Near the end of his struggle, he made me promise to finish the book. Luckily, he didn't make me say when, because it took another thirteen years.

In the drawer. Out of the drawer. My counselor at the Oklahoma City Vet Center, Peter Sharp, not surprisingly saw value in writing as therapy, and the thing in the drawer was often a topic of discussion. Then the man who for years had listened so patiently to redundant ramblings from my scarred psyche died suddenly from liver failure in 2011, inflicting an emotional shockwave that dogged me for months. In the wake of Peter's death, my unfulfilled promise to Paul tugged at me with renewed vigor. The note was due in full. I was tired of running. So I put everything on hold and pulled the beast from the drawer, this time vowing to end the standoff. No one was more surprised than me when it was finished seven months later. To these two men, I owe a debt that can never be repaid, not simply for prompting the completion of the manuscript, but for enriching my life in too many ways to list.

To those who may recognize themselves within these pages, I beg forgiveness for putting words in your mouths, for errors involving time, person, and place, and for other inaccuracies. My only defense is that I made an honest effort given the limitation of available resources and the passage of time. To the few I disparaged, I recognize that you were doing your jobs the best way you knew how. My criticisms reflect only the views of myself at the time and what I recall as the views of fellow soldiers.

Grateful acknowledgment is due my editor, Chris Evans, for his enthusiasm and expertise and for taking a chance on this work. A hearty salute is also due Eric Bergerud, accomplished military historian and author of two books on Vietnam, for his honest appraisal of the manuscript and his valuable advice. And finally, the woman in my life, the lovely and talented Shellee Graham, for her insights, her creative input, and above all for putting up with me.

INTRODUCTION

O ne question that baffles people to this day is why so many continued to answer the call once Vietnam seemingly became unwinnable. Yet the answer is not complicated. Some of us went because we still trusted our government and believed in America, mom, and apple pie. The rest did so because they were told to. We were, after all, Baby Boomers, and most of us were raised to believe that when your country calls, you go.

As an infantry private, my Vietnam War began almost five years after the first American combat units became operational there. Like others before me, I was issued a rifle and dispatched into the jungle to kill Vietnamese communists. That was my mission, period. Battlefield strategy and political maneuvering were beyond my realm. My focus was limited to grappling with a single, ever-pressing battlefield fundamental: live or die.

Live. Or die. I still believe that is the only motivation necessary for a soldier to fight hard and fight well, regardless of the cause or expected outcome. As General Patton declared, the objective is not to die for your country, but to make the other poor dumb bastard die for *his* country. Part of what men under fire do involves risking their lives to win battles. A larger part of what they do involves enhancing survival odds, most often at the expense of the enemy, though not always. True, there were villains among us in Vietnam, as there is in any population of size, but one thing is certain: virtually everyone who participated in combat operations there was prepared to do whatever it took to ensure the survival of themselves and those around them.

The following narrative is not revisionist. It makes no indictments, and it makes no attempt to explain the real reasons young Americans spent themselves in the steamy jungles of Southeast Asia. Its single purpose is to depict the above principles at work, to illustrate the sometimes valiant efforts of those who fought a war they were not permitted to win. I made a concerted effort to present my story in the context of what I knew and experienced at the time rather than from an analytical perspective based on what I learned later. To do this required keeping dialog and behavior at the level of kids barely out of high school. I thought this to be a more honest approach than imposing a maturity or sphere of knowledge that didn't yet exist. While most of the names were changed for obvious reasons, all of the people and events are real. Likewise, much of the dialog is based on what I remember of topical discussions and the personalities of those involved.

Two decades passed before America moved beyond the hawk-and-dove mentality tainting any attempt at objectivity and started looking at what really happened in Vietnam. Finally, during the first Gulf War, a now remorseful nation moved to atone for the persecution of Vietnam vets by lavishing affection on its current uniformed youth and showing a newfound respect for those who served in Southeast Asia. The lessons learned in Vietnam were by then clear, and many believed that the sacrifices made there would help ensure greater deliberation before sending our sons and daughters into the buzzsaw of war. While this has not quite proven out, what happened in Vietnam has ensured that our vital interests be more directly threatened and that a greater level of debate take place before mobilizing.

In that sense, the dead of Vietnam maintain a presence in America's consciousness. Considering that it was largely a draftee army fighting an unpopular war erratically prosecuted, the devotion to duty and accomplishments on the battlefield under such excruciatingly adverse conditions exemplified the proudest traditions of the U.S. military. While maybe not heroic, this in large part is their legacy, and a noble one it is.

It is this tradition and love of country that compel today's volunteers to accept the challenge, even as they are hamstrung by politicians and perilous rules of engagement. They enter the arena for the same reasons we did: mom, America, and apple pie. It is a calling, and one of the highest order—to become guardians of freedom. Perhaps some of them have been inspired by the grunts who slogged through the muck and misery of Vietnam.

I'd like to think so.

1

Snap, Crackle, Pop

I volunteered to serve. I saw a lot. Men died. Friends died.
I got hurt. It was shit. It was awesome. Yeah, I'd do it over.

—BILLY WALKABOUT*

Early March 1970. 25th Infantry Division. Northeast of Cu Chi.

Draped in ammo, five of us eased out of the perimeter in a slow shuffle and meandered into the grungy terrain, a treeless slab of spoiled, rugged ground sandwiched between Highway 1 and the Filhol plantation. We walked against a stiff breeze that scrubbed at dry, fractured skin and seemed to sand away at the sky, slowly erasing the remaining light and causing our pace to quicken. Broken stalks of brittle grass crunched under sun-bleached boots as strained eyes scanned ahead for deathtraps in our path. Mosquitoes, out for an early start, whined and veered against the wind in frustrated charges—truants from an orchestra of night sounds still warming up, waiting for actors to take the stage.

Smitty brought us to a halt at a scallop-shaped depression that looked like it could be a decaying sand trap on an ancient golf course. Stumps and

---

*Quoted in Stanley W. Beesley, *Vietnam: The Heartland Remembers* (Norman, OK: University of Oklahoma Press, 1987).

gnarled brush infested the outer edge, offering only scant concealment and even less real protection. Ridgeway studied the view, then dropped his gear and keyed the radio to report the location of our ambush patrol. The words were barely out of his mouth when a hissing sound caused heads to jerk around at the same instant an explosion flattened all of us face-first into the dirt. On the heels of the blast, smaller detonations cracked like cherry bombs, releasing a blizzard of jagged steel that filled the air. The deafening concussions jarred my senses and stabbed painfully at my ears.

"Cluster bombs!" Smitty yelled. "Stay down! Stay down!"

Ridgeway groped for the dropped radio, found it, and snatched at the handset. "This is Poorboy One! We've got artillery on our heads, right on top of us! You hear me? Get 'em off! Get 'em off!" But they kept coming, crashing down like lightning bolts, slinging dirt and scything the air, forcing us to dig with fingertips and toes, to claw and scratch our way into the earth as shrapnel whizzed and zipped, intent on slicing us up before we could soak into the soil and disappear.

"Turn 'em off, goddamnit! Turn 'em the fuck off!"

I cowered, terrorized by the thought that if they got much closer, we would be cut to pieces and that as seconds dragged by, our odds were losing ground.

Ridgeway continued to wail at the radio's handset: "They're still comin'! Get 'em stopped, damn you!"

He was answered with another thunderous airborne explosion that rattled skulls and sent a new batch of the grenade-size shells raining down. I heard the *whup-whup* of ragged metal chopping divots near our sand trap, and I scrunched down tighter, feeling the grit scour my chin. I could only hope that our tormentors would play through or just skip this par-five altogether.

We were splayed flat out, as low as it was possible to get, but escaping the bombs' lethal kiss had everything to do with luck and nothing else. They were designed to dismember whatever found itself in their kill zone, and we could only squirm and holler and hope. Private First Class Ridgeway continued to scream orders at the officer corps and curse their wives and mothers. The rest of us concentrated on searching for salvation by squiggling in the sand like tortured lizards.

Then—somewhere—somebody snapped their fingers and it stopped. Just like that.

Nobody moved.

Seconds inched by. In skeptical, stunned silence, we remained frozen, breath held, waiting for the next barrage. Smitty was the first one brave enough to get up. He came to his knees in a brazen act that I was sure would be construed as defiance by the invisible dispenser of death. The others sensed it, too, and we cringed at his arrogance.

Amazingly, nothing happened. We waited some more. After a few minutes, Ridgeway cautiously followed Smitty's lead, and one by one, the rest of us emerged from the soil a bit at a time—up, then down, then up— like frightened prairie dogs. When no punishment followed, we finally decided it was safe to go about the business of setting up.

The sky had gone from ugly gray to indigo while we'd been getting raked over the coals, leaving little time for putting out trip flares and pin- pointing landmarks, such as they were. As I arranged my position, I thought about the raw truth I'd just experienced, but I was too shaken to see the irony: my first taste of fire had come from the barrels of our own guns. All I could think of was the fact that I could actually die here in less time than it takes to blink, and the revelation was numbing. The confi- dence born of ignorance I'd carried so comfortably until now had just been flattened under the weight of emerging probabilities, cold odds that favored no one. The same question kept rolling over in my mind: How many near misses earned one trip to oblivion?

Squelch broke, interrupting the snowy static on the radio. A bland voice from the command post said, "Poorboy One, gimme a situation report. Repeat, gimme a sit-rep."

Ridgeway lunged for the radio. "I'll give you a fucking sit-rep," he growled.

Smitty cut him off. "Cool it, goddamnit. Just cool it." He took the handset and answered the call, then reminded us that we had made too much noise already and that we needed to get squared away before it was totally dark. There was general agreement to this proposal, even from Ridgeway, who still boiled with anger. "Those fuckers are gonna pay," he said, scowling at the radio.

I had been in the field only a week, and this was my second time out on ambush patrol, which had proved to be a perilous and miserable way to spend the night. The elements were harsh and anything could happen, as I'd just found out. There was no moon, and only the density of the light distinguished ground from sky. The stumps and wavering terrain created odd dark spots here and there, and the wind rustled the scraggly grass that grew like tall weeds. Our outpost was about five hundred meters outside the company's night defensive position in a no-man's-land that had undergone years of clearing and tunnel excavation but was still active with Viet Cong and a hotbed for boobytraps.

I stretched out until it was my turn for watch, though I didn't do much sleeping. Covering my face to avoid the bloodsuckers was like trying to breathe through a catcher's mitt. The wind had eased, and except for the chatter of bugs, the night was quiet when the radio was passed to me. I was exhausted, but got quick help in waking up from a squadron of winged prospectors intent on mining my neck for liquid ore. I answered a radio call for a sit-rep, then pulled a wrinkled Marlboro out of a bent pack and dug for my lighter. I fired it underneath my poncho liner, then uncovered and cupped it tight to hide the glow. The nicotine fix perked me up and the smoke discouraged the less hardy of the bloodletters.

After staring into the darkness for a couple of minutes, I thought I saw a white flash out of the corner of my eye. While I waited to see if it had been real or imagined, a couple of dull *whump*s and the popping of distant rifle fire drifted across the darkness, verifying it. It looked like 2nd Platoon's patrol, a half-klick away, had blown their ambush. Another grenade detonated in a sharp twinkle, followed by a parachute flare that streaked upward and burst in a dim yellow glow. A machine gun joined in, reinforced by more grenades, and red and green tracers were soon looping about, interlacing in a way that made me imagine a duel fought with defective Roman candles. It was definitely deep shit for somebody.

Smitty materialized in the darkness next to me. "This'll probably be over quick, and they may get flushed our way," he whispered. "Stay ready." The others were up now, assuming positions, and together we sat waiting, jaws tense, itchy fingers on triggers. Minutes later, the sound of chopper blades beating the air announced the arrival of a Cobra gunship, brought in to up the odds for our side.

We watched as a lethal downpour of red rain poured from the Cobra's minigun, dousing the action. When it was done, everything went dark. Again we waited. There were no sounds, no lights, no radio chatter on our net, no movement. Still, it was possible that survivors might stumble our way, careless in their retreat. If they did, we would be obliged to stuff a second dose of bad medicine down their throats. So we settled in for the long pull, watching and listening. For a while, I had to resist exaggerating minor noises into marching armies, but it became easier with time, and by the wee hours, the odds for contact had all but vanished. The only battle left to fight was the mighty struggle against stiffening joints and the slow saturation of muscles with fatigue. When the merciful dawn at last arrived, erasing the blackness and bygone threats, it was all I could do to straighten my legs and haul myself into a standing position. I was positive that somehow the earth's rotation had been slowed, adding extra hours to the ordeal.

We fired smokes, stretched our bones. No little men had crossed our kill zone, proving it had all been for nothing, and we agreed that basically we'd been flimflammed out of a night's sleep. We packed it up, and as soon as the sun pulled free of the horizon, we dragged ass back in, finding the encirclement of armored personnel carriers right where we had left them.

The perimeter was abuzz. 2nd Platoon's ambush patrol had wasted nine VC and suffered not a scratch, a feat that prompted Captain Littlefield to make vague promises of decorations. All eyes were on the winner's circle, and nothing was said about the attempted murder of Poorboy One by our own artillery. By now, it seemed pointless to bring up a subject already forgotten. Besides, it was time to move out.

I climbed bleary-eyed onto the clattering personnel carrier, aching with fatigue and churning with hunger, thinking it was just as well. Dwelling on negatives only eroded morale, and I had doubts that a mistake that deadly would be repeated anyway, at least with me as a target. With that thought in mind, I anxiously pried the lid off a can of beenie-weenies and dug in as the tracked vehicle lurched forward and began creeping across the wasteland toward the rising sun.

2

Have Gun, Will Travel

The general sense of vague and oppressive wonder grew upon me.
It was like a weary pilgrimage amongst hints for nightmares.

—JOSEPH CONRAD, *HEART OF DARKNESS*

Fast Forward: Nighttime, December 1970.
1st Cavalry Division. On watch somewhere
in the mountain jungle southeast of Song Be.

Smack!

I felt the greasy smear against my neck. My own blood. *Well spent,*
though, I thought. *There's now one less vampire in the world.* I wanted to
laugh out loud, but I was on watch, if you could call it that. I couldn't see
my hand in front of my face. I could smell it, but that's all. Another blood-
sucker buzzed my ear. I took a swing and missed. He circled, doubled back,
and made a drag-strip run straight down my ear canal.

Smack!

Three days. I'd missed a trip to Hawaii by *three* days. Had to have
ninety or less to pull out with the unit. That was the cutoff, no flex. So it
was off to the famous 1st Cavalry, along with Ranger. We ended up at LZ
Dragonhead on the lower edge of the Central Highlands. With a bit of
luck and a little salesmanship, we'd managed to stay together, right down to

7

the same squad. Now I sat in the moldy night jungle, thinking about nearly getting wasted by cluster bombs that time in the Filhol.

Leaving the 25th Infantry Division had been a hard pill to swallow. Only a couple of weeks had passed since Ranger and I lugged our duffel bags onto a Chinook and left Cu Chi base camp forever, putting it all behind us—the Filhol plantation, the Renegade Woods, Cambodia, the works. As the chopper lifted off, all I could think about was how it had all come and gone so fast, and I was struck by the weight of it. What would become of Cu Chi and the fire bases and other villages in our area of operations? What would become of all the places whose names had been burned into our memories?

I grieved over it all the way to Song Be, thinking about the thousands who had bled and died over the years in the Michelin and Filhol plantations, about the endless agony endured in the snarled underbrush of the Iron Triangle and within the tangles of the Boi Loi and Ho Bo Woods. All of these places had to be sitting heavy on the minds of every haggard 25th Division grunt who had sweat and cursed their way through these enemy strongholds. Now I would become one of the haunted. We had staked our claim and worked the land. Now we were giving it all back. And for what?

These realizations had put me in no hurry to strap on a rucksack and start playing ground-pounder again in somebody else's yard. The thing was, I had no choice. I had to get over it.

After a two-day orientation at the Division HQ at Bien Hoa, we headed for 2nd Brigade headquarters at Song Be, situated in the hill country sixty miles northeast of Cu Chi. We reported to 1st Battalion, 8th Cavalry, there on Thanksgiving Day. The lieutenant who signed us in rejected arguments for rear jobs based on our shortness, but agreed to send us to the same company. We stored gear, checked out rucksacks and weapons, then caught another Chinook headed for the boonies two hours before sundown. Our destination, LZ Dragonhead, was on a remote mountaintop somewhere in the sea of green humps to the southeast of the Song Be base camp.

Once airborne, the expanse of emerald we flew over could be seen stretching from one horizon to the other. Below, twisted rivers slithered through narrow mountain valleys, turned brightly platinum by the angled rays of the descending sun. Only occasional pockmarks from bombings marred an otherwise spectacular vista.

"Would you look at that," Ranger said. He was incredulous.

"This is gonna be a different war from mechanized infantry," I said, stretching for a better look.

"Can't wait to start humpin' those hills," he said.

"My bones ache already."

"At least we'll have shade."

Fire Support Base Dragonhead looked like a shaved head in a room full of Afros, perched prominently on top of the tallest hill in sight. We landed in a cloud of dust fifty yards outside the perimeter, splitting the distance between the fire base's ring of wire and the treeline. As soon as its cargo was off-loaded, the lumbering chopper lifted off and climbed fast.

We reported to the command bunker, where we were dispatched to A Company's 1st Platoon, apparently hardest up for help. We hooked up with two of our new platoonmates on the bunker line who were in transit. Steve Farber, from Iowa, was a machine gunner. Andy Brenn, from Louisiana, was a rifleman. We traded histories; then Ranger and I got busy packing our rucksacks and learning about the "Mob," as the platoon was known.

"Life here is a cycle of monotony and drudgery," Steve told us.

"Fifteen out, five in," Andy added. "There's guys here who've been in country seven months and never seen a PX."

"Roger that. Dragonhead is as close to the rear as we ever get."

"One company secures the artillery here at the LZ, and the rest of 'em are out there, all the time." Steve swept an outstretched arm from left to right, covering a few hundred square miles of rolling jungle. "For the most part, each platoon operates on its own. We hardly ever see the other guys except when we're back here."

"Everything is up and down," Andy said. "Mostly up. And the bugs'll make you crazy.

"There's no villages in our area, but there's not many VC, either. That's the good news. A lot of the guys have never been in a firefight."

I felt my brow twitch. In one way, this was welcome; on the other hand, a unit heavy with cherries could prove hazardous to my health.

"It's a world of jungle misery and long days of waiting to run into Mr. Cong," Steve added. "Like Andy said, enemy activity has been low."

Ranger said, "Have you guys ever heard of a thing called a stand-down? Where every couple months you store your weapons in the armory and have no duty, and sleep a lot? They happen at real base camps. They involve steaks and beer, shit like that."

"We've heard fairy tales about it," Andy said, "but nobody around here's been able to prove they actually exist. It's like UFOs. Show us one and we'll believe it."

Ranger and I just looked at each other.

"When do we sky up?" Ranger finally asked.

"Tomorrow. It's resupply day."

In the morning, I re-packed my rucksack, double-checking everything. When it was done, I had either stuffed into it or hung upon it a poncho, poncho liner, two pair of socks, a plastic bag to hold my wallet, writing pad and pen, two towels, toiletries, a Claymore mine with detonator, two canisters of smoke, four star-cluster flares, two bricks of C-4 explosive, a piece of rope, a mosquito net, a can of bug juice, a rifle cleaning kit, an abbreviated first-aid kit, a canteen cup and utensils, one trip flare, an entrenching tool, extra M16 ammo, nine C-ration meals, eight quarts of water, four grenades, and my steel helmet. I decided to keep the grenades inside to avoid having their pins pulled by tree branches. It was about forty-five pounds, give or take, and even though it figured to lighten up as I drank and ate my way toward resupply, I knew that what it would more likely do is get heavier the longer it was on my back.

That afternoon, we boarded a Huey that gained altitude quick, then set pitch and banked hard toward the crest of the hill. We sat on the floor's edge, legs hanging out, and for the moment, I found myself staring nearly straight down. There was no pull, but I didn't trust it. I'd always believed it was a bad idea to disrespect gravity, so I hung on tight for safe measure.

We leveled off high above the jungle. The sun, already low to the horizon, had left the ridgelines and valleys in deep shadow. The air had gotten cooler, and I let myself drift with it, knowing within minutes I would be absorbed into this postcard view only to find it rooted in evil.

The Huey dropped a few hundred feet, then slowed to a hover. I tightened my grip and strained my neck for a straight-down look, which convinced me right off that the pilot was lost. Below was a deep crevice between two hills with jagged ridges. The crack began at a highpoint near the vee of the converging ridgelines, then sloped down into a jungled ravine and disappeared beneath the canopy. No way he could get in there.

Flash Gordon moved the Huey forward a little, then held up, hovering. That's when I noticed a wisp of yellow smoke swirling up from the crease, right where the hills rose the sharpest on three sides. I felt my throat tighten. It was hard to believe I was going to die at the hands of a crazed delivery driver. I glanced at the others. They all looked bored, even Ranger. I couldn't believe it.

The pilot from hell then angled the front of the ship toward the top of the vee and dove for it, sending my stomach to the roof of my mouth. He swooped for the crevice, dropping fast, then pulled it back up hard and circled wide. I looked at Ranger, who was now as bug-eyed as me.

Whew! It's over, I thought. *He tried. Gave it his best shot.* I was sure he'd learned his lesson. I might have patted him on the back had he been within reach. That's when he stomped on the gas and made a run straight for the smoke, plunging downward so fast my insides floated free.

He couldn't make it. Halfway down the chute, outcroppings cut off his approach and he had to jerk it back up, barely clearing the treetops. He leveled off up high. This time, everybody was paying closer attention, but most of them still seemed unworried.

"Is this an everyday thing," Ranger yelled, "or are we gonna crash and burn?"

"It's a little hairy," Steve said. "But I've seen tighter LZs."

I just looked at him.

The Huey climbed again, higher and higher, until the hills below started losing definition. Then there was a cut in power and the chopper dropped like a falling elevator in a looping circle, one that got tighter with each revolution. We were directly over the deep end, sinking into the crease as the ship corkscrewed down and the hillsides rose up around us. My innards felt like they were in a blender, and I found myself staring at my knuckles, which had gone white from trying to force my fingers into the Huey's doorframe.

Figuring we were goners, I clamped my eyes shut. That's when the pilot pulled up severely, leveled off just above the timber, and glided effortlessly onto a thumbprint landing zone that allowed only a few yards between the tips of the rotor blades and the towering bamboo. I was astonished to see that we were actually on the ground.

Somehow I managed to get my nerves situated in a hurry, then hopped out casually, as if I were an old hand at such landings. We dropped our gear to help unload supplies, and when I got a look at the pilot, I smiled inside and thought, *Congratulations, shitbird, you got us here, but you'll never get out.*

Scraggly men in filthy fatigues drifted out of the treeline like seasoned hoboes and began rummaging through a bag of clean laundry, oblivious to the newcomers. Ranger and I found a level piece of ground to occupy while we waited to see what was next. The pilot, meanwhile, had the last laugh. He lifted off effortlessly, pivoted with hummingbird ease, then popped the clutch and climbed out of the pit at full tilt, clearing the upslope treetops with room to spare. In seconds he was gone.

We met our lieutenant, Russ Healy, and were assigned to 1st Squad, which meant we'd be sticking with our new buddies. Besides Steve the machine gunner and Andy, there were four others, including our squad leader, Larry Ralston. Casual introductions were made, and then we moved out. By now, the tiny landing zone was drenched in shadow. Following the LT's lead, the platoon picked up a narrow, overgrown footpath wiggling uphill into the undergrowth and started to climb. Hampered by the weight of the packs and the damp, slippery ground, we were forced to grip vines and bamboo stalks to keep our footing, and it took only minutes to break a good sweat. As luck would have it, Healy had the stamina of a mule and kept us climbing until it got so dark he had to stop.

"He likes to park on top of the tallest hill in the area," Steve said. "I'm sure he's pissed about not making the summit."

"Swell," Ranger said. He was dobbing his face with a clammy towel.

"Higher elevations mean better commo, but the fact is, Healy likes to prove that he can out-hump everybody else." Paul Daw was a tall, fair-skinned, bulky New Yorker with a scattering of freckles and a shock of unruly corn-colored hair that hung low across his forehead. He was a former machine gunner who had seen serious action, and that was welcome news. We had dropped our rucks and were in the midst of leveling out a hunk of the slope to sleep on.

"You get used to it," Denny said. Denny Drees was a Kentuckian with a quick smile and a manner of confidence that told me he was good in the jungle. "The only hard part sometimes is keeping up, especially when you're at the rear, walking drag."

We formed a loose perimeter, then set out trip flares and Claymores before getting guard assignments. By seven-thirty, it was pitch dark. I joined Ranger under the mosquito net we'd rigged up with our ponchos for shelter. I munched on some C-rats, then stretched out. I wasn't even aware I'd dozed off when I felt myself being nudged awake for guard. I crawled outside our micro tent, took the radio, and propped myself up in a sitting position against a tree. Unlike the flatlands around Cu Chi, the foliage here was literally within reach, and being on watch meant simply listening. The only skill it involved was the ability to stare into blackness for an hour without losing consciousness. Somehow I had to occupy my mind, so I did the natural thing, which was to replay past events. As I had just discovered by revisiting the Filhol, this passed the time, but it was also part of an ongoing effort to help me understand the why of it all.

Smack!

May you roast in hell, I thought. I flicked the limp little shit from my neck and dug for a smoke. I'd gotten decent mileage out of that friendly fire incident, as chilling as it was. It was nearly time to answer a call for a sit-rep, and that meant another fifteen minutes had passed. Not bad. Not bad at all.

I keyed the radio's handset twice when squelch broke, indicating the all-okay, then let my mind go idle just long enough to get blindsided by a flash flood of homesickness. At this stage of my tour, fighting it was useless, so I let it wash through, and before I knew it, the current had carried me all the way back. I didn't know how long the return trip would take, but I knew it would lay waste to the rest of this watch and as many others as I cared to indulge, assuming I could stay on track. More and more, I'd been having flashbacks to specific moments that hijacked my attention, even when I wanted to think about something else. I would have to work harder to keep the wheel steady.

Sitting in the dark in the sultry jungle surrounded by silence made it difficult to place myself back in the World, which now seemed as distant as another lifetime. But that's what I wanted to think about, and I believed that with a little concentration, I could make the leap.

3

Where Every Man's a Tiger

I think Frankie was the first killed. And the crazy thing, Don bought Frankie's car, an old '57 Chevrolet. Don joked around and said, "Well, I guess I'll be killed too." He kidded around about it, but in a way, I think deep down he really believed it. I took Don's death pretty hard.

—MARK HATFIELD*

Rewind: 3 July 1969. Oklahoma City. Reporting day.

It was a day I would think back on a thousand times. I woke up early, ate a hardy breakfast, and headed for downtown. When my mom tearfully dropped me off at the Oklahoma City induction center, I gave her a hug and a cheerful goodbye with the assurance that everything would be fine. After eight hours of classifying, sorting, and finalizing paperwork, the day's catch was shuttled by bus to the airport for an evening flight to Dallas. After a long layover, a Frontier twin-engine prop delivered two dozen of us to an airstrip in the southwestern Louisiana forest that carpets Fort Polk. We deplaned in a slow shuffle and filed onto a bus that hauled us to the reception station. There, a couple of sergeants stood waiting to maltreat new arrivals. It was 1:00 A.M., Independence Day, 1969. I was two months past my twentieth birthday.

---

*Quoted in Stanley W. Beesley, *Vietnam: The Heartland Remembers* (Norman, OK: University of Oklahoma Press, 1987).

Our ragtag group was impolitely shaped into a loose formation while the more aggressive of the two engaged in calculated badgerment of the new meat. We were standing on a parking lot next to a tree-lined field. The air was damp, the scent of pine needles rich.

Our antagonist strutted along the front row, stopped, then joined noses with the recruit standing stiffly on my right. The recruit's name was Greely. We'd met on the plane. Impulsively, I shifted my eyes, a move that was immediately picked up by enemy radar. The sergeant's steely-eyed gaze shifted, and he glared at me like a predator distracted from a kill. The inside of my mouth dried up as if sand had been slung across my tongue, and I refocused dead-ahead, struggling to become invisible. I could feel the burn of his death-stare on the side of my face.

The attack on Greely was resumed. "Is this here a pussy on yer face, pussy-boy? Answer me, boy!"

Greely, adorned with a fuzzy goatee, threw his shoulders back, jutted his chin, and squalled, "NO SIR, SIR!"

I chanced another glance by shifting my eyes and saw the runty sergeant's face twist into a grotesque mask. "SIR! Did you call me SIR!?" Hands on hips, bent at the waist, he blew stale breath in gusts while hurling epithets and degrading Greely's closest kin. Wormy vessels on his forehead bulged, straining to pop, and as Greely stood frozen in frightful confusion, I fully expected to be sprayed with miniature detonations of red mist.

Somehow Greely held up, and the maniacal assault soon fizzled. The sergeant continued down the line, imparting a variety of threats on other innocents until he and his accomplice judged the group adequately intimidated. We were marched to a small building where bedding was issued and then herded toward a barracks, flanked by our tormentors, who barked a mixture of directives and life's new truths into the night.

The lights were off when I finally stretched out on a narrow bunk, still dressed. The glowing dial on my Timex told me it was 3:00 A.M. I closed my eyes, replaying the day's events and contemplating the seriousness of my predicament. My destiny was now in the hands of strangers, and for the first time, I felt the full weight of it. A short gust of fear blew through me and sent a chill sparkling up my back. I pulled the sheet up snug and attempted to empty my mind by twisting my face into the thin pillow.

Sometime later, exhaustion sneaked in and I faded out, wondering drowsily if they were planning to give us the day off.

A dreamless three-hour sleep was terminated by white lights and menacing loud voices. Before I knew it, I was outside, standing in formation, yawning and rubbing my eyes. On the horizon, a brilliant sun squatted fatly, and following a breakfast of rubberized toast and runny eggs, we began the hurry-up-and-wait of in-processing. There were endless forms to fill out and innumerable tests to take. Our heads were shaved, pictures taken. Uniforms were issued, dog tags stamped. When there was no line to stand in, it was KP for as many hours as the cook decreed or gate guard all night.

After five days, names were read from a list, and a couple hundred of us—properly evaluated, categorized, and outfitted—were stuffed belligerently into a pair of tarpaulin-covered tractor-trailers and transported through a downpour to our basic training company at the other end of the post. Tailgates dropped as soon as the trucks crunched to a stop in the graveled compound, and a pair of angry Smokeys ordered us to fall in, backs to the road. Through pelting rain, I could see the ends of two-story, white-frame barracks positioned in a neat row at the rear of the compound. Beyond was a scattering of tall pines. To my left and right stood one-level buildings, separated by the lot we now occupied. That's all there was to it. There were no trees, no shrubs, no potential for shade. Just gravel and grass.

Dripping, we were hustled into the mess hall. Inside, a frail-looking corporal with glasses called roll under surveillance from the Smokeys, then turned it over to the first sergeant, a thin, hard-muscled man in his upper fifties who scowled at us like we were the sorriest representations of humans he'd ever been forced to cast eyes on. His name was Beck, and he spoke with such genuine disgust we might as well have been child rapists about to receive justice. He didn't bother getting in anyone's face. Instead, he simply made it clear that we were going to suffer mightily over the next eight weeks and that any non-hackers would be recycled without hesitation. I had long before psyched myself for the mind games and rigors of training, but the fact that Beck wasn't even a drill instructor and vowed to personally make our lives hell on earth was downright frightening.

When he was done, they divided us up. I was sent to 4th Platoon, where I joined fifty others in the upper tier standing rigid in front of double-decker bunks. Near the stairwell, a resident E-4 stood leaning casually against the wall, chewing thoughtfully on a toothpick as he sized us up. We were waiting for the man chosen to be our primary drill instructor, and his job as helper was to make sure our mouths stayed shut in the meantime.

Presently, our drill sergeant entered. He was tall, lean, black. He allowed that his name was Keever Sparks. He spelled out some rules, then informed us that he could run forever and that we would learn to also. No one challenged this claim. For a while, he paced, snorted, scowled. He looked us up and down, back to front, substituting guttural sounds for words. Nobody moved. I could feel sweat-drops snaking a ticklish path down my side, but I didn't dare flinch. I could almost hear the heat. At one end of the room, an ancient floor fan whirred and clinked in a wasteful effort to shuffle the heavy air.

Two more assistants entered the room and ordered duffel bags and pockets emptied, then commenced to seize things not army-issue, like key chains and prescription drugs. It was their way of demonstrating that whatever civil rights we had once enjoyed had been revoked.

Dominion established, Sparks left. The underlings stayed on to teach footlocker-packing and bed-making, lessons that ate up the rest of the day.

At the evening formation, First Sergeant Beck itemized a long list of things guaranteed to trigger his wrath, then sent us to the chow line in order of status—regular army enlistees first, reservists second, National Guard recruits third, and draftees last. After eating while being yelled at, we spit-shined the barracks for inspection, passing on the third try, then, with the day's activities concluded, hit the rack, late.

At 4:30 A.M., Sparks flipped the lights on, slapped the sleep out of us by kicking over a cluster of trash cans, and began the process of manufacturing can-do soldiers. We were ordered to get dressed, get our bunks made, clean up his mess, and be outside in six minutes. He then stomped out, booting an overlooked can at the exit. It would prove to be a mad scramble each day to get this done and be outside before blowing whistles sent us racing to formation in the company compound.

Training commenced. The smell of sweat and evergreen filled our nostrils as we grimaced, grunted, cursed, and groaned. Horizontal ladders bloodied palms, PT tortured muscles. The scorching sun reddened skin and sapped strength, knocking down half a dozen men a day. This was the routine, wear and tear be damned. After a couple of weeks, most of us learned to suffer the heat and respond to orders as obediently as slobbering canines. To our good fortune, Beck left after the first week, never to return.

Elsewhere, it became a summer packed with happenings that would permanently burn themselves into America's consciousness. Astronauts walked on the moon for the first time, and Hurricane Camille flattened the Mississippi coast. In California, killers led by a ghoul named Charles Manson slaughtered a house full of people, and on a farm near Woodstock, New York, a whopping collection of hippies and dropouts converged for a rock-'n'-roll orgy unlike anything ever seen.

News of all this drifted through, but our trainee noses were pressed too firmly to the grindstone to give it much notice. Of importance was keeping Sparks happy and surviving the heat and physical abuse. He made it his business to ensure that we stayed focused on matters of greater concern than events in the outside world, such as maintaining the gleam on the barracks floor and conditioning our bowels to jettison shit during three-minute latrine breaks.

When it was done, I marched peacock proud with my buddies across the parade field—new graduates reviewed by the brass. Ahead was advanced training, then probably Vietnam, but that was in the ever-changeable future. The two guarantees were that autumn would bring cooler temperatures and the award of one stripe elevating me to Private E-2 would push my earnings a notch above the seventy-eight dollars a month I now collected. Trying to plan beyond those truths was a waste. What mattered was that basic training was finished. I was an authentic soldier now. Combat ready.

My new orders directed me to infantry AIT (Advanced Individual Training), right down the street at Fort Polk's notorious Tigerland. As I entered the area, I passed a colorful billboard that read:

TIGERLAND
HOME OF THE VIETNAM COMBAT INFANTRYMAN

It looked a whole lot like where I'd just come from, and I got the feeling I might be headed for another eight weeks of hard labor.

At the initial formation, the first sergeant made it all come true and then some. His name was Grimes. He was a hulking, leather-skinned Airborne Ranger with hash marks to the floor, combat experience in three wars, and the disposition of an annoyed rhino. His first promise was to spend most waking hours in the pissed-off position, and he left little doubt that his singular objective was to coach the winning team each and every cycle. That fact would overshadow everything and dictate the quality of our lives. Delta Company would outshine every other company in the land of tigers or be damned. Finishing second to "Brand X," as he labeled the competition, was forbidden. It was that simple. Unlike Beck, whom I had pegged to be a sadist, Grimes at least had a motive.

Each day began with the company chant, screamed at the top of our lungs: "DELTA-THREE-THREE! WHERE-EVERY-MAN'S-A-TIGER! A-BIG-FUCKIN'-TIGER-WITH-A-DICK-THIS-LONG!"

Though I wouldn't have thought it possible, the regimen was more grueling than Basic, both physically and mentally. Walking in the company area was forbidden. Except when we were in the field, the prelude to every meal was a forty-yard low-crawl followed by a trip through the horizontal ladder and ten pull-ups on a bar over the mess hall door. In addition to staff drill instructors, we were harassed by E-5 "Shake-'n'-Bake" buck sergeants fresh out of NCO school getting their on-the-job training. Even though First Sergeant Grimes should have been behind a desk, he regularly stalked the compound, looking for opportunities to nail unsuspecting recruits. The thought of what he might unleash if we failed to measure up to Brand X was enough to maintain a fever pitch.

Weekend passes were grudgingly doled out after the first three weeks and became automatic thereafter, assuming one's uniform passed inspection and the company as a whole hadn't disappointed the Man. Nearby Leesville had plenty of barstools to park butts on, and that's where Friday and Saturday nights were spent with my bunkmate, Jerry Rhoads. From inside dim, smelly lounges, we forged what I knew would be a lifelong friendship while shooing prostitutes and solving the problems of nations, all the while becoming too mush-brained to remember what we had been through or to care about where we were headed.

At graduation, I expected orders for Nam. Instead, after a two-week leave, I was dispatched to Fort Benning, Georgia. A group of us had been given the choice of attending either NCO school or dog handler's school there. Both schools were supposedly voluntary, but low numbers had forced conscription. Jerry had signed on with the dogs. The last thing I wanted was more training of any kind, so I chose the twelve-week NCO school, where they promised we could opt out after five weeks if we didn't like it. It turned out to be little more than a continuation of AIT and included an additional eight weeks for OJT with an infantry AIT company after graduation. It was too much, so I respectfully resigned in January, right after Christmas break. I didn't care about being a buck sergeant. I was anxious to get on with it, to do my year in the jungle and get my life back, assuming I still had one.

Once new orders were cut, they gave me fourteen days back on the block to prepare myself for the journey to the jungle. I used it wisely, surrounding myself with old friends and empty beer bottles. More than once, I thought about Ronnie High, a former running buddy who had told me the night before leaving for Vietnam in 1968 that he didn't think he was coming back. He had quietly but earnestly uttered those words as a small group of us sobered up with muddy coffee in the dimly lit Lee's Skyline Restaurant, a twenty-four-hour trucker hangout on the outskirts of Oklahoma City.

Hearing this from him had been hard to believe. Ronnie was rough-and-tumble, a man's man, quitting school out of boredom when he was sixteen, then breaking horses for a living until he could get into the Marine Corps at seventeen. Everybody loved Ronnie. He was tough as nails but had a heart as big as his pick-up truck and he loved to laugh. But somewhere along the way, a death premonition clobbered him like an iron bar to the skull, and no amount of talk could change his thinking. I supposed he only told me so he could get it off his chest before shipping out. That was in early summer. Near the end of August, he took a stitching of machine-gun rounds while trying to help wounded buddies in Quang Tri Province. He was eighteen years old. Back on the block, me and the rest of the crew were still in school, doing the weekend thing, making our moves, groovin' to cool sounds. Just being kids. News of his death smacked us back like a swift kick in the teeth. Whether he'd known it was coming or whether it was coincidence didn't really matter. He was dead, and it was more sobering than the strongest cup of Lee's coffee ever brewed. I had been shaking my head over it ever since.

Now, a year and a half later, it was my turn to go. But unlike Ronnie, whom I tended to believe had somehow really *known*, my confidence was high and I was resolute, even though as it got down to the nitty-gritty, a teaser of self-doubt bobbed to the surface a time or two. I was also nagged by a need to be certain it was the right thing to do. I wanted to know that my role in this drama had a genuine purpose. But in the end, I realized that it didn't make any difference. The fact was, I had no influence and I had no say. To keep analyzing it was useless. I could change nothing. What mattered now was that I marshal my strength, that I order up the right frame of mind and lock in. I believed my survival depended on it.

4

Over the Hill
and through the Woods

It was an evil wind that blew you hither,
Soldier, to this strange bed—
A tempest brewed from the world's malignant weather.

—PHYLLIS MCGINLEY, "SOLDIER ASLEEP"

February 1970. Sunny California.

I expected a California sky smeared with smog, but instead it was clear, the air crisp. San Francisco's temperature was mid-sixties, comfort-cool, and the effect was pleasant, elevating my spirits. I stood with a gathering of others outside the airport waiting on a bus from Oakland Army Base. We were huddled together like strangers in an elevator. Except for shuffling feet and awkward comments, there was little interaction.

I tried to keep my thoughts neutral, but it didn't last. Polk popped up behind my eyes, and before I knew it, I was mentally flipping through my basic training yearbook, speculating on who would not celebrate another birthday or how many previous occupants of my bunk were now bones in the ground. I was about to fly out of America, maybe for good, and the devil's advocate inside clamored for attention. There was no question that getting on that plane willingly could cost me my life. But such logic was swiftly trumped by the ever-vigilant inner voice insisting that *Even so, you still have to go.*

I knew it was true. I had been programmed with duty-honor-country almost from the minute I squalled into the world. I just wasn't wired to seriously consider alternatives. Nor could I deny the allure of the danger and a chance to measure up to other generations of warriors. It might have been an unpopular war, but it was the only one I had. It was this reasoning that allowed me to keep lingering ambivalence in its place. Fully embracing the conviction that I had no choice was a sure-shot backup.

The bus pulled up, air brakes hissing. A fat, bushy-browed sergeant stepped out and called names from a roster, checking them off as we boarded. Inside, only the chattering engine interfered with silence, and when the seats were filled, the bus lurched forward and snaked its way toward Oakland Army Base. My nerves had settled, but as I watched storefronts and civilian traffic pass by, I couldn't help comparing the bus, whose gullet we stuffed, to a shrewd predator grown fat from prowling the same bountiful trail time and again.

Inside the base's fence, the doors to the bus flapped open and another waiting sergeant lined us up, then explained the rules in a spew of words that robbed him of approximately sixty seconds. After drawing a breath, he pointed to a concrete barracks where we would stash our bags and advised us that work details would be assigned to fill idle time. He concluded by adding that no passes of any kind would be issued. Period.

War-worn veterans, most of them there for out-processing, didn't stay long and kept mostly to themselves. I tried to avoid them, but it wasn't always possible. On my first journey to the PX, I stopped to secure a snack from the vending machines and found myself standing next to a gangly Spec-4 wearing dress greens and a deep tan. He was chomping on a Snickers.

"On your way to Nam, man?" he asked.

I had hoped to be ignored. "Afraid so." I dug for a quarter.

"When ya leave?" The chaw of caramel and nuts in his cheek muffled the question.

"Not sure yet. Tomorrow maybe." And instead of keeping my mouth shut, I said, "On your way home?"

He took a big bite. "Yeah, but I'll be goin' back in about five days. This is my third trip home in eight months." He turned to the machine, contemplating another selection.

I could have said, "Uh huh," and moved on. Instead, I looked him straight in the eye and said, "How can you do that?"

He chuckled and shook his head, as if my reaction was expected.

"Body escort," he said, then just let it hang.

"Body escort?" I said. I'd never heard of it.

"Yeah. You know. He jerked a lever to retrieve a Zagnut, then turned to face me. "See, whenever a dude gets wasted, they send an escort home with the body to tell his family what an inspiration he was and how he was hero. It's a great opportunity to escape the Zone."

He flipped the Snickers wrapper into a can, swallowed, and started on the Zagnut. "I keep getting picked because I'm tight with a dude in Graves Registration for our brigade." He paused to wipe away a chunk of chocolate clinging to his lip. I just stood there, stupidly.

"Hell, I don't even know these guys," he went on in a confidential tone, "but it gets me back to the World for a few days. With luck, I'll pick up a couple more free rides before I rotate." He grinned triumphantly. "It's like R & R, man!"

I couldn't put a sentence together, so I mumbled something unintelligible and drifted off. Back at the barracks, I found myself feeling riled, both at him and myself. The morbid bastard had bragged about it, and I just stood there like a dummy. Bewildered, I forced the episode from my mind with a cat nap, but questions lingered. Is everybody in Nam willing to grab any opportunity to gain an advantage? Would I become like him?

After two days, a group of us were moved into a sprawling, self-contained, one-level building with partitioned bays, a facility we were not permitted to leave. Essentially, we were locked down. Two days later, my name was announced at the daily cattle call, and late that afternoon, I boarded a bus destined for nearby Travis Air Force. It was dark outside when we got there. Inside, the small lobby was sprinkled with civilians, most of them waiting to welcome home vets. Curious, they stared, as if the zoo's newest species had just paraded through. They must have forgotten, or were maybe remembering, the day their own sons went away. Soon a commotion outside diverted their attention, and a pair of double doors whapped open, delivering a flood of noisy returnees that quickly consumed the room. Envious newbie eyes locked on them as they swarmed in, but there was no chance for interaction. They were preoccupied, and we were hustled out-side as fast as the gate cleared. I didn't look back.

On board, an hour passed while fuel was added and a fresh crew checked in, a quiet time of reflection and nail biting. We were about to be hurled into a harsh alien world, and backtracking was no longer a possibil-ity. For me, it was actually settling: I no longer had to debate the pros and cons. Eyes closed and head back, I was starring in my first firefight when the slow whine of turbine engines sparked murmurs inside. I brought my seat up when we started rolling, and while announcements were made, the Boeing 707 swung onto the runway and accelerated in a strong pull. The nose came up, suppressing gravity with a smooth, steady push, and we climbed fast. From the hushed cabin, I turned to look out the window and watched the colored lights below fade into blackness.

The sun's sharp rays angled in through the portholes, and I could tell we were getting close by the contagious restlessness creeping through the plane. I couldn't see a thing other than silky ocean below, but I was fidgety, brought on by a mix of dread and exhilaration that caroused around my insides like cheap whiskey.

When the plane broke the coast, it caused pile-ups at window positions. Surrounded by other heads, I pasted my face to the glass and for the first time took a good look at the place I had heard about since I was fifteen. Below, I saw a disorganized quiltwork of paddies marbled with pockmarked splotches of jungle and intersecting waterways. I studied the land intently, as if waiting for something to happen. I detected no movement, no smoke, no hints of battle, but I knew that unseen horrors percolated somewhere within the lush woodlands. Somewhere, unseen from above, patrols from both sides navigated stealthily through the thickness, maneuvering for advantage. Maybe the glint of our plane was seen by them as we passed overhead. Such a short distance now separated us, and realizing I would soon join them caused a flash of queasiness in my stomach.

The ground angled out of view when the plane cut power and dropped in a bank before leveling on its final approach. Soon the rising ground rushed by, faster and faster, until finally, seventeen hours out of Oakland, concrete met screeching rubber to announce our arrival at Bien Hoa, South Vietnam.

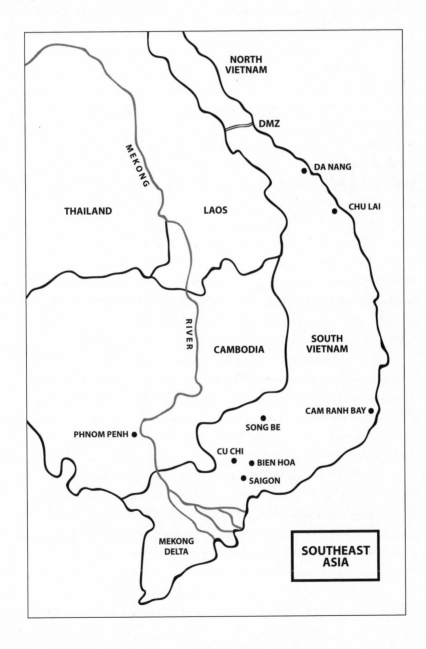

The small fortified airstrip I had constructed in my mind was nowhere in sight. Instead of a couple of buildings and a few people standing by to pass out rifles, I saw a modern military complex. Interlocking runways and massive steel hangars proclaimed their permanence. Trucks, heavy equipment, and storage buildings consumed the landscape, and scattered across the tarmac in wobbly heat waves was a war's worth of parked jet fighters. Dozens of shirtless men scurried about, tending to the planes and shuttling supplies.

I gawked at all this until the jet rolled to a stop and the aisles jammed up. The doors popped open, and when my turn came, I ducked through the exit door to follow the other stiff-legged, lump-throated soldiers, shading my eyes against the glare. Vietnam welcomed me with a blast of heat and a smell that raced up my nostrils like a poison menace, making me wince and shake my head. The odor seemed to be a blend of spoiled food, open latrines, diesel exhaust, gunpowder, and who knew what else. Getting used to it would be a chore. None of this had been included with the cozy, sanitary, living-room side of the war I had always known.

Squinting against the sun, we were led into a shady, cavernous hangar where a lieutenant imitating a traffic cop directed us to a far corner. We huddled up there until a sergeant came along and took charge, and after our bags were offloaded, we were ushered outside into the heat to board buses destined for nearby Long Bien.

The first thing I noticed was that glass in the bus's windows had been replaced with expanded metal, no doubt to ward off hurled objects. It made me wonder how safe we were, stuffed unarmed inside a mobile cage as we chugged down a two-lane blacktop littered with Vietnamese pedestrians. It was easy to picture a sneering old woman in command of an automatic rifle riddling us with hot lead.

But except for occasional glances, the Vietnamese ignored us. They walked and bicycled at a lethargic but measured pace, as if part of an ill-defined exodus, and it was difficult to imagine any of them having an important destination. They wore black silk pajamas or baggy dungarees with faded khaki or checked shirts, and nearly all of them pushed a cart or carried cargo of some kind, such as bundled sticks and wicker baskets. The twang of their whiny speech was somehow annoying, but it seemed to fit with the environment of the war and the putrid odor that soiled the humid air.

The 90th Replacement Company at Long Bien was primarily a way station, a place where those in transition either delighted or despaired, depending on their direction of travel. We were delivered there just in time for the afternoon formation, and after a brief orientation, they handed out booklets itemizing rules of conduct and showed us where to take cover in the event of a rocket attack. Following that, the first order of business was to make sure we all had something to do.

My first assignment as an infantryman trained to kill my country's enemies was to find a broom and sweep out a nearby Quonset hut. Inside, to my dismay, departing troops had assembled for a briefing. Wearing stateside fatigues, pale skin, and shiny boots, I self-consciously worked my way through the gathering of rowdy, boisterous men. I sneaked looks at their sun-bleached fatigues and tanned faces—faces weathered in a way that spoke of hard times and hidden agony, all concealed behind forced grins and laughter with a phony ring to it. Except for an occasional dismissive glance, I was ignored, and when I finished up, I shuffled back to my barracks, glad to get away but suddenly eager to be as seasoned as they were. How long would it take? When could I start?

I'd been in country only six hours, and already I'd learned that the value of virtually everything was measured against the calendar. Outside of rank, the pecking order was dictated by time in country. Traditional standards were obsolete, and judgments, it seemed, were made mostly on the basis of instinct. A real grunt could tell where a man had been and for how long simply by the condition of his boots and his disposition. Newcomers were the equivalent of dog turds that real warriors had to periodically scrape from their boots. The act of showing up for the war did not establish even good intentions.

I was into my third day of menial tasks when my name appeared on a roster for the 25th Infantry Division at Cu Chi. I had no idea where Cu Chi was and had never heard of the 25th, but it sounded like home just the same. I was ready to hang my hat where there was some sort of permanence and was eager to get there. It was a short hop by cargo plane, and when we landed, I found myself on a base of impressive size and scope.

Five of us jumped into a truck, and on the way to the replacement station, the driver gave us a quick tour. I saw the division headquarters building and a PX the size of a K-Mart. We passed a post office, a restaurant, a hospital, and a couple of service clubs. Higher-ups lived in detached, air-conditioned hootches landscaped with flowers and shrubbery. A network of tidy asphalt roads crisscrossed the compound, and outside the high earthen berm, endless rolls of concertina wire circled a six-mile perimeter, all of it embedded with Claymore mines, trip flares, and barrels of explosive Fougasse. Evenly spaced bunkers and guard towers watched over the scrub-covered plain extending in every direction. They even sprayed to keep mosquitoes out.

The first thing the instructor told us at in-country orientation was to forget everything we had been told about Vietnam in stateside training. This came as no surprise but made me wonder why they didn't just teach us the real thing in Basic and AIT. We learned what to expect in the way of booby traps, the elements, and the enemy in our area of operations. When that was done, we received our promised promotion to E-3 (Private First Class) and were dispatched to units.

My new orders directed me to 2nd Battalion (M), 22nd Infantry. The "M" stood for mechanized, meaning I'd been assigned to a battalion of armored personnel carriers, or APCs, also known as "tracks." It was an unexpected twist, and I wasn't sure what to make of it, other than thinking that riding had to be better than walking, didn't it?

Battalion HQ was right off the main drag that halved Cu Chi. Out front, a decommissioned APC sat next to a sign that read:

HEADQUARTERS
2/22 INF.
TRIPLE DEUCE

Three of us were dropped off. Inside, a clerk handed off our orders to the battalion executive officer, a major, and we were shortly doled out. I was headed for Alpha Company, so I hoisted my bag and walked across the compound toward a row of tin-roofed buildings. I signed in at the orderly room, then plodded over to one of the barracks, where a few men were napping at one end—transients and medical hold-backs, I soon learned.

I picked a bunk near the middle and stretched out to await the afternoon formation. Afterward, I walked over to the enlisted men's club, hoping to find some Schlitz, and ran into one of the guys I'd come to Triple Deuce with. His name was Weatherby, and he was now a member of Charlie Company. I ordered a brew, settling for Pabst, and sucked it down while he told me the story of how the gleaming APC in front of battalion headquarters had ended up there.

"It rolled over a boobytrapped bomb up in the Boi Loi Woods last summer," he said. "Boom! Killed all eight on board." He made an exploding gesture with his hands and stared at it in wonder.

"Eight?" I said, incredulous. "Jesus. How could the damn thing still be in one piece?"

"Have you seen the inside of it?"

I told him I hadn't, but maintained doubt about the story he'd heard.

He waved me off. "You just have to see it. Come by tomorrow and we'll go over for a look."

I nodded. "If I'm still here, I'll be by."

The lights were out when I got back to the barracks, so I eased the screen door open and tiptoed to my bunk. I was bone-tired, but I couldn't sleep. I stared at the shadowy ceiling and thought about the eight dead men. Gone. In a split second. Maybe mechanized infantry wasn't so great after all.

In the morning, after formation and chow, I walked over to Battalion HQ with Weatherby. I looked around to see if anyone was watching, then hoisted myself up the side and peered over the edge of the APC's open cargo hatch.

I was not prepared for what I saw. The entire floor was gone, as if a massive fist had been violently driven through it from below. Only jagged shards of curled steel lining the interior walls remained. The force of the blast must have lifted the whole thing head high. I got down quick, suddenly feeling like a trespasser, and took a few steps back, amazed at how deceiving appearances can be. Sparkling fresh paint concealed the truth inside the way a smile might disguise a killer's intentions. What was once a feared war machine had been transformed into an icon of death masquerading as a mascot. Ironically, the damp, exposed earth below had given life to a patch of thriving wildflowers that stretched toward the sun.

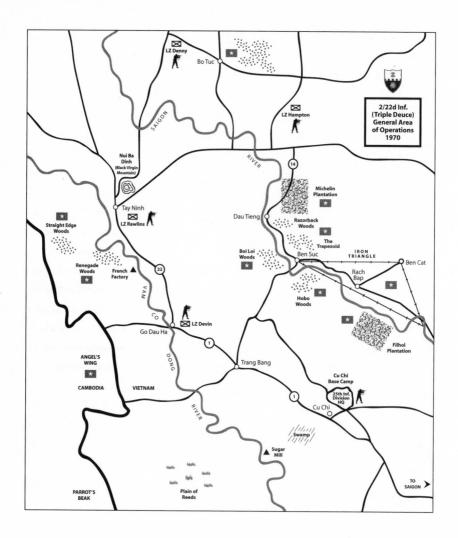

That afternoon, I reported to the supply room and the armory and traded my duffel bag for field gear and a weapon, then followed four others on a short walk to the airstrip. While we waited, I watched heat waves rise from the concrete in ripples and wiped sweat from my face. Little was said, reminding me that I was still considered an invisible man. I had come to accept my standing. In their eyes, little could be gained wasting time on a new guy who was unknown to them and who brought nothing to the table—no experience, no collateral, no down payment. I didn't have any questions anyway, so I wasn't feeling put down. I had heard all the talk and I'd had all the training. Today I would start living it. No more preparation, no more anticipation. It was the first day of my war, and I was ready to meet it head on.

I looked up at the popping sound made by the incoming chopper and watched it drift in, thinking, *This is it,* and before I knew it, a thumping in my chest joined a swarm of butterflies in my gut to bring the confidence I'd just felt to a grinding halt. Incomplete thoughts bounced around like careening bumper cars, turning a relatively calm mind into a pile-up. I took some deep breaths to let it all untangle and was left holding a manageable load of simple, ordinary fear flavored with a strange sense of bravado. When I added it up, it seemed about right for the moment.

The Chinook rattled in, stropping the air harder and louder, and a sergeant with a bag of mail told me to kneel down and get a grip on my stuff. It was good advice as the rotor wash kicked up a typhoon surface wind that blew dirt and debris all over the strip. I shielded myself from the sandblasting as best I could while the massive twin-bladed bird squatted heavily on the pavement, jet engines roaring. The back ramp came down in a hydraulic whine, signaling passengers to hustle aboard, and we scurried inside, quickly strapping ourselves into the web seats lining the cargo hold.

Once the ramp was up and the throttles advanced, the vibrating hulk lifted off with an impatient lurch, skimming the pavement in a slow climb. Within seconds, we were outside the wire, leaving Cu Chi in the distance.

5

Jungle Fever

*The jungle animalizes people. After awhile you
feel like your insides are exposed, like one big festering sore
contaminated by the filth and the rot.*

—ANONYMOUS VETERAN

Fast Forward: December 1970. 1st Cavalry Division. Somewhere in the mountain jungle southeast of Song Be.

Smack!

My time machine had a flaw—it didn't account for the distraction of bugs jerking me back to the present. I now knew what creeping insanity felt like. The insects were a sinister scourge devoted to making me a screaming lunatic. They had been bad in the Triple Deuce. Here in 1st Cavalry-land, they were a torment. Tonight the mosquitoes used a decoy: one would buzz my ear while others slipped in silently from the other side. Spikes would be driven deep and sucking mightily before I even felt the prick.

Smack!

I slapped my neck so hard the resulting welt provided a buffet line for the neighborhood. I finished my watch, sacked out, and braced for a new day in the oozing jungle. The replay of my days with the 25th would have to wait.

35

Steve and the boys had not lied about the lay of the land. Everything was up and down and the jungle so meshed with bamboo and vines in places that it had to be hacked through with machetes. There was no avoiding the leeches, relentless in their quest for blood. Up your leg, under your shirt, sitting, standing, walking, it made no difference. Constantly, they inched their way up fatigue pants, seeking the warm meat beneath the fabric. When filled up, they turned purple-plump and sluggish, delightedly gorged to several times their normal size. The bleeding holes they left festered, scabbed, itched. I was convinced the evil bastards were put on the planet to finish off minds already on the brink.

The daily routine was to be up at first light and on the move in thirty minutes, trading one population of bugs for another. We spent more time than I considered healthy following streams, knee-deep in water flanked on both sides by sharply rising ground. Hoisting ourselves up hills using vines and branches became the routine, and it took acrobatic balance to maintain footing without having your rucksack flop over your head from leaning too far forward. I guzzled a gallon of water a day and fell dead asleep half an hour past dark. There was no apparent pattern to our movements. If an actual objective existed, we evidently had no need to know about it.

I found the beauty of the shadowy jungle undeniable. It was lush, green, mystical, damp. At the same time, it was an object of hate, a steamy incubator of cruel elements designed to scrape away a man's sanity. Lately, few enemy had caroused here. Most of the inhabitants were Montagnards, or "Yards," as they were called, indigenous jungle dwellers who had migrated from India centuries ago. They kept mostly to themselves and were not usually bothered by the Vietnamese. They lived in primitive mountain camps, and their allegiance was mostly to themselves, though some served as volunteers at U.S. Special Forces camps.

Since the U.S. wasn't supposed to use booby traps, we called such devices "mechanical ambushes." I set my first one with Sergeant Ralston on a leafy trail two hundred feet downslope from our night defensive position. The mechanical ambush we created was a Claymore mine rigged to a tripwire—as simple as it gets but bloody lethal. This was routine, but to hear Andy tell it, they hadn't killed so much as a monkey in the last two months. "Some of these guys have never fired their rifles," he told me, "and I'd be surprised if more than a handful have qualified for a CIB."

It was a reminder that I was prowling Indian Country with a bunch of rookies, and he smiled when he saw the look on my face.

"You're not helping my confidence much," I said.

"Just saying what you've pretty much figured out already," he answered.

I thought about that the next day while meandering down yet another well-worn path. I thought about my freedom bird, too. Dragonhead was in the flight pattern of commercial air traffic. Sometimes from hilltops we'd see an airliner high overhead, hauling home the lucky bastards who'd made it out. We couldn't see jack from the jungle. In fact, sometimes we couldn't glimpse the sky at all. In places, even the ground cover was so thick it had to be chopped away just to create sleeping positions.

"Can't get shittier than this," Ranger said. We struggled to pull ourselves up a muddy trail in an effort to reach the top of Healy's choice before dark.

"Sure it could," I huffed. "Gooks up above could start rolling grenades down the slope."

"Wise ass."

"You gotta look at the bright side, amigo."

"I'll remember that the next time your feet come out from under you and you start cussing like a wild man."

"Yeah, well, don't hold your breath. I think I see the top of this greasy fucker now, as a matter of fact."

It wasn't the top, but close enough to it and level enough that for once Healy called it done. We set up around the trunk of a gnarled Banyan the size of a Redwood. It was a good spot with good commo and ground that wasn't too lumpy. The only drawback was the discovery of a massive spider web spanning the overhang directly over Mob 1's position, which looked strong enough to rescue a high-wire act. The bamboo spider that engineered it was poised at the outer edge of the web. He was only partially visible, but he looked big enough to audition for a sci-fi movie, and I regarded his domain with the same reverence of a kid who suspects alligators have found their way under his bed. My plan was to keep as much distance from him as possible. I could only hope that if we minded our P's and Q's, he might not use us for a snack. For now, he sat motionless, as if waiting to see what our intentions were regarding his turf.

Then Denny walks up and says, "Look at the *size* of that mother. Let's fuck with it."

My face twitched, and I turned to him. "Are you crazy?" As far as I was concerned, the spider was lord of that tree. Its knobby stick legs, banded yellow and black, were as long as those on some eating-sized crabs I'd seen on Florida beaches, and its onyx-colored body was the size of a small mouse. That was enough for me.

"Go ahead," Andy said, "but if he jumps on your face and chews your nose off, you won't get no Purple Heart."

Denny ignored our warnings and unsheathed his machete. As he stepped lightly toward the web, the spider retreated a half step, sensing danger. He was now almost out of view. Undaunted, Denny reached up, extending his arm, and gently tested the web with the flat of the machete's blade. The white mesh moved in, then sprung back when released, like a net of stretched rubber bands. He turned toward us and grinned.

"Look how strong that fucker is. It's incredible." He reached up again, even higher, and pressed the machete hard against the web. He let up and then started to push again. This time, the spider streaked out in a blur of yellow and black. Denny jerked back so fast he dropped the machete and tripped over his own feet, falling flat on his back.

"Shit!" he squeaked. "Did you see that? Did you see that shit?"

Steve and Ranger were both suppressing laughs. The lieutenant wandered up and told everybody to shut up and get busy. I went back to organizing my gear, keeping a close eye on the web all the while. There was no retreat in the spider this time. He stood center stage until dark, ready to face all comers. Our sleeping position was far too close, and I dozed off only after imagining various scenarios of the spider exacting revenge. As usual, Ranger was sawing logs in about thirty seconds.

At first light, the feel of something on my face jerked me awake. I whipped my hand up frantically, only to find a big floppy leech latched to my lower lip. I sat up and quickly popped it loose, almost retching at the thought that I could have slept with my mouth open.

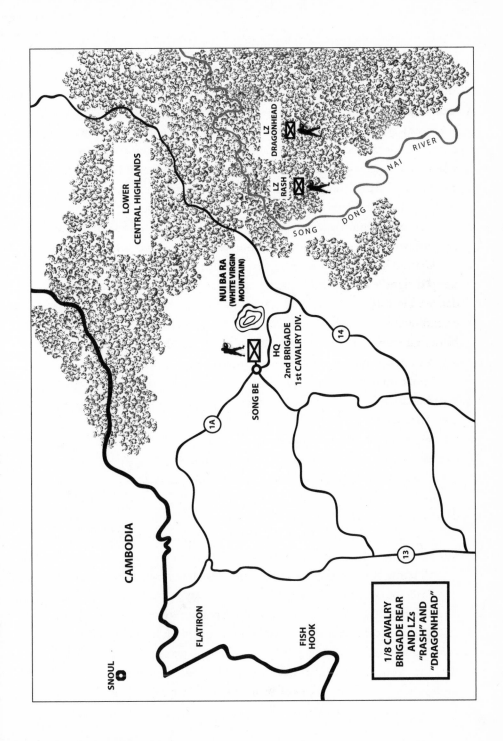

LZ DRAGONHEAD

LZ RASH

NAI RIVER

SONG DONG

LOWER CENTRAL HIGHLANDS

NUI BA RA (WHITE VIRGIN MOUNTAIN)

HQ 2nd BRIGADE 1st CAVALRY DIV.

SONG BE

14

1A

13

CAMBODIA

SNOUL

FLATIRON

FISH HOOK

1/8 CAVALRY BRIGADE REAR AND LZs "RASH" AND "DRAGONHEAD"

Lately, it had begun to rain about the time Healy started looking for a hill to camp on. The tempo of the season was picking up, and when we were finally due to rotate into Dragonhead, a short soaking every afternoon was as certain as the coming sunset. On the morning the choppers were scheduled, we climbed-slid-fell down a mud-slicked slope and then went to work cutting a landing zone. We busted ass to finish by noon, but the Hueys were late, and by the time we landed at Dragonhead, evening chow was history. If that wasn't enough, a full alert was ordered just in time to rob us of a night's sleep.

I met our company commander, Captain Isaacs, for the first time. He seemed like a meat-and-potatoes kind of officer just muddling through his tour like everybody else in these God-forsaken mountains. He wasn't very personable, but the important thing was I could find no chip on his shoulder.

The next four days were spent pulling guard and filling sandbags. "Five in" had shaped up to be not much better than "fifteen out." By the time we skied-up again, I was feeling the need to draw a calendar on my helmet.

"This is some kind of joke, no?"

My fatigue shirt was sopping. It had just rained for twenty minutes, as it had right about four-thirty on the last three afternoons.

"It's payback," Steve said.

"Payback?"

"Yeah, for when we bitch about the heat. That's why we get a few buckets on us at the end of the day."

"So we spend the night shivering our asses off and begging for sunrise?"

"Ten-four, bro."

The hill we'd just started up was so steep and slippery that when Andy lost footing, he dominoed Steve and Ranger behind him. After they recovered, we pushed on, and in spite of being wet, I sweat buckets. My hands were cut from snatching at branches, and the leeches, stimulated by the rain, lusted for greater shares of blood. I was having thoughts of mutiny when we finally reached Healy's chosen spot and dropped our gear.

At that elevation, sunset brought a cool-down, turning wet fatigues clammy-cold. As darkness settled in, I prepared myself for another night of bug-infested hell, but as it turned out, I was too exhausted to be robbed of sleep. My only difficulty was trying to keep my teeth from clattering while on watch. In the morning, we slid down the other side of the hill and began another mindless day of tramping through the undergrowth. The steamy jungle heat was enough that even Ranger moaned about it. "Damn, it's a hot bastard," he groused. "Where's the stinkin' rain now?"

"Shut up, man," I said. "You're pissin' off the rain gods. Now we'll get dumped on twice as hard."

"Screw the rain gods, man. I'm dyin' here."

"Well, that's just great. I hope you get frostbite tonight, fucker."

A halt was called to cut an LZ for resupply, and once the choppers dropped their loads, we feasted on a cornucopia of just-delivered treats from the World before moving out. My own box from home included tuna, crackers, canned pudding, and comic books—everybody's favorites. Even the lieutenant agreed that it was better to gobble it now than to hump it, and it was late by the time we saddled up. Even so, Healy managed to sniff out the tallest peak in the range. Thanks to the daily deluge, however, we were forced to hold up on a semi-level spot a bit short of the summit. This left the lieutenant feeling cranky, but I figured he'd be pressed to find anybody within shouting distance who gave a shit.

It was a mostly flat spot, just above a saddle—a slight dip that leveled off before sloping up again toward the top of the hill. It wasn't an ideal defensive position, but in my book, it would do just peachy considering the time of day, the weather, and the lack of interest the Cong apparently had for either us or this forgotten rain forest. Because of the terrain, we had to space sleeping positions farther apart than usual. Ranger and I ended up almost isolated on a little protrusion that overlooked the saddle below.

Ranger heard it first, a rustling sound in the trees twenty yards below our position. I was busy organizing my rucksack before it got totally dark or another squall rolled in. He snuffed his cigarette and nudged me, pointing. We got on our bellies and stared at the underbrush. For a second, everything was still, and then I heard it, too—the sound of twigs popping, as if stepped on with considerable weight. It couldn't be a Yard; they were

smarter than to move about this time of day. We eased our rifles into position and strained to see through the thickness.

More crackles, but still no movement. The light was really getting low,
and there was a thin haze in the boughs. There was no wind, not even a
fluttering breeze, and the leaves were so motionless they could've been part
of a mural. Adrenaline pumping, we waited. New sounds followed—more
distinct, closer together, closer to us.

"Look!" Ranger whispered. He jabbed a finger. Part of the overhang
near the center of the saddle swayed, and I caught a fleeting glimpse of
dark fabric and something metallic through a crack in the greenery.

I drew down with my M16, tightening my grip and locking every
muscle to keep a true aim. "I'm gonna waste him the next time he shows,"
I whispered. I was totally focused, my mind devoid of emotion and any
thoughts other than making the kill. There were no images of grandeur, no
fear, nothing. He could have smelled our smoke or heard us and was working to pinpoint our location. We couldn't just let him go.

"Hold up!" Ranger said. "We gotta get the LT first. He'll have our
heads if we don't." And before I could answer, he scurried off to find
Healy.

The jungle was silent now, and I had to decide whether to wait for the
lieutenant or not. If I got another chance, it would almost surely be the
last. Yet if I let loose with my M16, it would give away our position, kill or
no kill, and we would have to pack up and move in the dark.

Down below, branches moved, and I saw a blurred profile emerge into
a bare spot, moving from my right to left. In the dying light, it was little
more than a silhouette, but it was an upright figure, and it was carrying
something. For a second, the figure paused, as if on alert, and I had a
decent shot. I drew a breath and slowly squeezed a sweaty finger against the
trigger.

Without a sound, Ranger appeared next to me. "Don't fire! Don't fire!"
he whispered.

I jerked a glance at him, then looked back to the woods. My target had
disappeared. I turned to look at him, feeling the anger rush up. "I just saw
the son of a bitch. Right there," I said, pointing.

"Healy said no firing till he gets here."

I couldn't believe it. "Well, where the hell is he?" I scanned the saddle. The jungle was quiet. Seconds ticked by with no movement, no sounds. Game over.

"Shit." I went limp.

Healy materialized in a crouch. "What's the situation?" he asked casually.

I looked at him. "We just saw a dink, lieutenant, but he's gone now."

Healy's expression didn't change. "It was probably a rock ape," he said. "I heard one pass by my position a few minutes ago. Happens all the time."

He was never going to believe it. In his experience, it was more far-fetched to encounter actual enemy combatants than a mythical creature hardly anybody believed really existed. Then again, maybe he thought rock apes were common primates.

"I'm pretty sure about what I saw down there," I said.

"Hard to tell in the jungle," he answered. "Especially in this light. I wouldn't worry about it." Then he left.

I sucked down a warm soda and stretched out, for the first time in a while feeling the old fear of being stalked. It was a reminder that I was still a long way from being home free. Somewhere in those woods, one of the enemy would now live to fight another day, courtesy of Healy.

I wanted to fume over it but couldn't get it working, so I swept it from my mind and went to sleep with just one thought roaming the halls: sixty-two and a wake-up.

———•———

The rain persisted with daily dousings, most often just minutes before shelters could be rigged. Leech scabs and bites hardened during the day, only to get soft and weepy from clammy skin and mildewed fatigues. I'd been scuzzier before but had never been this wet for this long. I began thinking more and more about warm sand on sunny beaches. All the while, the bugs flourished. The little cans of army-issue bug juice we packed contained a potent liquid that looked like creosote and smelled like strong solvent. We used it around our sleeping position as a barrier against crawlers, and that worked pretty good but wasn't foolproof. After another day of fighting mud and leeches, we applied a liberal dose of the nasty stuff out-side our shelter. I had just drifted off when my mind, then my eyes, popped awake. Whatever it was was long and squiggly and moving. CENTIPEDE! I kicked the air and swung at my lower leg, then started beating my bedding like a rug.

Ranger bolted upright, only half awake. "What the hell you doin'?"

"I think there's a big-ass centipede in here," I said, "but I don't know if I got him or not."

He was quiet for a minute, the way a sleepy mind works when trying to process words. After a minute, he started rearranging the netting around our drooping little hootch. He yawned, then just sat there staring at nothing.

"We gotta find that fucker," I said.

"Fuck it," he said. "Don't worry about it." He then flopped back down and scrunched up under his poncho liner.

I patted the ground all around until there was nothing left to do but give up. "I hope he bites your dick," I said, then laid down cautiously, eyes open wide.

I was still awake when I was nudged by Denny and handed the radio. I sat up and moved to the opening of our shelter, draped my poncho liner over my head, and fired a smoke.

With me it was insects; with Ranger it was snakes. Just a couple of days ago while walking drag, we'd come face to face with a bamboo viper, one of the so-called "two-steppers," which, once it bit you, was all you got before you dropped, according to legend. Ranger jumped back when he saw it. "Holy shit, look at that! That's a two-stepper, man!" I looked, and what I saw was a small green snake about two feet long. Having come from the land of rattlesnakes and copperheads, the little viper hardly looked fearsome.

"What's the big deal?" I said. "It's just a little green snake."

His eyes were buggy. "A little snake?" he said. His lips had barely moved, as if repeating such an insult might draw the snake's wrath.

"Yeah, a little fucking snake. You want me to kill it?" Without waiting for an answer, I unsheathed my bayonet, leaned over, and hacked it in two.

"Come on," I said. "Now we gotta catch up."

Ranger spent the next hundred yards insisting that the correct way to deal with Mr. Two-Step was to run and, if there was no avenue of escape, to let the snake decide if you get to live, not the other way around.

I snuffed the Marlboro and shuddered, thinking again about the centipede. The jungle was as black as pitch and as quiet as the inside of a cellar except for a "fuck you" lizard somewhere in the mulch calling out to me. "Fuck you, too," I said under my breath, then I broke squelch to answer a sit-rep. The cussing from the lizard was enough to keep me conscious until it was time to wake up Paul and pass the radio. When I hit the deck, I faded fast, figuring that if the centipede came back and gnawed a hunk out of my ass, I might at least get medevaced.

The morning was spent following Healy down trails and ridgelines into a long valley. We pulled up at noon. While we rested, 3rd Platoon materialized out of the treeline, and together we waited for a squadron of choppers to haul the bunch of us to an under-construction fire-support base called Rash.

"We'll be there about three easy ones," Healy announced, "guarding engineers until the perimeter is secure."

I thought about asking why higher-up needed another fort in an uncontested wilderness, but I knew there would be no answer, so I focused instead on the distant sound of choppers thumping their way across the hills. Men got to their feet and hoisted rucks when the first vee of slicks came into view over the farthest ridgeline. I watched as they descended with the contour of the land, suddenly feeling old and as weathered as those men at Long Bien I'd wanted so much to be like. Thinking back on that caused a little jolt as I realized I had reached their level long ago without taking notice. True enough, I now had my own secrets stashed behind weary eyes. I had seen things noncombatants could never fully grasp, things either too personal to tell or impossible to fully express.

At the lieutenant's signal, we moved out, filing through the breeze-bent elephant grass toward the arriving helicopters.

6

How to Make It Rain Fire

War is the ultimate reality-based horror show.

—COL. DAVID HACKWORTH

December 1970. 1st Cavalry Division. LZ Rash.

Rash was mud soup, a half-finished mess of an LZ being gouged out of a jungle hilltop with a view that went for miles. A few bunkers and makeshift huts were in place, and that's about it. There was no berm, no concertina wire, no sheltered sleeping positions—at least not for visitors—no mess tent, nothing. A temporary ammo dump was not much more than a ditch. The treeline had been bulldozed back fifty yards or so. Splintered tree stumps and fallen trunks were strewn everywhere, and piles of debris had been pushed together into massive deadfalls. Three dozer operators and a demolitions team were at work on a clump of protruding jungle, and men on motorized flatbed carts called mules stayed busy retrieving supplies and explosives from a primitive chopper pad outside the perimeter. Water-filled tire tracks crisscrossed the compound, which for the most part was ankle-deep in brown sludge. Puddles dotted the naked hilltop like spots on a Dalmatian.

Ranger and I searched out and claimed one of the few semi-firm spots on our assigned portion of the perimeter, then got busy rigging a shelter using our ponchos. We drove some stakes into the soft earth and strung it up tight. We then dug an industrial-strength drainage ditch all the way around, just the way we'd been taught in basic training. When we were satisfied it could withstand a typhoon, we plopped our asses down and happily munched canned food while we watched the sun set.

Technically, we were on guard around the clock and therefore not obliged to fill sandbags or perform other chores. That made the prospect of three days at Rash better duty than three days at Dragonhead, all things considered. We spent the first full day cleaning weapons, improving our hootch, and reading the latest shipment of comic books my mom had sent from the World. Outside the perimeter, the dozers—called Rome plows—clanked, squealed, and red-lined their engines as stubborn trees cracked and popped in surrender. Down the line, shirtless, sweating slave-troops toted box after box of Bangalore torpedoes out to the jungle wall where they were linked into miniature dynamite pipelines for blasting away the growth, one thin strip at a whack. By quitting time, which was when the sun touched the canopy, it looked as if the jungle had been shoved back about another twenty feet.

The rain started at dusk, and the run-off trench we'd dug around our improvised pup tent was at flood stage so fast we could only watch in disbelief. Soon rivulets of dark water snaked their way inside, so we grabbed entrenching tools, dashed outside, and went after the ditch like civil defensemen desperate to save a town. But the more we carved on the ditch, the more it crumbled, and when we finally gave up, all we'd accomplished was getting drenched. Back inside, once-dry poncho liners were sopped, evidence that what we had believed to be a waterproof shelter was no match for the monsoon of Vietnam.

By midnight, I was in a fetal position. My jaw ached from chattering teeth, and I was so wet and so fucking cold I promised myself that if I survived Vietnam, I would never, ever be cold again. I drew my knees up tighter and stared dumbly at black nothingness, trying to think of something to take my mind away. But the best I could come up with was a run-in with a different kind of rain back in the Triple Deuce. It was a painful memory, but once it reared its head, I was stuck with it.

It had been hot then, even after dark, and the storm that rolled through was brutal. We were somewhere near Trung Lap, and I was on watch when the thunderheads first rumbled, pushed by cyclone winds and crackling flashes of white that illuminated the landscape for miles. When it hit, the violence of it drove the whole squad inside the personnel carrier. Exhausted men, packed in close, curled up and hunkered down like pups under a porch, too tired to care that they could be crushed by a falling sky any second.

Staying topside was a waste, so I retreated to the driver's seat and lowered the hatch until there was only a slit left to see out through. It would have been a hard sell to even call it being on watch, but there it was. The curtain of rain was so dense that everything beyond the front of the track was blurred. The first lightning bolt to drop in close slammed the ground with such force it could have been a detonating rocket, and I recoiled. More followed, and sheet lightning strobed the treeline in frenzied flashes. One direct hit, I thought, and even the dinks won't be able to scavenge anything worthwhile.

Gradually, the rain slacked and the storm moved on, pushed by the kind of rolling thunder that rattles windows. Intermittent chain lightning fractured the sky like brilliant cracked glass, and I was awestruck by its beauty. I raised the hatch some and watched hypnotically while the men behind me, dead out, only snorted and shifted, too skilled at war sleep to be roused. Outside, I tracked another approaching wall cloud, fueled by strengthening sparks of current and its own inner turmoil. It rolled and boiled, working up a head. As I watched its approach, the overall scene made me feel small and completely insignificant, twisting my emotions in a way that sent me straight into a slump. Without resistance, I surrendered to it, and within minutes, it seeped in deep. Feelings of fatigue and loneliness overwhelmed, saturating me in sadness, but it somehow fit nicely with the ache in my bones—the result of eighteen-hour days and restless, interrupted nights.

As the light show intensified, I lit a cigarette and drifted willingly in the emptiness I felt, a void that matched the hollow feeling I'd carried since, well, since always, it now seemed. The difference was that for the first time, I could feel the faith that had kept my spirit propped up bending sharply under the weight of an invading, nameless sorrow. It seemed headed for collapse, but I had no strength with which to stop it, or even try. I floated along instead, in a perverse way feeling that this despairing corner of the world is where I deserved to be.

The image of a lost love skittered through my mind and swiftly booted my heart across the empty space inside. Just as quickly, I felt tears mixing with errant raindrops on my face. Outside, pulsing clouds edged closer, flickering with the promise of punishment. The wind howled. I wiped my face with a filthy sleeve and reached for another smoke. I saw her asleep in a warm bed light years from here. I saw her enjoying her carefree girlhood, disconnected from things larger than her own vanity, oblivious to the horrors of this place called Vietnam and the suffering endured by its captives. If only she could know. If only she could see. I was in her past now, but I still could not bear to picture her with someone else.

Opportunities to wallow in self-pity were rare, and I was not going to be denied. I welcomed the pain. Outside, monster, wind-driven drops—scouts for the main force—pelted the track's deck in anger. I scrunched lower, took a deep drag, and waited for the next sit-rep.

———•———

An icy drip from the incessant pattering on our plastic shelter snapped me back to LZ Rash. It had found entrance into my waistband and snaked a path south, causing me to squirm. I gritted my aching teeth and shuddered, so uncomfortable that I tried to get lost in mental anguish again as a trade-off. I was ready to swap anything, figuring I could tolerate any ordeal if it meant being dry. But it was no dice, and all I could do was coil up on my mushy bedding like a banished snake until morning came and the sun could save my soul. By then, my freedom bird would be another notch up in line and I could tick off another hard-earned day. That, by God, was worth something. So I squished and shivered my way to sunrise. Ranger, whom I now suspected of having reptilian innards, slept straight through.

I spent the day baking myself into a stiff but toasty state, then helped Ranger re-vamp our pathetic shelter. The dozers dozed and the bomb squad bombed, blowing down and pushing back hunks of the hedgerow. By five, the sun was headed for the ridgeline and still there wasn't a cloud in the sky. I reasoned it was some sort of trick, but decided not to risk messing it up with negative thoughts. We deserved one dry night. Not even the devil could argue that.

The hills cooled fast, and by dusk, we lounged in pleasantly cool air, grateful to be in a place without leeches and other crawlers. Even the mosquitoes were lackluster in their aggression. Around nine, word was passed to prepare for a mad minute. Not a bad idea, when I thought about it. I hadn't test-fired my rifle since coming to the Cav, and if there were any bad guys in the bushes, it would give them reason to re-think their plans for the evening.

At the signal, the entire perimeter blasted away with small arms and machine guns, peppering the jungle and rubbish heaps in a deafening roar of murderous searing lead. Tracers sliced across the empty space outside the perimeter in an extravaganza of glowing crimson. It was invigorating, assuring that anything lurking in the woods had just been hammered into hash. When the echoes died and smoking barrels cooled, we went back to sipping beverages in small congregations and enjoying the night breeze, glad to be anywhere but burrowed down under a tarp in a torrential rain.

I stood next to a half-built bunker with Steve, speculating that if the sky stayed clear, the rising moon might be bright enough to read by. He seemed distracted, then nudged me and pointed. "Do you see that?" he asked.

I followed his outstretched arm but didn't see anything. I did notice that Ranger and Andy, standing nearby, were also pointing.

"Come on," Steve said, and we walked over.

"You guys see that?" Andy said.

I looked out past the berm toward the treeline, and then I saw it. There was a small light flickering. It looked like a fire ignited by the mad minute. Not unusual, except that with all the rain we'd had no other fires had started, and this one's flames, now growing fast, seemed far too healthy.

"What the hell is that?" he repeated.

I looked around. Another gathering of puzzled men were now staring and pointing, too. Then I glanced sideways, back toward the CP, to see if anybody with rank was paying attention.

"Maybe an ammo box from—" Ranger started to say, but he never finished.

An invisible force hit me so hard that in the space of a half-second, I was slapped backwards into the mud, as if I'd been strapped to the bail of a sprung rat trap. I never heard the explosion. The shockwave got there first and knocked my five senses into the slop next to me.

It didn't seem possible, but I became aware that I could still think. Even so, I presumed myself dead. I had no idea what that involved, but it appeared certain. The silent, silky blackness surrounding me was decorated with psychedelic orange polka-dots. In my mind's eye, I squinted to get a better understanding of it and discovered that they were actually little red fireballs. Now it made sense: I was in flight, passing through an asteroid belt on my way to God-knows-where. I knew it couldn't be heaven because after a few seconds, the asteroid fragments began pelting me and they stung like hell. My life wasn't flashing before my eyes, but then I figured a lot of things probably don't happen the way we expect when we finally drop our last load. None of it added up, but I was too transfixed on the stoning to devote thought to it.

Another fireball clipped my shoulder, followed by one that grazed my scalp and spun my eyes into better focus. The next one hit me square in the forehead and knocked out some of the fog, causing an idea to zip through a circuit: maybe I wasn't in flight after all. In fact, maybe I was still on the ground. And damned if it didn't prove out when I felt something pressing against my back. It had to be the earth! The pellets from hell were some-how raining down from overhead. That meant I could be alive. If true, the next thing I needed to do was find a way to dodge the fireballs so my resur-rection could stay on course. On the other hand, if the whole thing turned out to be an afterlife hallucination, which was still a good bet, my worries were for nothing. But I couldn't trust it. After all, it was a situation where reason didn't have a lot of credibility.

Finally, I made a command decision: I was alive! I didn't try to figure out how; I just believed it. This was confirmed only seconds later when I heard muffled voices. I raised my head a little, and in that instant, the grid completely unlocked, as if a switch had been tripped. What had been hap-pening in slow motion zipped forward to regular speed, and the glowing globs came rocketing down. I cringed and threw an arm over my face. Luckily, it took only a couple of seconds in real time for the last of them to splat into the mud and fizzle.

I sat up. Woozy. Looked about. I saw other men getting to their feet. There was mud on my face and shirt. I realized there must have been some kind of explosion. All at once, I felt damn lucky to be breathing. I spotted one of the burned-out asteroids and leaned in for a look. It was about the size of a ping-pong ball and appeared to be a dirt clod that had been scorched to the point it was almost black. After further examination, I realized that it was indeed a singed mud ball. How can it rain burning mud balls? I glanced around, afraid that Doc would see what I was doing and have my daffy ass shipped to the goofy ward until a team of clinicians decided I was sane.

I got to my feet, ready to deny everything.

Ranger saw me wobbling in place and slogged unsteadily toward me.

"Are you okay?" he said.

I started to say, "I don't know what you mean." What came out was, "It's hailing fire. Swear to God. Fucking little mud balls with flames shooting out of them—"

"The Bangalores blew. Andy and them figured it out. Remember all those crates that were delivered on the chopper pad today?"

"They kicked my ass."

"Are you listening?"

"What?"

"The Bangalores. Nobody ever brought the sons-a-bitches in from the chopper pad."

I rubbed my forehead, caressing a fireball abrasion.

"There was a shitload of them out there. Must have been three or four dozen boxes. It's a flippin' miracle it didn't go up during the mad minute."

"Uh, okay." I was still trying to grasp it all.

"My guess is that the CO of this pig sty just got his ass in a sling. He's damn lucky nobody got killed."

I looked toward the part of the perimeter closest to the helipad. Part of it had disappeared.

"What about those guys over there?" I finally said, pointing. The conversation seemed to be clearing my head.

"They got the worst of it. Paul took a piece of shrapnel, but the rest of our guys are okay. One of the engineers was hauled out on a litter."

I checked myself for lacerations. There weren't any. "Did you see this?" I said, picking up one of the little clods.

"Yeah. Can you imagine how much heat it takes to make mud glow? I thought I was in the fucking Twilight Zone."

Healy showed up. He told us that the guy on the litter had fractured his shoulder when a wall of sandbags fell on him. Paul would join him on the dustoff. The rest of the casualties, he said, were mainly bumps and bruises.

For the first time, I noticed the moon, rising high and shining bright, but I no longer cared about reading. A pulsing pain at the base of my skull convinced me to head for the rack, so I shuffled back to our shelter, which was drooping badly but holding, and stretched out. I counted the throbs until I fell asleep, then dreamed about flying.

Sunrise revealed the rest of the ugly truth. Every structure on the ground-zero side of the perimeter had been pushed over. An exact replica of a bomb crater had replaced the ground next to the chopper pad. The explosives evidently had been low enough to the ground to be missed during the mad minute. It may have been a single round or a ricochet that nicked a crate and ignited the fire. Maybe the flames found their way to some blasting caps. It was puzzling, but I supposed it was a moot point, in any case.

"Get this," Ranger said. "From what I hear, the deputy division commander is supposed to make an inspection here today." He munched cheese and crackers while staring at the destruction.

"Bad news for somebody's career," I said. "Can I have one of those?" The sight of food had my stomach growling.

"He might get by with blaming it on the dinks," he said, "but it'll take a professional liar and a bunch of accomplices to pull it off."

"Won't make any difference," I said. "Somebody'll rat him out."

I left long enough to retrieve a box of rations, then hurried back to watch the action.

The Rome plows fired up and gunned their engines. They clanked right past us, then swiveled and chuffed toward the crater, where they started pushing dirt into the hole. I looked around. The rest of the engineers were working like maniacs to undo the damage. Even the officers had their sleeves rolled up, rushing to put Humpty together again. The bunch of them checked the sky constantly, like burglars watching for headlights. While the suspense mounted, we strolled casually back to our area to work on our own digs and wait for the showdown.

They didn't make it. At the sound of choppers, we eased back over for the arrival of the brass. The general's helicopter settled to the ground right next to the half-filled crater and the part of the base that still looked like a tornadoed mobile-home park. He and his entourage climbed out slowly, taking in the scene, and for several minutes the whole cast of characters just stood there, staring at each other.

7

Time Out, Kick Out, Bug Out

A pint of sweat will save a gallon of blood.
—GEN. GEORGE S. PATTON

New Year's 1970. 1st Cavalry Division. LZ Dragonhead.

Christmas brought Bob Hope to Bien Hoa. Ranger and I had the privilege, being shortest in the platoon. Paul was back, so we didn't feel overly guilty about it. When we got back to Dragonhead, having glimpsed the great one from seats about two hundred yards away, the company had arrived from the field. On New Year's Eve, we all celebrated surviving the year by dispatching a dozen cases of star clusters and parachute flares donated by the taxpayers.

At sunrise, a slightly hung-over lieutenant from the supply branch handed Ranger the keys to a mule and started us hauling goods in from the chopper pad. Easy duty. We hit him up for rear jobs, but he said he wouldn't even admit to having openings until an officer, namely our lieutenant, recommended us to him. We knew what the chances of that were.

Later, prowling the LZ for somebody with beer to share, we hooked into a well-stocked group of Four-Deuce mortarmen willing to sell us all we could carry at their cost. We decided to drink our fill first, so we plopped down on ammo crates next to their mortar pit and commenced to shoot the shit. It didn't take long to realize we had struck an alliance with a bunch of space cadets, men sequestered on Dragonhead so long they had morphed into LZ schizzos. For them, everyday was a rubber stamp of the day before: practice dry-fire missions, clean equipment, and restack or replace existing sandbags. Their only diversions were playing tag with two ornery squirrel monkeys named Crossbow and Tomcat and inhaling happy-smoke while fantasizing about the freedom birds passing by overhead. For the most part, they spoke in riddles and incomplete sentences.

In the course of the evening, Ranger and I determined that our days in the field should be over. It just wasn't fair for us to be endangered by the rookie factor and the tactics Healy employed outside the wire. It wasn't arrogance, just a fact. Later, I encountered Healy at a piss tube and, swaying only slightly, launched my pitch, which immediately devolved into begging him for LZ jobs. Somehow it seemed best to let the liquor do the talking.

It was a waste. At sack time, I broke the news to Ranger, who was already stretched out. "Fuck it" was all he said. He then rolled over and in seconds was snorting and drooling. I sulked for all of five minutes, when I could no longer keep my eyes open.

In the morning, I had a conversation with a rather affable chopper pilot while hoisting cases of C's onto his Huey. He was a captain and was looking for a door gunner, somebody with machine-gun experience who'd seen some shit. As much I wanted the last laugh on Healy, I told him that the glory sounded good but that I was too freakin' short to get my balls blown off for the privilege of sleeping at a real base camp and having a chance to chase Donut Dollies. If I'd had nine months to go and was looking at probably getting killed anyway, it would've been tempting, but now it was out of the question. So I said thanks but no thanks.

I made it a point to smile big at Lieutenant Healy when we mounted choppers to sky up. "Happy fuckin' New Year, LT!" He gave me a funny look but didn't say anything. Figuring on a twenty-day drop, I was down to thirty-four and wake-up, so I tried to think of this rotation as my last fifteen out.

We followed streams for two days, then went ass-sideways into the jungle to rendezvous with resupply. It took all day to hack through a half klick of bamboo mesh, which still left the chore of cutting an LZ. As a general rule, pilots didn't need much of a reason not to land, so we risked a "kick-out" every time a pad was too small or not level enough, something Healy tried to avoid. So he egged us on, coaching the construction as if it were in a wood-chopping contest, noise discipline be damned.

It may have been short-timers syndrome or just healthy paranoia, but I was really getting bugged over his hard-on for stream-walking roulette and generally behaving as if we owned the place. We made enough noise to cause every dink within two klicks to cock an ear, and I reasoned I stood a good chance of ending up buzzard bait if even a handful VC happened to be passing through. *All I'm trying to do here is survive a few more days,* I thought, *and he's breaking however many rules it takes to make sure I leave in a rubber bag.* I had to find a way to make my profile lower.

We heard the chopper along the hills just after the LZ was finished. I had sprawled out to rest, shirt soaked, waiting for the cool blow of the rotor wash to lower my skin temperature. The Huey appeared overhead and stopped, scoping us out from fifty feet up. The pilot backed it up a little, braked, moved sideways some, then hovered, as if something didn't cut muster. For a couple of minutes, we watched, getting that uneasy feeling as the smoke canister popped during his approach thinned into wispy vapors. All eyes were now on the chopper. I heard Sergeant Ralston say, "What's his problem? He'd better not give it the boot," just when the goods started coming out.

Huh?

Our stuff! Men sprang to their feet. Fingers jabbed at the sky. "HEY MOTHERFUCKER!"

On the heels of the C-rations came a tarpaulin full of clothes that tumbled awkwardly until it unraveled at treetop level and dumped most of its contents into a nearby creek. Two care packages detonated in a spray of sundries within the bamboo stalks and vanished, followed by a final case of rations that landed dead center of the LZ with a smack and a bounce. The chopper then set pitch and sailed smoothly away, mission accomplished.

It took an hour of scavenging to recover enough stuff to see us through the next three days. We filled canteens in the stream. Healy shrugged it off, saying we probably didn't give them enough clearance to avoid the kick-out. The important thing, he said, was that we find a good hill quick and get to the top of it. We just stared after him.

"Assholes," somebody mumbled. "Nam sucks," another added.

We didn't come close to finishing the climb. Healy's hill was a bastard, its slope so steep and slimy it was all we could do to pull ourselves halfway up. Moods were dark. It had just rained. The resupply pilot had fucked us over. We were wet, the light was nearly gone, and now this. Sleeping positions would have to be dug into the side of the incline to keep from sliding off, so it was out with the entrenching tools to hack at the earth in what light remained.

I set my shovel's blade at a right angle to the handle and used it like a hoe to chop up some ground quick. The soft soil gouged out easily in heavy wedges. *The first good thing that's happened all day,* I thought. *Yes sir, this won't take but a couple minutes. I'll get me a nice level spot and heat up some—*

Whoa! What the hell is that? I'd opened up a little tunnel, like a snake or a mole would make. I stooped down for a closer look. I didn't like it, but what could I do? I stood up for another swing, cutting deeper into the turf, then stopped again, thinking I detected movement within the dirt. I squatted, peered, then poked at the ground. Some loose granules started moving around and out popped a gleaming black scorpion of a size I wouldn't have thought possible.

"Ahhh!" I jumped back, lost my footing, and skidded downhill on one knee. A small tree stopped my descent with no small amount of pain. "Shit! Fucking son of a bitch!"

"What the hell?" Ranger hustled over. Steve and Paul heard the commotion and followed. I pulled myself up and pointed at the nest. To our amazement, a second scorpion scampered from the hole, then a third. They came out quick, the way eels dart from ocean caves. They were bigger than any crawdad I'd ever plucked from a creek.

"Damn," Paul said. "Look at the size of those fuckers." Nothing seemed to rile Paul. Most of the time we didn't even know he was there. He was slowly chewing gum and seemed genuinely spellbound. Forced into the open, the scorpions had formed a perimeter, pincers raised, stingers twitching, as if prepared to make a fight of it.

"Kiss my ass," Steve said. "The bugs over here are as crazy as the dinks."

For a few seconds, we just stood there, fixated. Finally, I snapped out of it and said, "Get 'em!" Steve blind-sided one, slicing it in half with his spade. The other two started running in circles.

"Get 'em!" I squawked. This was my sleeping position. There could be no survivors. Calculating speed and distance, Paul slowly raised a boot and squished number two, although it took four hard stomps to get it done. Number three then rushed for the hole in retreat, heading my way. In desperation, I commenced a wild chopping frenzy that guillotined him cleanly somewhere around the fifth swing.

When it was done, Ranger scooped up the body parts and heaved the whole mess into the brush. Everybody but me relaxed. I stared at the hole intently, waiting.

"I doubt if there's any more in there," he said.

"Maybe not in *that* nest," Paul added. "There's probably more close by, though. Just the same, I'd dig that out good if I were you, Ross. A dude in 2nd Platoon got stung by one of them black bastards while he was asleep, and—"

"Save it, Daw. I don't wanna know."

"—by the time he stopped hoppin' around like he'd been stuck with a bayonet his arm had swelled up like a melon.

"C'mon, man."

"Before the dustoff got there, he was barfin' up his insides."

"Thanks, brother. Thanks a lot."

Ralston showed up with the roster for watch. "Thought everybody was settled in by now," he said. I didn't bother to answer.

At this point, it was nearly dark. *Great,* I thought. *Just great. We're in the middle of a scorpion breeding ground, I can't see shit, and if I get stung, I'm gonna fucking die because a medevac couldn't get in here if Christ himself called for it.* I attempted to dig the rest of the tunnel out of the ground, then smoothed everything off and patted it down good. I waited, watching for rustles in the dirt, but the light was gone and I had to give up. While everybody else sacked out, I ate cold canned meat and tried not to think about it.

For now, sleep was unlikely, so I cut a deal with Denny to take first watch and then did what worked best to make the time pass—revisit old haunts for the umpteenth time. I was confident that if I did it enough, everything would ultimately make sense. Until then, it would poke at me, making me feel like a fugitive, suggesting that I might someday be the subject of an inquisition. I figured if I replayed it another hundred times or so, I would at least discover some clues to the whole mystery. Maybe.

8

Spider Holes
and Boogymen

I asked myself what I was doing there, with a sensation of panic in my heart as though I had blundered into a place of cruel and absurd mysteries not fit for a human being to behold.

—JOSEPH CONRAD, *HEART OF DARKNESS*

Rewind: Late February 1970. 25th Infantry Division. Cu Chi Base Camp.

It only took a minute to find the mental bookmark from the last time I played memory lane. I was departing Cu Chi's airstrip to join the company in the field for the first time, glad to be getting my tour underway but suitably apprehensive. My nerves had settled a bit once the Chinook was airborne, helped some by the lofty view. Below me, the rutty land was a concoction of washes and brush, looking like a deformed desert with no purpose, even as an objective in war. I had to wonder what the mission in this wasteland could be, though I supposed it didn't much matter. It was a short hop, and as the chopper floated down toward Alpha Company's night laager position, the armored personnel carriers—an assemblage of green steel boxes arranged in an irregular circle—stood out conspicuously, contrasting sharply with the open range.

I scurried down the dust-choked ramp and headed for the perimeter. The others drifted off to their platoons, leaving me to find my way, so I approached a grunt who was intently hacking at a stubborn piece of ground. He glanced up, saw I was a replacement, and, with an annoyed look, tilted his head and said, "CP's over there"—then renewed his attack on the rooty earth as if I'd never existed. I mumbled a thanks and moved on.

At the command post, I found Captain Littlefield. He looked more like a grizzled street cop than an army officer. He was short and stout, with wavy black hair and a square, lined face. Cold eyes suggested a lack of tolerance. Without wasting words, he assigned me to 1-4 track—1st Platoon, 4th Squad, stationed across the perimeter.

As I made my way, I was struck by how different these APCs looked than the stateside specimens I'd seen in training. These were dirt-smeared, scarred, and modified to suit conditions. Some had been gouged by shrapnel, and most had names painted on their sides. They were manned by grimy, tarnished grunts, most in sleeveless fatigue shirts or no shirts at all. The captain's track and the mortar and mechanics tracks served as a hub to the outer perimeter, where the line platoons, with four tracks each, formed a circle. A twelve-by-seven-foot section of chain link had been erected in front of each APC, held up by steel poles temporarily driven into the ground. Farther out, Claymore mines linked to the tracks with electric wires aimed their savage blasts at the empty spaces beyond. Here and there were hastily dug garbage sumps and latrines consisting of stacked sandbags for seats. The air was stale and hot and smelled like piss and sweat.

I reported to 1-4's squad leader, a skinny black sergeant named Emmons, who seemed indifferent to my arrival. "You the FNG we were supposed to get two weeks ago?" he asked.

"Looks that way," I answered. I knew that FNG meant "Fuckin' New Guy," and that it came with the territory. I wasn't bothered by it.

He gave me the once over, then looked past me. "We're diggin' in for the night," he said, pointing. "Find yourself a spot in that area over there and get to it."

I dropped my gear in a sandy depression thirty feet behind the APC and scooped out a shallow sleeping position. Others had done the same, and I wandered back to the track to meet some of them. 4th Squad was known as "The Rottin 8." *Sounds about right,* I thought. I exchanged nods and a few handshakes and met our platoon leader, Lt. Mike Decker, who was due to rotate out in a few days. There wasn't much in the way of chat, so I hung around awkwardly until Emmons took notice and assigned me a chore. Cu Chi was close enough that the Chinook had brought along hot food. I filled paper plates until everyone was fed, then got some for myself, already feeling antsy to get through the get-acquainted phase.

By dark, everybody had settled in. They sat atop the track and mingled on the ground. A few were sacked out. Thin layers of cigarette smoke hung in the dead air, and miniature clouds of gnats and mosquitoes swirled. The sounds of men moving about and the murmur of conversation was occasionally punctuated with the crack of hands slapping fresh bites. Lightning bugs drifted aimlessly, doing what they could to oppose the darkness.

Odd man out, I returned to my spot in the bumpy wash. Seated on my plastic poncho, I considered options for getting comfortable. I had just cupped and lit a Marlboro when an up-close voice jerked my heart into my throat: "Hey." I whipped around to see the shadowy face of our driver, John Keinroth, staring down at me. I sat up straight, tried to act casual, and offered him a smoke, hoping he hadn't heard the crashing cymbals inside my chest that had twanged every skin surface from the scalp down. Evidently, I was more uptight than I realized.

"Since I make most of the rules, I thought I'd get with you and go over a few things." He came to a squat and fired his smoke down low, casting a weak glow on his scruffy face. He was tall, angular, oval-faced, and underweight. Large black glasses sat heavily on his thin nose, and coarse stubble explained where shaving ranked on his priority board.

He spoke matter-of-factly. "First thing is, don't go get on anybody's nerves by pretending to know anything. FNGs can't know anything. Nothing to be ashamed about, just a fact. So for now, just watch, listen, and try not to fuck up." He turned his head and spit. "I don't know what you expected, but out here, we're always short-handed. The textbook shit they teach back in the World is a joke. We have to make do with what we've got. Mostly you'll walk behind the track with the other grunts. Sometimes you'll ride. It just depends on where we are and what we're up to. During contact, everybody is on the ground but me and the gunners. Emmons gives orders under fire. Otherwise, it's my track and what I say goes. I use the grenade launcher. We have a gunner for the Fifty and one for the side-mounted Sixty. Everybody else uses their rifle."

He talked on. I listened. He told me to never let any body parts hang over the side of the track when mounted unless I didn't mind losing them. Shrapnel from mines and booby traps was slung right up the sides with the speed and cutting edge of a mower blade. Bunking inside the track was reserved for the .50 gunner, also known as the track commander or TC, the driver, and the squad leader.

When all the business was out of the way, he told me he was from Iowa and, at twenty-three, was the oldest in the squad, a fact he was reminded of more often than he liked. If I had any doubt in any situation, he said, help was only a holler away. "With our platoon, it's all for one and one for all," he said. "Most often, it works good that way. Not always, but most often."

I wanted to assure him that I was a team guy, no problem, but I just nodded instead.

"Now follow me," he said. He led me to a spot about halfway between our track and the CP, where a piece of warped and splintered plywood lay on the ground. He shoved the plywood with his boot and revealed a hole in the ground about eighteen inches in diameter.

For a second, I couldn't believe my eyes. "Is that a tunnel entrance?" I said.

"It's an old one," he answered, "but it hasn't been cleared, at least not by us."

I didn't know what to say. I could only wonder why it hadn't been checked or destroyed before the company camped around it.

"The CO wants us to monitor it tonight with a flashlight each time we change guard. So when you finish your watch, check it out before you crash."

My expression told him what I was thinking. "We didn't get an explanation. But that's what he wants, so that's what we gotta do."

I was too new to question anything. Maybe it was a joke or a test. But there was no mistaking what the hole was.

"Just shine a light in it?"

"Roger. But do it down low so it can't be seen above ground."

"Got it."

From there, we walked over to the track, and he showed me how to respond to calls for situation reports, or sit-reps, while on guard, and pointed out who would relieve me after my watch. He stayed topside with a few others while I shuffled back to my sleeping position, not wanting to wear out my welcome.

I dozed off late, sweaty and bitten, only to be awakened by Mike Abbott, a baby-faced kid with thick black hair and eyebrows to match. He had a Cheshire cat grin that said, "What, me worry?" We had talked earlier for a minute, and he immediately dubbed me "the Rook," for rookie. I could tell he had a devious bent, but sensed that he could be trusted. I also knew we would get along. He vanished into the darkness as soon as I was on my feet.

I trudged over to the APC, boarded, and dropped in behind the big .50-caliber machine gun. I found a Claymore clacker (hand detonator) draped over each side of the turret, a radio handset, a Starlight night-vision scope, and John's M79 grenade launcher slung on the gun shield, loaded but breach open. A belt of .50-cal slugs snaked into the gun from a metal can placed in a holder mounted to its left side. It looked like serious business.

I gave my eyes a rub, then commenced to watch in earnest, feeling privileged to be entrusted with such magnificent weaponry. With all this, who could get close? It was enough raw power to give me a rush, and I had no trouble imagining myself the vanguard of an entire army. *My, my,* I thought. *The destruction I could cause with the flick of a wrist. Get the women and children off the streets, people. I am cock o' the walk, and woe to all who stand in my way. Yessiree.*

I was saved from this B movie script by the weak crackle of static on the radio and a buzz in my ear. I slapped at the mosquito's prick, then stretched my eyes open wide and resumed scanning the terrain. When my vision fully adjusted, what I saw was a complicated mix of oblique shapes and gray-black hues whose densities stretched and oozed if I stared at one spot too long. I knew that wasn't the way to employ night vision, but I couldn't help focusing time and again on the most prominent spots. I had to be sure they were fixed objects. It was a good thing, because soon enough some of them began to throb, fade, and sway, causing me to stare even harder. I answered the first call for a sit-rep by breaking squelch twice, signaling all okay, even though things were not okay. I was near positive that some of those murky shapes were closer than before. I fixated on one in particular that seemed to be more pronounced than it had just minutes ago. My pulse quickened and my mouth dried up at the realization that I could be virtually face-to-face with creeping Viet Cong.

All the swagger I'd just felt dissolved in a brisk wave of fear as sparks tried to ignite a flash fire of panic. Hoping to head it off, I looked away and concentrated on forcing reality back into the equation. I knew I had the firepower. What I didn't know was when to use it. If I messed this up, I might never be trusted.

What had all this looked like before? Was there a stump there or not? I felt a fist swell up in my throat, pushing me to decide something quick. A twitchy finger lightly tapped one of the Claymore clackers, and I began to gently lift the grenade launcher from its slung position with my free hand, wishing like hell there was somebody here to give me some guidance. Then I remembered the Starlight scope, and I grabbed for it, letting go of the M79 and the clacker. I stuck it to my face and twisted the controls from one extreme to the other, only to discover that with no moon and a hazy sky it was virtually useless. All I could see was a screen filled with sparkles against a green background, so I put it down.

My eyes stabbed at the darkness. Things looked about the same, but I couldn't be sure. An inner voice urged me to reset the alarm, to investigate calmly. I resisted. If seeing was believing, I was positive that at least one of the silhouettes had shifted over some and inched forward. It was bigger, blacker.

I cupped an ear but heard nothing. I glanced away, looked back. No change. I had to be sure, so I repeated the process half a dozen times, each time forcing myself to count slowly to twenty. The silhouettes held their positions. Time passed. Finally, I relaxed. The aggressor shadows were stationary and had been all along—otherwise, they would have been on top of me by now. For the moment at least, I was safe. I was back in charge and feeling more self-assured. I decided to use the time I had left to practice the night-vision techniques I'd learned in training and to get accustomed to the subtle nocturnal sounds around me. I figured that with dedication I could fine-tune these skills in a week or two. If I didn't, there could be a price to pay.

I worked on it, but soon became bored. An hour is a god-awful long time to sit and look at nothing, and toward the end of my watch, fatigue took over, tugging with irresistible pull. Staying awake was now the challenge, and it became less plausible as silent black minutes inched by. For the third time, squelch broke on the radio and a whispered voice reached out and said, "One-Four, gimme a sit-rep." I broke squelch in reply, then fought back mightily as an evil mastermind hung the weight of a thousand planets from my lids. It took inhuman effort to keep them from slamming shut. In just thirty minutes, I'd taken the slide from frenzied vigilance into a lethargic mire of false confidence and deflated tension, two thugs vowing to beat me unconscious.

After what seemed like another two hours, the final fifteen minutes passed. It was time to climb down and wake up Steve Ridgeway. Then I remembered I had to investigate the hole first, and that brought me fully awake. There was no getting around it, so I grabbed the flashlight clipped to the gun shield and lowered myself to the ground. Within the perimeter, it was completely dark and silent. It was as if the place was abandoned. I no longer thought for a second that this was a test. With nobody around to yuk it up, there would be no point. I stepped lightly toward the spot where the plywood was, feeling myself knot up inside at the prospect of uncovering it and presenting my head as a target. I couldn't understand why they hadn't just backed a track on top of it. How it helped to check it once an hour in a way that basically amounted to offering a sacrifice was beyond me. Such questions had no answers, so I took a deep breath and gently slid the covering to the side. Keeping a safe distance, I knelt and edged the flashlight over the opening, making sure it was pointed down, and flicked on the beam. Nothing happened, so with my heart thumping, I craned my neck for a peek inside. I did it quick, and when no shots rang out, I ventured a more extended look. All I saw was a dusty hole about five feet deep with an abrupt elbow leading to who knew where.

When it was done, I replaced the plywood and quietly made my way back, hoping such strange assignments wouldn't be a habit with Littlefield.

I gave Steve a gentle shake, but his body resisted, and I had to do it again and again, afraid that at some point he might come up swinging. Finally, he sat up, gave me a puzzled look, ruffled his hair, and asked me if

I'd heard or seen anything. I handed him the flashlight and with a yawn said no, everything was quiet.

Once he was on his feet and moving toward the track, I blissfully crawled under the thin material of my poncho liner and turned all systems off. Sleep rushed in, and as I slipped away under the buzz of the blood-suckers, I thought I heard the distant faint thunder of artillery fire. *That's somebody else's war,* I thought, then allowed myself a little inward smile and checked off the first day.

9

RIF

Today I felt pass over me a breath of wind
from the wings of madness.

—CHARLES BAUDELAIRE

March 1970. 25th Infantry Division.
Filhol Area of Operations.

We patrolled a wilderness they called the Filhol (pronounced *fill-hole*), named for the nearby Filhol rubber plantation. The local VC's specialty here was hit-and-run ambushes and setting booby traps. Our mission was to RIF—conduct reconnaissance-in-force—which was a more civilized term for "search and destroy." The idea was to keep the enemy from reinfesting an area that was once home to the most extensive tunnel complex in the country. Over the years, the terrain had been bombed, burned, razed, and defoliated until reaching its current state. Other duties involved securing fire-support bases and serving as a reactionary force to ground units who needed help stomping Asian ass. At night, ambush patrols (APs, for short) consisting of five to eight men as well as three-man listening posts (LPs) were sent out to try and snare encroaching Cong. My seat on the track, when I was allowed to ride, was a square wooden ammo box on the right rear of the top deck behind Ridgeway. Similar seats surrounded the outer perimeter.

Mostly, I trudged along behind the track with the other peons, where I learned how the sun fries things and how dust replaces oxygen. When we rode, I sought to understand our true role in this drama by asking rookie questions and getting short answers from John and our .50 gunner, Wayne McDonald, an assertive Kentuckian from a well-bred family who had no difficulty expressing his opinions.

"There's more goin' on here than meets the eye, right?" I said to anyone listening. It was the third day of sun and dust punishment, and I had been thinking how good it would be to move on, to change pace, to find *shade.*

We had stopped for chow. John sat stoop-shouldered on the rim of the driver's hatch, glasses low on his nose to keep sweat drops off the lenses. He looked up, moving only his eyes, and said, "Right."

"Beaucoup booby traps out here," Ridgeway added. He was munching on a fast-melting chocolate disk from a B-2 food unit and made the remark offhandedly, suggesting that knowing such things was universally understood.

"We ever gonna go anyplace besides here?"

McDonald, his words muffled by a cheek jammed with rations, said, "We'll be doing a lot of shit, man. We just came back from the Boi Loi Woods over by the Iron Triangle, which you probably never heard of, and in the next month or two, we'll likely be all over Three Corps like rats through Swiss cheese." He stopped to lick his fingers, then studied the results.

"You probably think rif'n' the Filhol is duller than sittin' watch or burnin' shit," Donnie Roberts put in. He was a boxy, freckle-spattered redhead who manned the M60 machine gun and, next to Emmons, was shortest in the squad. "But don't think what Steve just said don't mean nothin'. Just before you got here, One-Three tripped a boobytrapped one-five-five arty round over by the Trapezoid that killed three, and last month, a track with First of the Fifth Mech rolled over a boobytrapped seven-hundred-and-fifty-pound bomb up in the Michelin Plantation. Pow! Wasted every man on board." He made an exploding gesture with his arms, followed by a dead stare that made me wish I'd kept my mouth shut.

"Chances are, we'll escort a convoy to Tay Ninh before long or pull security for the arty at LZ Devin," John said. "Or they may move us up on the border to shake some cages. Things don't stay the same for long."

He was right. I saw my first dead body an hour later. We had mounted up and were creeping along in a dusty column when my eye was drawn to a blackened object lying on the parched earth that looked like a rotted log. When I realized it was a dead Vietnamese, my impulse was to alert somebody, as if something that significant should be reported. Then I realized that others had seen it, too, but paid no more attention than they would driving past roadkill back in the World. What would have been a serious discovery back home was of no importance here, especially when the corpse was as decomposed as this one. He had twisted and shriveled up to the point he looked more like an oversized serving of beef jerky than a human being.

I suited up for my inaugural AP that night, along with another newbie from our squad, Willie Pearce, an eighteen-year-old black from Michigan with a thin mustache and a personality so reserved he came to be known as Invisible Willie. We followed four others into the scrubby terrain at sunset. I carried my M16, fifteen magazines, a Claymore mine, grenades, a towel, and a poncho with liner. We had an M60 machine gun along and a radio. There were no trails here, but the area was known for punji pits and other crude booby traps like explosive cans filled with nails, glass, and other objects designed to gouge, blind, castrate, and even kill their victims. There were also tunnels, though most were inactive.

The chosen spot for the ambush site was about six hundred meters from the security of the company. There was no cover of any kind, only thin concealment within the tall grass and scattered scrub brush. Because of this, we couldn't risk standing up. It was all hands and knees. Once a sit-rep had been called in to establish our position, Claymores were set and a watch list made up. Roberts was the senior grunt, and he kept me next to him. Darkness brought a light breeze and a starry, moonless sky. One spot on the far horizon emitted dim light, which I assumed was a village on Highway 1, maybe Trang Bang or Go Dau Ha.

I had third watch, and when the time came, I had no trouble staying awake. Mosquitoes were abundant, and I was jittery anyway, imagining what it would be like to spot a contingent of VC wandering our way. Staring across the shadowy ground lit only by ambient starlight was eerie. Halfway into my watch, I heard a few faint notes of Vietnamese music drifting on the breeze. *Where the hell is that coming from?* I thought. *Are there VC walking around out here with radios?* Now spooked, I pricked my ears and concentrated on sounds. Bits of oriental music continued to wisp by, but they sounded far away, as if they'd been carried on the wind a great distance. I thought of waking Roberts, but decided not to. Then I heard an unnatural sound close by and stiffened. I made myself wait. I looked. I saw nothing. A moment later, I heard it again. That was enough. I hadn't yet learned the difference between natural and threatening noises and wasn't about to chance it. I shook Donnie's leg hard, and he came up on one elbow.

"I think there's movement out there!" I whispered excitedly.

My words had been louder than I realized, and he immediately grabbed my arm and said, "Shut up!" He then quietly rousted the others. We waited. And listened. There was nothing. It was a false alarm. After five minutes, they all went back to sleep. I answered a call for a sit-rep and resumed staring into the night, feeling like a dope for being excitable and hoping my FNG jitters hadn't pissed everybody off. Errant notes of ghostly music continued to float my way until it was time to pass the radio. Even then, sleep didn't come easily. Ducking the bugs meant keeping my face covered, and the price I paid was a river of sweat. When daylight came, the best I had managed was a few hours.

On the way in, I brought up the subject of the mystery music, but I don't think anyone believed me.

———•———

We marched on miserably to nowhere, and by the end of my first week in the field, I was convinced that anywhere had to be better than here. The fact that I was too inexperienced to know better wasn't lost on me—I just craved relief from the broiler.

We got a new platoon leader, 2nd Lt. Joe Yearout. He was a big man—narrow at the top, wider at the waist—who hailed from New Jersey. He wasn't new to Vietnam, but was new to the field. He was married, person-able, and made a genuine effort to be accepted. It was obvious even to me that 1st Platoon had lucked out.

Beyond the outer reaches of the Filhol area of operations, the waste-land gave way to cultivation. Mingling with parched rice paddies and a scattering of hootches were clusters of *trees*. It was a quasi-oasis, tended by leathery, hunchbacked farmers who toiled relentlessly to wrench a lean bounty from the stingy earth. Assorted livestock and dirty, bare-assed chil-dren further civilized the area. It looked so peaceful I expected it would be skipped for a more likely target, maybe the nearby Ho Bo Woods. But instead, we took a breather in the shade and then prepared to do our day's work right there.

We dismounted and started a slow walk behind the tracks, looking for who-knows-what. The dry season was at its peak, and the dust kicked up by the treads soon frosted our skin and fatigues with grime. The sun, mostly unobstructed, hammered down, generating a free flow of sweat that wormed pathways through the dust until our cheeks and necks were road-mapped with miniature rivers of mud. After two hours, it was hard to remember what fresh air tasted like.

The APCs stopped at the discovery of a small pond nestled in some frail saplings. The captain wanted to take a look, so while waiting, we climbed aboard in search of better air. Littlefield rolled up and dismounted to study the stagnant brown water. He decided it would be a good idea to search it and assigned the task to Lieutenant Yearout, who happened to be standing alongside 1-4 at the time.

The LT looked up at us. "I guess we're elected. Any volunteers?"

John was the first to speak up. "Come on, lieutenant. This is dumber than when we laagered around a tunnel entrance."

The LT just looked at the ground, listening patiently.

McDonald frowned and snorted. "His quirks are gonna get somebody wasted one day." Apparently, the captain had a history of ill-conceived ideas.

Ridgeway started to take his turn, but the lieutenant held up a hand. "Look, guys, I didn't say I agreed with it, but since dinks have been known to store caches underwater, it's a valid order, so let's get going."

Joe Yearout had earned the respect of the platoon straightaway. He treated us like equals and wasn't above getting dirt on his hands or even pulling guard at night, qualities that earned loyalty fast. He seemed to have more common sense than the average officer fresh from OCS, and while he had already recognized that Captain Littlefield was a man with flaws, there was only so much he could do.

The debate ended, and in short order, six of us sloshed into the water up to our armpits and formed a line, silently begging for an absence of explosives or punji stakes with each adventurous step in the squishy muck below. We waded across slow and easy and, in fifteen minutes, completed the chore, emerging from the slop with only sopping fatigues and the makings of a grudge for the CO. On the plus side, the water had cooled us down some and managed to wash away part of the baked-on crust.

The company mounted up and moved out in the direction of the huts. The tracks came up on line, then slowed to a crawl while we lighted small hunks of C-4 explosive and commenced to commit agricultural homicide by pitching them out behind the APCs as we clanked and churned our way across the semi-fertile turf. Two hours of this mutilated a lot of soil and burned a lot of ground cover, but only detonated a couple of booby traps. Mostly, it pissed off the peasants, who were not shy in voicing their outrage. We had no sooner stopped to rest when two squawking old women ran from a hootch and chewed us out up close while threatening our tracks with sticks. Their men folk, far afield, showed support by pumping clenched fists and waving farm implements in a way that made me think of dancing witch doctors. I wondered what the point was until Ridgeway explained that landowners who somehow coexist with concealed explosives planted all over their fields can't be trusted or sympathized with.

We set up for the night some distance away. Once the trip flares and Claymores were out, the RPG screen up, and the track dusted down, C-rations were bartered for and consumed. Our platoon sergeant, Roger Pitt, appeared at dusk.

"Y'all got your trip flares set?" he asked.

"Yep." Nobody looked up.

"Got your Claymores out? RPG screen squared away?"

"Yep."

"Be sure and double-check everything and dig in before dark."

"Yeah, we know."

It was a quiz he administered daily. From what I'd observed, Pitt was a tolerated pest. He was generally pleasant but had a bent for nagging, and he must have thought most of us had skulls packed with lumpy grits. He was a lifer, too, which answered a lot.

Darkness brought the usual night fears and higher bug density, two villains that pilfered sleep and scraped at edgy nerves. At midnight, I found myself still wide awake, slapping mosquitoes and sweating. The little bastards were in my ears, up my nose, anywhere they could suck juice—buzzing, buzzing, buzzing. I covered my face as long as I could stand it, but within minutes, I was drowning in my own sweat.

I was convinced they knew this.

———•———

Dave Santa-Cruz, 3rd Squad's .50 gunner, agreed. "Even gook bugs hate Americans."

We sat eating a breakfast of canned rations.

"There it is," I mumbled. I was picking up lingo fast.

I had connected with Dave on my second day out when he had seen me sitting by myself and lumbered over, clutching a pair of sodas and a good-old-boy grin. He was a six-footer of wiry construction with a flawless Hispanic complexion, onyx hair, and brown eyes that suggested inner calm.

"It's a shit job, but somebody's got to do it," he had said, extending an arm while scouting for a place to sit.

"Thanks." I accepted the pop and offered a smoke. "What's a shit job?"

"Trying to convince new guys they're not lower than maggot dung." He waved off the cigarette.

We leaned back against the track. I took a pull on the soda and considered the relative ease of a larvae's life. "Your job's already done," I said with a half grin.

"I thought you should know it's a good idea to make yourself known around the platoon. There may be times when you'll have to rely on people outside your squad, and it helps to know who you can count on . . . and vise versa."

"I hope to be considered reliable by everybody."

"Just don't come on too fast. And don't be quick to judge. It takes a while to sort things out and size people up."

I looked at him, realizing there was a lesson being laid out.

"Take your squad leader. Emmons knows his job, he's just not very friendly, never has been, and he's hard to get to know. He's a doper, too, and that makes him suspicious by nature. The rest of your squad is all right. You'll see for yourself the next time we make contact."

He had said it easily, the way someone would talk about ordinary things. He tilted his head for a final gulp, crushed the can, and took aim at a small garbage sump. "Not much room here for mistakes," he added, concentrating on the toss. "The main thing is for everybody to know that you can be counted on. So if you bust ass, most of the others will do the same for you. If you sham, or make fucking up a habit, or become a whiner, they won't take major risks to cover your back."

The can sailed in a perfect arc into the sump.

"Sham?" I didn't know the word.

"Shirking responsibility. Shammers try to make things easy for themselves, even if it means making things harder for others."

"Ah," I said. "That won't be a problem." I had already figured out that dependability meant everything, prerequisites nothing. Until he measured up, a West Pointer would get no more respect than a private who couldn't remember whether he finished eighth grade or ninth. FNGs, regardless of rank, were generally considered untrustworthy and potentially dangerous. I knew that I would have to prove myself as opportunities presented themselves. There was no other way.

"Hey!" Dave called out to a short, dark-haired grunt with a Clark Gable mustache who was headed our way from 3rd Squad's track.

"This is Jim Shukas," Dave said, "one of the shortest dudes in the platoon. Everything you need to know about Nam is inside his head."

"If I was that smart," Jim said, "I'd be gone already." We exchanged nods. "The main thing is to not rely on people like me for all the answers."

"See what I mean?" Dave said.

"Gotta go," Jim said. "Time to hound Littlefield for a rear job again."

Dave was from San Jose. He'd been in country five months. He had only one goal beyond surviving Nam: to buy an MG convertible and use his GI Bill to go to college. 1st Platoon, he told me, was considered the company's "A" team, and for that reason, it got called on more than the others. "Just something to be aware of," he said.

I was surprised by how open he'd been in that first conversation, but glad to know I'd met someone I could really talk to.

With breakfast out of the way, we got underway, moving toward the rising sun. The company had been in the field for three weeks with no rain and no rumors of a new mission. The dust billowed and the sun blazed, and dispositions were on the downslide. To top it off, at midday we linked up with a company of South Vietnamese (ARVNs) and had to haul a platoon of them around with us for the day. This did nothing to improve attitudes.

Two of them rode on 1-4. They sat scrunched up on the rear of the track, jabbering a mile a minute in a language that seemed made up entirely of vowels. This constant chatter further aggravated already frayed nerves.

"Keep your valuables in sight and watch those dudes close," Roberts told me. "They'll steal you blind, and if there's a way, they'll get somebody killed."

"That bad, huh?" Even if he was exaggerating, I would take his word for it. I eyeballed them.

"Check it out," Ridgeway said.

I wanted to ask some questions, but decided not to.

"If there's one thing I hate," McDonald added, "it's rif'n' with untrained idiots who don't give a shit."

I figured that about covered it, so I did my best to ignore them.

The Vietnamese had laid their weapons down and swung their legs out to dangle over the side of the track, dangerous acts both. All the while, they pumped their jaws at each other, occasionally meeting my gaze with a smile or nod, as though in agreement with whatever I was thinking.

We discovered some dilapidated relics of long-ago enemy emplacements and abandoned hidey-holes, none of which appeared active. With the tracks on line, we stopped near a withered grove of trees, where a cache of some sort had been discovered by 3rd Platoon. While they searched, we rested. I glanced at the sun, lit a cigarette, and reached for my canteen. I was squinting at the sky and guzzling greedily when machine-gun fire cut the air, causing me to gag and slop water down my front.

We looked around, but it was too far down the line to tell what had happened. John upped the speaker volume just as the radio crackled. "Coupla dinks sprang from a bunker," an unidentified voice said. "3rd Platoon knocked their peckers off."

The lieutenant moseyed over after a few minutes. "They found a nice little ammo and food cache along with another dead VC," he said. "Dinks never got a round off."

Maybe all of this would put Littlefield in a good mood. Maybe we'd even stay in the shade awhile longer. So far, we had collected three bodies, some goods, and hadn't had any problems from the ARVN freeloaders. Not bad for half a day's outing.

Instead, we pushed on. The tracks were spread apart, still on line, creeping along at pedestrian speed. I had a towel over my head to help deflect the glare, but it didn't help. It was shaping up to be a long afternoon when an explosion ripped the dull air in a bone-rattling crack. I flinched so hard I teetered and almost fell through the cargo hatch. I looked around fretfully, trying to determine what had happened as 1-4 ground to a halt.

Sergeant Emmons, head set on, stood up and turned around. "One-One tripped a booby trap. Everybody stay put."

Once again, lack of experience twirled uneasily in my gut. It could've been a land mine, an incoming mortar, or a tossed grenade, and I couldn't have said which. If it had been the onset of an ambush, I wouldn't have known which way to shoot. I also realized that the slightest hesitation could leave me punched full of holes. I would have to learn how to react in these situations and be quick about it.

When the smoke cleared word came down that 1-1 had three for dustoff and tread damage. The captain broadcast an order that nobody dismount just as I looked toward 1-2 and saw a pair of ARVNs slip to the ground as smoothly as snakes from a tree and strike out across the minefield, their apparent quest to visit a buddy on another track. 1-2's squad leader hollered at them, but they only looked back and played dumb with a shrug. A few steps later, they both went vertical, sucked up in the plume of an ear-piercing blast that shook the ground and spewed dirt in every direction.

They each hit the deck with a thud. One of them barely moved. His slashed-up sidekick, sprawled nearby, managed to get to his feet, wobble a bit, then stagger a few steps before falling down again. He tried to get up, couldn't, then just sat there, staring in wonder at his bloody legs. Scorched pieces of tattered fatigues littered the ground.

The captain's voice boomed over the track's radio speaker. "What's going on over there? I told everybody to freeze!"

Lieutenant Yearout answered. "A couple of ARVNs got blown up, sir. One of 'em looks awful."

"Say again?"

"I said a couple of—"

"Lieutenant," he interrupted, "get your medic over there and have him, only him, treat the casualties. Nobody else. Is that clear? No one else!"

Doc Santana, our medic, lowered himself from 1-3 and made his way to the scene of the slaughter, kneeling beside the more mangled of the two. He plugged some holes using bandages about the size of a wallet, then went to work on a leg that looked like a ham stolen from the rotisserie and chewed frantically by starving dogs. Little fountains of blood fizzed here and there, and groans of agony emphasized the depth of the man's pain. Every so often, he'd extend a quivering arm, as if reaching for the hand of God, and it was anybody's guess whether blood or piss had soaked what was left of this trousers. I had to doubt the wisdom of Doc's gallant effort. There was no way the guy was going to survive.

By the time he had done what he could, a medevac rolled in, rotors smacking the sky. Doc helped the more ambulatory of the two onto a lowered litter. He finished plugging leaks in the other one, and when the litter returned he worked his hands under the dying man's back and flexed for the heave-ho. It took two awkward tries to load the wheezing, slippery wreckage onto the stretcher. When it was done, he sat back for a minute and rested, his blood-coated hands dangling over his knees, sweat steadily dripping from his brow. The chopper cranked in its cargo, set pitch, then whisked away to the re-assembly plant a mangled mass that only moments before had been a fundamentally defect-free human being.

When it was over, I realized I was still staring at the wet spot in the dirt. I hadn't been prepared for a crash course in human anatomy, and I found myself transfixed. I was struck by the savagery of it, but at the same time, I felt a sense of detachment that comes with relative safety, as if such things only happened to others. I was learning and learning fast, and so far, not at my own expense.

Littlefield's voice broke the trance. "Mechanics only on the ground. Any ARVNs try to dismount, break their legs."

The lieutenant's track was made operable and we moved out. Roberts, for one, ranted about it the rest of the day, encouraged by nods and grunts and "Right ons." He was right. Their recklessness had cost the ARVNs plenty and jeopardized everybody else. I knew why the South Vietnamese weren't straining themselves to help us win their war, but why they were so careless was a mystery.

Word came down later that the mangled South Vietnamese gave his last gasp sometime before touchdown at Cu Chi.

10

Kiss of Fire

AKs rip the night
Senses take flight
Death walks the land
Points a bony hand
Who's turn tonight?

—RONNIE CRONE, "NIGHTS"

March 1970. 25th Infantry Division. Near the Hobo Woods.

My clothes faded and my skin color went from white to red to brown. My dogtags got demoted to a place within the laces of my non-polished boots, and I learned to make passable goulash from outcast C-rations. I requisitioned my own floppy bush hat and acquired a small steel ammo box to store toothbrush, mail, and wallet. A tubular aluminum bracelet hung fashionably from my right wrist and most of my fatigue shirts were now sleeveless. Wearing underwear, a sure ticket for crotch fungus, was a thing of the past.

I sat on the track with Abbott, John, Smitty from 1-3, and his buddy Carl, watching the sun swell and stretch as it mashed itself into the horizon.

Abbott took a long sip on his soda, then answered my question about how come we hadn't been killing gooks. "It's like this, Rook," he said. "The dinks are crafty little rodents. They don't stay in one place long enough to

83

get a good fix on 'em. All we can do is chase 'em and harass 'em till they give it up and go into hiding or go someplace else."

"Then we start looking for them all over again," Carl said. He was a lanky country boy who had never learned a mean word. He seemed to take whatever came his way with a nod and a smile, and he had a habit of running a hand through his wheat-colored hair when he talked.

"It's called the perpetual-motion strategy," Smitty said. "It's designed to keep us in gookville forever." Casey Smith was classic California—blond, golden, blue-eyed. If it hadn't been for rules, he'd have brought along a surfboard in case we conquered a beach. He was smart and confident but a thinker who was nearly impossible to rile. The word "LOVE" in swirling pink letters adorned the stock of his M16.

"Forever chasing gooks," John said tiredly, more to himself than anyone.

"Forever for you and the Rook, maybe, but not for me," Abbott said, perking up.

"Here it comes," Carl said, shaking his head.

An accordion grin split Abbott's face and his thick brows began to dance. "In exactly ninety-nine days, I am leaving this shithole for good."

John fired a warning look. "Don't start it, asswipe. And stop staring at me with that Howdy Doody happy-face."

"Dig it. Ninety-eight and a wake-up. You are lookin' at a two-digit midget. I'm gettin' so short I can't hold a long conversation."

John, eight months from salvation, leaned forward and said stonily, "Ninety-eight and a wake-up don't . . . mean . . . nothin'."

"Ninety-nine days, old man. Ninety-nine days." Now it was a jingle. "Any day now I'll be needin' a ladder to get on and off this track."

"Keep it up, by God, and the day your chopper's due, I'm gonna drive off and leave your ass when you squat for one of your short-timer shits. And knock off the 'old man' crap."

"Oooooh, big threat, old man."

John lurched, but Mike hopped off the track, still laughing. Too tired to give chase, John settled back and pulled a Winston from a crumpled pack. "Just be thinking about that long hump back to Cu Chi, Mikey-boy," he hollered over his shoulder.

The company was somewhere north of Trung Lap, scouring the wilderness that skirted the Hobo Woods. Enemy lurked, proven in the wee hours that night when an AP from 2nd Platoon killed four VC that slinked by their position. The next day, a sizable cache was found, but without any VC to go with it. An hour was killed waiting for choppers to make the trip and haul off the bounty. From there, it was more of the same: roaming no-man's-land like cops on patrol.

And the beat goes on. Yeah, the beat goes on. Sonny and Cher hung in my head like that until we had worked our way back to an area northeast of Cu Chi, where it was announced that the company was headed to secure LZ Devin, the fire-support base just off Highway 1. At this, I felt a wave of relief. We had just gotten word that our sister company, Charlie, lost an entire squad to a booby-trapped 250-pound bomb, the most dreaded kind of news. Getting out of the field could only improve the state of our nerves.

I had spent considerable time perfecting my image of this mythical artillery base, and with orders to rotate with Bravo at the little outpost near the village of Go Dau Ha, I was elated at the prospect of better digs, even if it was temporary.

My fantasy LZ Devin was a place of hot food and cold beverages, where men go when higher-ups act on the knowledge that human endurance has limits. It was a place without bugs, where breezes rustled shade trees and where time was set aside for naps. My LZ Devin was a place that would soothe what ailed me.

When we entered the gate, what I saw instead looked like an on-location Hollywood movie set. Somehow we had been transported to North Africa and were about to be cast in a remake of *Tobruk*. There was no other explanation for what confronted me. The so-called base we clanked in to, only fifteen miles from Cu Chi, was a decrepit, sun-bleached eyesore no more than a hundred yards across. Its main components were deteriorating sandbags and drooping concertina wire holding up rusty tin cans. The hazy air inside did not circulate. It stood motionless and heavy, like transparent rubber, too thick to draw fully into the lungs. Eroding bunkers with frayed skins leaked sand from wavy walls, and resident artillerymen looked like demented sun-worshiping mutants, wearing only boots and shorts and hats and dazed expressions. The surrounding terrain was desert and scrub from here to eternity; only the dunes were missing. Overhead, a smirking sun glowed white-hot, urging us to park and sit a spell.

As soon as the tracks were parked, they cracked the whip and organized us into chain gangs charged with filling sandbags and replacing old wire while impersonating broiled trout. For several days in a row, my glands set new records for pumping out salt, and I came to realize that without the oxygen-deprived shade of a grimy bunker and access to the outdoor shower, I stood a fair chance of being transformed into a six-foot serving of overcooked sausage. At least in the Filhol, we could cause air flow with movement. Here, we were a collection of Cool Hand Lukes confined to the Box—never mind that we already had our minds right.

Emmons left. His replacement was Stan Spencer, an FNG shake-'n'-bake sergeant with what quickly proved to be a hard head. Emmons had been surly but respected. Spencer, wasting no time, showed a preference for stubbornness where simple common sense would do. Luckily, the structure of the squad imposed limits on power, which would help, but because he equated rank with uncompromising authority, he had trouble with the concept of shared say-so. I speculated that he would be told to either get with the program or get fucked sooner rather than later.

The days at Devin became a blur as we toiled under the sun, spitting sand and lacerating knuckles on concertina. The upshot, if it could be called that, was that Spencer soon found the wisdom in toning it down, though he still showed difficulty when making weighty decisions, such as whose turn it was to burn shit.

March had become April, and a respectable rebuild of Devin's outer perimeter was well underway when word came down that a Ranger team sent to recon the Renegade Woods had landed smack in the jaws of an NVA Regiment and ended up in dire straits. The lieutenant called us together at sunset with the news that we were headed up there in the morning.

"The Wolfhounds moved in yesterday, and it's been a dogfight," he said. "We'll be on-station initially as a backup." That's all for now. Get your weapons cleaned and top off your tanks."

This got a reaction from those in the know, who had trouble digesting the notion that the Hounds would need help squaring away anything they ran into.

"I'm way too short for this shit," Roberts said. Nods and sounds of agreement followed. Only McDonald seemed unimpressed. "Don't start shakin' in your boots yet," he said. "Could be somethin', could be nothin'. We won't know till we get there."

I asked John about it. He described the Renegades as a maze of wooded thickets and clearings that was a known incubator and operational hub for the NVA. It hugged the Vam Co Dong River on the east and was close to the Cambodian border to the west. Triple Deuce had ransacked the place more than once. As for our part in what was going down, he stood with McDonald. We would have to wait and see. I wanted to conjure up some expectations, but couldn't get a foothold. Even so, the prospect of seeing action for the first time was energizing, and any reason to get out of Devin, even to a dangerous unknown destination, was welcome.

Being ground pounders, we weren't privy to much, including the size or extent of any operation. We were only there to knock 'em down and count bodies. Questions were always asked, but answers were usually short and vague. We were the dogs; higher-ups held our chains, and when they said, "Sic 'em!" and turned us loose, we charged. Ignorance is bliss, they say, and it would be many years before I learned the whole story of what happened in the Renegade Woods during the first week of April 1970.

It had begun with two Ranger teams, a total of thirteen men, who were dispatched to evaluate reports of new enemy activity there. The two Hueys they rode were escorted by a Cobra gunship and a light observation helicopter (a LOH, or "Loach"). Their insertion point was a clearing that contained two bomb craters, a well, a dead tree, and some fresh footprints. From the LZ, one team stepped off toward the western treeline, led by the team leader (a lieutenant) and two others. They had moved only a few meters when machine-gun fire snapped from the bushes. One of the Rangers was hit and the handset on the lieutenant's radio was shattered. The third man's weapon was ruined by a ricochet. The lieutenant and the weaponless team member managed to take out the machine gun with grenades, but before they could access better cover, new fire erupted from the brush to their front and flank. They were seriously outnumbered and dangerously exposed. Knowing they would die in place if they didn't move, the three of them scrabbled to the east.

The assistant team leader used his radio to request fire from the Cobra on the western treeline and to ask for reinforcements. The lieutenant decided to split the teams, using one to provide covering fire while he led the other into the eastern treeline in hopes of maneuvering around the NVA. It had an effect, and the incoming tapered off momentarily. The Cobra made strafing passes while the choppers that had dropped the Rangers into the frying pan circled back with the intent of picking up the wounded, but the ground fire was too intense. They hauled ass to Cu Chi to get help instead.

The lieutenant's team made it to the eastern treeline, but they were immediately hit from all directions by withering fire that ripped through the underbrush. The other team was chased into one of the bomb craters by heavy fire that flashed from the northern treeline, killing their team leader and his sergeant when an RPG slammed into them. Their radioman was left badly wounded and the only remaining radio was destroyed. The rest of the team was isolated, pinned down, and bleeding.

In the face of a grim reality, the lieutenant ordered his team back into the clearing so they could consolidate in the crater. Firing on the run, they scrambled into the open. Along the way, the lieutenant managed to grab the wounded radioman and drag him along. Miraculously, they tumbled into the pit without taking additional hits.

From the lip of the crater, the Rangers laid out a high volume of fire, destroying the RPG team and one of the NVA machine-gun positions. Even so, they were easy pickings. They had nowhere to go and were running dangerously low on ammo. The lieutenant salvaged the handset from the mangled radio, which enabled him to fix his own and re-establish commo with the choppers. He called for more air support, a reactionary force, and a medevac.

The Cobra chucked the last of its rockets into the woods, but stayed on station, hoping its presence alone would help keep NVA heads down. The Loach expended all of its machine-gun rounds, then prepared to try to extract the wounded Ranger, figuring to leave one of its gunners on the ground to make room. That plan was aborted when the two Hueys, now as far toward Cu Chi as the old French Factory, realized there was not time to get there and back and turned around. They would attempt an extraction of the entire team or go down trying.

At the crater, the Rangers' situation was critical, with fire coming from all sides. One of their M60 machine guns had exhausted its ammo, including belts scavenged from the dead, and the gunner was reduced to using his standard issue Colt .45. Their M79 grenade launcher had also run dry, and the remaining machine gun soon jammed. In an idiotic display of bravery, an NVA soldier stepped into the open to toss a grenade. He was killed instead by GI hand grenades, but they were running out of those as well.

The firefight had raged for nearly an hour at this point, and annihilation loomed. Overhead, the Cobra and the Loach circled impotently. But before the NVA could cash in, one of the returning Hueys appeared over the treetops and swooped in brazenly, touching down within fifteen feet of the crater. Knowing it was do or die, the lieutenant ordered everybody aboard, even though the chopper was taking hits and could explode or be rushed at any second. The door gunners helped even things up by hosing the woods around them with a steady cracking staccato of machine-gun fire.

Using maximum torque and suffering severe vertical vibration, the pilot got the bird airborne with a mighty struggle and turned toward Cu Chi. On board were eleven Rangers and a crew of four, some of them clinging to the skids. They had to land at Trang Bang to provide first aid to the more seriously wounded Ranger, but it was a vain effort. He would later die from his wounds. The two dead had been left behind for recovery by a reactionary force.

The 2/27th Wolfhounds, the division's junkyard dogs, immediately invaded the neighborhood to retrieve the dead and start some shit. They weren't disappointed. In fact, like the Rangers, they bit off all the NVA they could chew. Company C troops were ambushed within minutes of insertion as their platoons followed separate paths toward the Ranger contact area, suffering several killed and multiple wounded. They were pinned down and stayed that way for six hours. Two Huey gunships arrived to save the day, but one of them was promptly shot down. Luckily, it made a soft landing and its crew was rescued by the other gunship. Company B was then inserted to reinforce their buddies, but they, too, were ambushed and temporarily pinned down when snipers killed their lead element's RTO and their FO. Ultimately, the Wolfhounds were forced into a fighting withdrawal as ammo ran low. Artillery fire rained in, and while Wolfhounds Company A was inserted nearby, the other two, B and C, consolidated for the night and were resupplied as the sun was about to set. Gunships and flare ships remained on-station during the night, but there was no additional contact.

April 3 began with air strikes and a napalm fire bath on selected targets. Ground action was persistent but involved small pockets of NVA. The Wolfhounds, reinforced by Bravo Company of Triple Deuce, finally reached the Ranger contact area. After recovering the dead, all three Wolfhound companies established a perimeter there from which to operate, ringed by the Triple Deuce APCs. Afternoon sweeps produced large caches of ammunition and documents identifying the opposition as the 271 NVA Regiment. More contact followed, but the North Vietnamese were temporarily fragmented and got the short end of the stick in these engagements.

On the morning of April 4, Company A, Triple Deuce, was deployed to join the fray, rumbling out of LZ Devin at sunrise. That night, Wolfhound Companies A and B consolidated in a large clearing, from which they later split up into platoon-size ambush patrols. B Company chose a nearby clearing, with 1st Platoon set up in an L-shape behind a low dike at the clearing entrance. The other platoons were in the same clearing to the north and northeast of them. Just after dark, 1st Platoon detected movement and then saw an unidentified element moving toward them from the west. Their lieutenant sought clearance to make sure they weren't friendlies, but was soon informed by his men that it was in fact a massive column of heavily armed NVA. The lieutenant initially ordered his men to lay low and let them pass. The enemy troops were so close that they stepped over the wires strung between the ambushers and their Claymore mines. At one point they paused for nearly a full minute to let stragglers catch up, standing just a few feet from the Wolfhound platoon. The column of NVA now stretched for three hundred yards. As the rear element finally entered the clearing, the Wolfhound platoon leader ordered his men to shift to the opposite side of the dike and open fire on the column as it slowly disappeared into the woods to the east. Their sister platoons nearby simultaneously unleashed a crossfire and a savage battle ensued.

Company A, Triple Deuce, standing by outside the woods, was called to react.

———•———

En route to the Renegades the morning of April 4, we underlings knew only that the Rangers and the Wolfhounds had tangled with the NVA and at some point might need help. Nothing more. We crossed the Vam Co Dong River bridge at Go Dau Ha where the road forked and followed the pavement west for a few miles before swinging north into the outback. Once in the area, we set up a perimeter and waited to see what would happen next.

Energy levels were high. It was hot, but there was no bitching. C-rats were brought topside and in a few seconds greedy hands had snatched the cartons bare. This sparked a session of bartering between 1-3 and 1-4, led by McDonald and Smitty. I knew I was out of my league, so I just watched. Carl was hoarding canned peaches, but it wasn't enough for a buyout of the beans and franks held by Shukas, who was not swayed. Mike then advised Ridgeway that if the two of them held out with their pound cake and fruit cocktail, they could end up in the driver's seat. Dave Santa-Cruz told Mike he was crazy and that more likely he and Ridgeway would wind up with ham & motherfuckers. At that point, all bets were off, and everybody settled for what they already had in hand.

"Nam sucks," Smitty proclaimed. He worked a P-38 can opener around a tin of boned chicken.

Shukas and Doc, mouths full, grunted agreement. Others nodded. I wanted to ask questions about the Renegades, then decided to wait. For now, Smitty had said it all.

We stayed in a so-called blocking position outside the woods until late afternoon, then shifted to a night defensive position closer to the treeline. A short rainstorm rolled in, turning the ground we occupied soggy, but moved on in time for fatigues to dry before nightfall. The lieutenant called a meeting after chow to share another crumb of information.

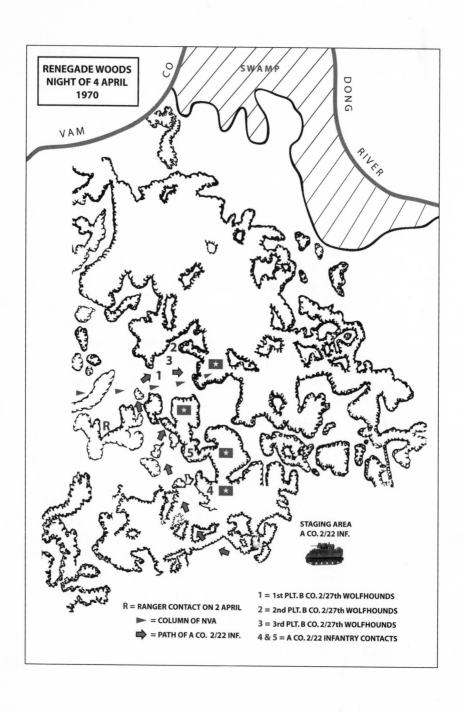

RENEGADE WOODS
NIGHT OF 4 APRIL
1970

CO

SWAMP

DONG

VAM

RIVER

2

3

1

R

5

4

STAGING AREA
A CO. 2/22 INF.

R = RANGER CONTACT ON 2 APRIL

= COLUMN OF NVA

= PATH OF A CO. 2/22 INF.

1 = 1st PLT. B CO. 2/27th WOLFHOUNDS
2 = 2nd PLT. B CO. 2/27th WOLFHOUNDS
3 = 3rd PLT. B CO. 2/27th WOLFHOUNDS
4 & 5 = A CO. 2/22 INFANTRY CONTACTS

"We're here to react, and from the look of things, it won't be a long wait."

There were murmurs. I saw Dave nudge Smitty.

"There really four hundred gooks in there like we heard, lieutenant?" McDonald said it plain and simple, as if curious more than anything.

"Nobody's stopped to count, but there's beaucoup. And they're the kind with uniforms and guns that shoot straight. The Wolfhounds have been knocking heads with them off and on for three days."

We cleaned weapons and watched the horizon coax the sun toward a new day someplace else. As twilight turned to dusk, my stomach got queasy and twitched with nervousness. Nobody had to tell me I was on deck to be shot at.

I busied myself re-cleaning my weapon and dusting off magazines, even though I felt more like a pretender than a real player. Conflicting emotions broke like rotten eggs thrown against my insides, and I didn't know which ones to heed and which to ignore. It was as if I had just been pulled out of the stands and shoved into the bullpen with pros who assumed I belonged there. The truth was, I didn't know if I could measure up. I felt about as much confidence here as I would facing down Fergie Jenkins from the batter's box at Wrigley Field.

Trip flares, RPG screens, and Claymores stayed on board. Rumors, flavored with bits of fact, spread around the perimeter like unreported brush fires. All the while we sat, waiting. It got dark. A lot of cigarettes were smoked.

Dave and Jim drifted over from 1-3, stirring air that swirled with mosquitoes. Next to me, McDonald applied oil lovingly to his machine gun, as if in a different world. He looked up at Dave with a twisted grin.

"Between the two of us, we're gonna bust some fuckin' heads, right, Santa-Cruz?"

Dave simply smiled and gave a cursory thumbs up. Shukas didn't react at all. I figured it must be standard McDonald bravado, and I tried to think of something off the subject to say when Sergeant Pitt appeared.

"Commo working okay?" he asked.

"Loud and clear," John answered.

"McDonald, is your Fifty in top shape?"

"Is a frog's ass waterproof?"

Invisible Willie laughed at this, and so did I.

"A yes or no will do."

"Roger-dodger, Sergeant Roger. It is clean, oiled, and ready to grind up gooks. The entire squad, in fact, is ready to rumble."

"Good. Now listen up. The Hounds have set up platoon-size ambushes, so it's only a matter of time. We'll be point platoon. Keinroth, how much night driving experience have you had?"

John rubbed his chin. "Night driving? Hmmm. That would be, let's see . . . zero. Yep, zero. I guess it'll have to do, though, won't it?"

Sergeant Pitt didn't find this funny, though I wasn't sure it was meant to be.

Pitt moved out, leaving behind a silence that hung there for a minute like a noose. Mike swept it aside by calling after him. "Better make sure old man Keinroth cleans those Coke bottles hangin' across his nose if he's drivin'."

Pitt just shook his head and kept going.

"I'm gonna get the sumbitch!" John growled.

Abbott was already on the move, circling behind 1-3. "Come on, grandpa," he said.

John sprang, but was stopped cold by faint popping sounds and tracers spitting out of the canopy a good ways off. All hands scrambled on deck, zippering flak jackets and strapping down helmets. Engines cranked and came alive. Tarnished Zippos were pulled out for last-cigarette rituals.

Jaws clamped, we waited for the word. Five pulse-throbbing minutes ticked off. I felt my teeth grind and strained to keep my nerves holstered. Meanwhile, the firefight spread. Still we waited, and watched, and stirred. They wouldn't give us a go. Just when I thought my jaw might fracture, the lieutenant's voice crackled over the track's speaker from 1-1 and cut the tension like a machete through bamboo. "Let's roll, First Platoon."

The track lurched forward and clattered toward the treeline abreast of 1-1. We then swung left to traverse the curtain of undergrowth. I wasn't sure if this maneuver was a proven tactic or if we were sticking our chins out, but at this point, I supposed, it didn't matter. As we moved along, I gazed into the darkness, trying to swallow a knot slowly clogging my throat. After a few minutes, we executed a right face and churned a new path directly toward the woods.

We plowed into the thicket and were met with a web of vines and branches that nearly jerked the bunch of us off the deck. Only ten feet separated our tracks, but we couldn't see each other through the snarl. It was all we could manage to hold onto gear while stiff-arming the foliage. John kept it slow, and after a minute, we pulled loose into a clearing. 1-1 was to our left front. We broke through another hedgerow, less stubborn this time, and John accelerated to catch up, but halfway across the opening, waiting North Vietnamese welcomed us to their hideout with a spray of sizzling fire that streaked out of the treeline in a horizontal shower.

Incoming rounds pinged the track like hail against glass. My stomach jerked, and instinctively, I plunged inside the open cargo hatch with the others. After a couple of seconds, I realized I was staring at everybody else's knees. For a minute, I couldn't comprehend why they would stand there fully exposed from the armpits up. Hot brass flew everywhere. The roar was deafening.

My circuits were scrambled up like backlash on a well-oiled casting reel, so I acted on the only thought maneuvering through the tangle: *Shoot back!* I sucked in some fast breaths to ease the ball-peen hammer bashing my chest from the inside and stood up. Somehow we had gotten trapped inside a fireworks factory ignited by arsonists. I flinched against the brilliant green streaks darting toward me through the glowing red of our counterfire. Lead flew from McDonald's .50 in heavy thuds. Roberts stitched the underbrush with his M60. On each side of me, fountains of brass flipped through the air in wiggly arcs from M16s on full auto. I started firing like a lunatic, taking orders from the voice of a drill sergeant shouting inside my head. Bullets popped and ricocheted like swarms of electrified bees, but I refused to duck. Now that I had put my chips on the table, I was welded in position and fixated on playing out the hand.

I expended six clips before it struck me that it took longer to change out than to empty, and I forced myself to use short bursts instead, more carefully aiming at the source of the enemy fire. The slower pace helped my head clear. It also allowed the reality of what was happening to catch up with me, unleashing a surge of fear that broadsided me with the force of a dump truck through a red light. The tiny green missiles indiscriminately whizzing by were capable of burning a path from one side of my skull to the other at roughly 3,000 feet per second, and thinking about dying in a split second here and now numbed my churning innards like Novocaine.

Yet all I could do was keep firing. 1-2 and 1-3 were in the woods just to our rear, adding their two cents. The rest of the company was out of sight and earshot.

Flares went up from 1-1 to our front.

Spencer took the clue. "Get some flares up!" he hollered. Mike ducked below and grabbed a handful of star clusters. He popped a few and resumed firing.

"Throw me some Sixty ammo!" Roberts yelled.

Mike ducked below again and hauled up a can of rounds. AKs cracked like strings of Black-Cats. I heard McDonald yell, "Motherfuckerrrrs!" Apparently, he was fed up with their refusal to be bullied by his .50 and figured a cussing out might help. John stood in the driver's hatch, methodically plunking grenade rounds. He said nothing, asked for nothing. He fired, reloaded, and fired with the speed of a seasoned assembly worker, blowing out chunks of trees.

"More Fifty ammo!" McDonald was barely heard through the racket.

"More ammo, goddamnit!" The .50 stopped.

"Gimme some fuckin' ammo!"

Ridgeway hoisted him a box from a rack on the deck, and while McDonald reloaded, it occurred to me there had been no order to dismount and take up firing positions. The answer came at a lull in the firing when John dropped into the driver's seat and we started moving again. The ambush was an obvious attempt to keep us from our primary objective, and Littlefield wasn't going to be sidetracked indefinitely.

New rounds flashed from the .50, and we all stayed tight on the trigger until we crashed through the next hedgerow. By then, the incoming had dried up. The whole episode had lasted about five minutes. The waltz was over, at least on that dance floor.

We kept moving. My ears rang fiercely. The only other sounds were the rattle of diesel engines and the clicks and clacks of reloading.

"Everybody okay?" Spencer's voice sounded muffled. I couldn't tell if my ears were stopped up or if he actually thought he might give away our position by speaking up. Amazingly, nobody on the track was hit. 1-2 and 1-3 tracks closed the distance in the next clearing.

Rottin "8" No. II.
LZ Devin.

Author (center)
at Fort Polk,
Louisiana,
summer 1969.

A "Zippo" works out in the Filhol area of operations near Cu Chi.

155mm mobile howitzer fires artillery from LZ Devin.

Staging area outside the Renegade Woods.

Morning sweep in Renegade Woods following action on April 4, 1970.

3rd Squad's APC in Go Dau Ha village. Dave Santa-Cruz in center of photo.

Members of 1st Platoon's 3rd and 4th Squads at LZ Devin. Author kneeling center.

Demo man (author), sets a charge on an unexploded 155mm artillery round.

Red ant nest common to wooded areas like the Renegade Woods.

An evening storm brews in the Filhol area of operations.

Interrogation of Viet Cong prisoner in the Filhol AO. 1-3 track is in immediate background, with Dave Santa-Cruz behind the .50-caliber machine gun.

APCs of the Triple Deuce en route to Cambodia on 5 May 1970.

Huey helicopters at a pickup zone near Cambodia.

Locals work the land in the shadow of Nui Ba Dinh mountain near Tay Ninh.

1-3 track works its way toward the Rach Cai Bach River en route to Cambodia.

Engineers work to complete a floatation bridge across the Rach Cai Bach.

The lieutenant gives the forward-ho signal as 1st Platoon tracks prepare to cross the bridge.

Engineers watch as dozens of tracked vehicles cross the 100-foot-long bridge into Cambodia.

Author on 1-4 track as it crosses the river into Cambodia.

Some tracks in the 1/5th Mech were mounted with miniguns in place of .50-caliber machine guns.

NVA encampment torched by Alpha Company, Triple Deuce, just inside Cambodia.

A much-needed breather is taken at an Alpha Company bivouac in an abandoned Cambodian village.

Alpha Company moves across the Cambodian landscape in columns of two.

One of Charlie Company's APCs is airlifted out following an ambush.

Escorting a convoy of artillerymen near Krek, Cambodia.

Typical Cambodian hootch, this one vacated due to fighting between U.S. and NVA forces.

Alpha Company moves into a valley north of Krek, Cambodia, en route to the "body farm," an NVA basecamp destroyed by U.S. B-52 bombers.

NVA shot by Alpha Company's lead track on Ambush Alley. Note Chicom grenade on belt.

One of approximately 150 dead NVA at the "body farm," this one killed by a falling tree.

Typical view of Ambush Alley, south of Krek, Cambodia.

Taking shelter from the rain, near Krek, Cambodia.

Portable bridge brought in to span a muddy creek bed near the south end of Ambush Alley.

One of numerous Charlie Company APCs destroyed by RPG fire along Ambush Alley.

NVA bunker discovered near Krek, Cambodia.

Damage inflicted by an RPG on Alpha Company's "Maniacs" in Cambodia.

An NVA prisoner taken on Ambush Alley not far from Krek, Cambodia.

The sharp crack of AK fire lashed out of the brush in another stream. It looked to be an exact repeat, as if somebody had rewound the film in hopes of improving the plot. John went back to launching aerodynamic grenades while McDonald pumped .50-cal slugs into the brush like a one-man wrecking crew. Streaks of red and green intertwined through the blackness like levitating pick-up sticks, zigzagging erratically.

"Fuck!" I blurted out. The relief I'd just felt had been stolen. Now I was pissed off. The little shits must have calculated avenues of approach and then waited for whoever came along. They were probably dug in, too. That would explain how they'd hung with us for more than a minute or two.

Spencer yelled to get the sky lit up. Ridgeway shoved a fistful of parachute flares at me and I fired them off. The light brightened the clearing but made the shadows from the trees longer and darker. At least we could see how the treeline was configured. Somebody tossed a hissing canister of red smoke that hit the ground and billowed thickly. The incoming slacked off, and we could hear the thump of rotors coming our way. Somebody had been in touch with a roving Cobra, and as the smoke swirled and spread, what was left of the shooting dwindled to a quick stop, like a faucet cranked closed in a hurry.

Lieutenant Yearout was on the horn. "Get moving. Our buddies up there need some room."

The buzz of a minigun ripped the air like a well-greased chainsaw in our wake, pulverizing the jungle floor with shimmering columns of red that cascaded down in a vivid display of horror art. I wanted to cheer, but realized it would be a rookie move. Besides, the job on the ground wasn't done.

Our machine guns raked a couple more hedgerows, but were answered with silence. I figured the NVA blocking units had finally headed for deep cover under the torrent of murderous fire. Up-trail, the original firefight persisted, vomiting its leftovers skyward, and we upped the pace. Word was passed that a platoon of Wolfhounds had ambushed a column of two hundred NVA and were barely holding on. Damn good thing that we were closing the gap.

"Hey, Ross, you did all right," Ridgeway yelled. "You, too, Willie."

"Thanks," I said. Willie just nodded. On the surface, I may have looked as calm as Audie Murphy, but inside my nerves whipped and sparked like downed power lines. I knew it was going to take some time for all this agony and ecstasy to ease off.

"How about reloading some magazines?" McDonald interjected. "There might just be a gook or two still at large."

I saw Spencer glare at McDonald, realizing the slack in his leadership had just been taken up. "That means everybody," he added half-heartedly.

A quick inventory revealed that thirteen of my twenty-two clips were dry. I grabbed a box of rounds from below and got busy replenishing magazines while the tracks navigated the constricted corridors that crisscrossed the thickets.

We were close to the trapped Wolfhounds, and the LT held us up long enough to get his bearings, then turned toward a weak spot in the treeline. Tracks from other platoons materialized behind us.

McDonald looked back over his shoulder. "Hey, Ross, you still with us?"

"I'm still here."

"You may not be rookie this time tomorrow."

"I'll settle for still being a rookie."

"Don't worry about it. We got 'em by the balls. All we gotta do now is squeeeze!"

I admired his confidence, but couldn't even think about puffing up my own chest.

We muscled our way into the next clearing and again pulled up. The Wolfhounds were one clearing away, just around a bend. The likely source of fire keeping them pinned down was to our right flank at about one o'clock, so we let it rip, walloping the woods with an avalanche of lead that I later reckoned would leave NVA survivors hard pressed to exaggerate when writing their memoirs.

Our guns perforated the thickets for couple of minutes, wrecking trees and battering Ho Chi Minh's best. Communist rounds dried up fast, and once the cease-fire order was given, there wasn't a sound except for sporadic pops coming from the abused woods.

Flares went up. We waited. McDonald, his gun smoking, craned his neck around, hyped like a pill popper. "Got-damn, that was righteous! We'll find bodies there tomorrow, guar-un-fuckin'-teed." He swiveled back around and the track jerked forward. I snapped in a new clip, still not ready to celebrate.

Our tracks pushed into the contested woodland just far enough to test resistance and check for pockets of NVA playing possum. None was found, but we did glimpse a scattering of discarded gear. It looked like the NVA had abandoned the Wolfhounds and, for the moment, the idea of unifying their piss-ant country.

From there, we swung to the left through a narrow passage and continued into the defended clearing. As we rolled in under wobbly flarelight, the beleaguered Wolfhounds came into view. They were strung out along an old dike that cut across the clearing. It was a poor excuse for cover, and they had crowded up to it like piglets latched to a sow's belly. As we formed a barrier between the dike and the treeline, they loosened their grip and came to life a few at a time. They had been only minutes from firing dry, and they glanced around warily, as if untrusting of their good fortune. Once those doubts dissipated, they got up and greeted us like emissaries from a merciful God. Their platoon leader approached 1-1 with a grin splitting his face and borrowed a line from an old movie: "Boy, are we glad to see you guys."

We dismounted, mingled. Littlefield joined the two lieutenants.

The Wolfhounds had half a dozen wounded; our company had two. Dustoffs were called and a mad minute was ordered. Once again, the treeline was thrashed, just for good measure. When it was done, we shared ammo, water, and sodas with the exhausted and dehydrated Hounds. By the time everybody was back in fighting shape, the medevacs arrived, escorted by two more Cobras. The jungle popped and belched from the latest whipping, but it was better safe than sorry. With so many NVA, a counterattack was not out of the question.

The Wolfhounds regrouped. The tracks were rearranged into a more secure perimeter, and we continued to pummel the bushes with mad minutes every hour until daylight.

At sunup, a general sweep was conducted. The underbrush to the front and flank of the Wolfhounds looked like an army surplus store hit by an Oklahoma twister. Bullet-riddled NVA were found, along with multiple blood trails. Slung all the way through the next hedgerow was an assortment of gear ranging from sandals and pistol belts to backpacks and weapons. Later on, nine bodies and two RPG launchers were found at the site of our first contact.

We returned to our blocking position outside the woods and spent the afternoon resting. With my first firefight tucked under my belt, I felt thankful for surviving and for not fucking up. I also marveled at the exhilaration I'd felt once we linked with the Wolfhounds. I knew it was a feeling that few would ever experience. The army trains recruits to think they're invincible. I now understood why some of them come to believe it.

Our rest was short. Not long before sundown, word was passed to expect a human-wave attack sometime during the night. It wasn't explained where the information came from, but after what we'd already witnessed, there were few doubters in the peanut gallery. All APCs toting 90mm recoilless rifles commenced digging foxholes between the tracks to set them up. That included 1-4, which squarely faced the woods, so we got busy. Four of us toiled for an hour digging a substantial pit, using the pitched dirt to create a berm in front of the position. We scrounged a spare tripod, disengaged the M60 from the track, and mounted the machine gun on the berm next to a wooden crate full of ammo. We set the recoilless rifle up beside the pit with a stack of Flechette rounds next to it. I had seen a pack of the little steel Flechette darts back at Devin and had no trouble believing the tales of VC being completely shredded by their blasts.

I should have been reassured. Instead, the idea of needing the 90 shoved the elation I'd been basking in completely off the stage, replacing it with horrific images of hand-to-hand combat while being overrun. Our weapons only gave us leverage as long as the heathens were held back. If the perimeter was breached, we could forget air support, grenades, Claymores, and everything else but rifles and possibly machine guns. From there, it would quickly boil down to a knife fight. The thought of hundreds of suicidal NVA charging out of the treeline like stampeding buffalo was just plain terrifying.

Guard was quadrupled, with one sentry behind the .50 and three in each foxhole to man machine guns and recoilless rifles. We doubled up on trip flares and Claymores and sent out no listening posts or APs.

I ended up in the pit with Mike and Steve for a three-hour watch, though time was not a factor. Even afterward, I was so wired I barely dozed. When darkness finally began to fade on the eastern horizon, the likelihood of an attack faded with it, and my over-tensed muscles finally relaxed. Sleep came quickly but briefly while the perimeter guards remained alert until full sunrise. For reasons known only to Littlefield, no mad minutes had been ordered during the night.

A full sweep of the woods was soon underway and continued throughout the day. This time, the clearings were mostly avoided in favor of breaking brush. Some of it was so congested with wait-a-minute vines that all of us took a beating. Walking would have been better, but there was too much real estate to cover for a dismounted recon to be practical.

"Stop goddamnit! Stop!"

I looked through the switches in my face and saw Steve teetering, his upper body in the grip of looping vines. Another two feet of progress and he would've been pulled off the deck. John held up until Steve freed himself and we inched on. After an hour of ducking and dodging through the unyielding tangle, attitudes had pretty much gone south. At least we had shade.

Eventually, the double canopy thinned. A short break was called so we could clear debris from the tracks and regroup. Once underway, thinking the worst was over, we hadn't moved another hundred yards when the track bulled into a hedgerow and dislodged a nest of tree-dwelling red ants that drenched us in a fiery shower.

"Ants! Son of a bitch!"

They swarmed over us, biting anywhere they found skin. I'd heard about them, but couldn't believe what I saw. There were thousands of them, maybe tens of thousands, and they were as angry as yellow-jackets on the warpath.

Men jumped to the ground, tearing at their clothes. Half the squad was soon naked, cussing and slapping like maniacs. The LT didn't have to get on the horn to know what had happened. His track was close enough to bear witness. A halt was called until things got under control and 1-4's deck had been swept off. For the rest of the day, we spent more time killing the hundreds still underfoot than watching out for NVA.

The North Vietnamese, meanwhile, had evidently withdrawn to their Cambodian sanctuary. The Renegades was a wrap, and we returned to Devin the next day. As bad as that was, it was better than being shot or eaten alive.

11

Walk Loudly and Carry a Big Stick

Vietnam was the first war ever fought without any censorship. Without censorship, things can get terribly confused in the public mind.

—GENERAL WILLIAM WESTMORELAND

April 1970. 25th Infantry Division. Go Dau Ha.

You could almost spit on Go Dau Ha from LZ Devin. It was a sizable ramshackle village at the juncture of Highways 1 and 22. Its only strategic importance was a bridge over the Vam Co Dong River which the VC used regularly for demolition practice. The platoon was dispatched there to secure the bridge until engineers showed up to fix the most recent damage. "Go-to-hell," as the ville was known, was a typical Vietnamese shantytown, with crumbling stucco buildings and tin-roof shacks supported by an economy that relied heavily on street-vendor profits and black marketeers. The main drag began where the bridge ended.

While Abbott and Ridgeway scavenged through a case of Cs in search of the least revolting meals, McDonald spotted an old gimp-legged Vietnamese hawking sandwiches on a nearby corner.

"Hey, papa-san, over here," he called, waving his arm in a wide circle.

The old geezer looked up, then hobbled over excitedly, pushing a rickety cart piled high with meats and vegetables. His wide grin exposed stumpy black teeth.

"How much for the deluxe submarine?"

"Special to numba one GI. One dolla."

"Too much. I'll give ya fifty piaster."

"No. No can do." The smile disappeared. He shook his head back and forth, like a child rejecting what would likely be forced on him anyway. "One dolla MPC, no piaster."

McDonald rubbed his chin, mulling it over. "Yeah, well . . . okay," he conceded, as if prepared to call the whole thing off. "But I want the works, got it? Everything." Then he held up a hand. "Check that. Everything but the crushed glass." He laughed at the joke. The Asian's smile returned, but it was a notch less friendly.

Ridgeway followed, signaling the old man.

"How you want sandwich?" he asked, eager to please at the prospect of multiple sales.

"Same-same," Steve said, "only no cucumbers and no mayo."

When it was done, our well-spent money had put the Vietnamese in a position to take the afternoon off. Between bites, little kids tried to sell us everything from questionable soda pop and trinkets to their frumpy sisters. I noticed a group of slouching, slick-haired adolescents—sleeves rolled up, cigarettes dangling—propped against a store front like a turf gang with nothing to fight over.

Ridgeway was checking them out, too.

"I wonder why nobody's told those draft dodgers their country needs them," he said.

"I wonder why nobody's told 'em James Dean is dead," McDonald said, his mouth stuffed.

"Every one of those punks are probably VC," Spencer added. He was carefully examining the contents of his lunch.

"Don't doubt it," Mike said.

"Can't trust any of 'em," John summed up, "young or old."

I stopped chewing. "Then why are we eating their damn sandwiches?" I stared at my sub as if it were a pipe bomb.

Abbott chomped down. "Cause we're hungry and these subs are outstanding." He let out a long burp. "Besides, they know we'd break their bones if they fucked with the food."

"Still can't trust the filthy mothers," McDonald advised. He then gob-bled the final three inches of his sub in one bite, chewing so hard I thought he might lose part of the finger he pushed it in with.

For reasons never explained, the platoon ended up spending the night inside an ARVN compound. It was a sad excuse for a fort, making Devin look modern in comparison. The bunkers were literally falling apart, and the piss tubes stunk so bad it was almost impossible to stand over one long enough to take a leak. Rodents, ignored by the Vietnamese, went about their business openly and unafraid. When it was time to bed down, my only choice was to find a bare spot of ground and give myself up to it. The place was smelly and depressing, and I hated the idea of staying even one night. I used my flak jacket for a pillow and spread out my poncho liner for a mat. After settling in on my back, I stared at the heavens until I dozed off. Sometime later, I was awakened when I sensed a warm weight on top of me. This brought me fully conscious, and I opened my eyes to find myself staring straight into the face of a rat the size of a housecat sitting on my chest, whiskers twitching. I was too stunned to move, and that was just as well, because after a few seconds he tromped across my left shoulder, brushing my face with his tail, and skittered off. I sat up and for the next half hour thought about what I could do to avoid sleep. I jerked awake just before sunrise, wondering how I had given up at some point without knowing it.

The first thing I noticed back at Devin was that no shade had been installed. This was countered by a warm-water dousing under the makeshift showers. Later, when dark settled over the land, a stiff breeze rose up to help hold the bugs back. For the first time since rotating there, it was almost tolerable.

I took a walk with 3rd Squad's Carl Petrowski and Jim Shukas on a quest to buy some weed from the company sniper, a Chicagoan named Renfro currently holed up in 2nd Platoon. Thin and blond, Kerry Renfro seemed to enjoy playing the part of a stone-cold hit man. From the get-go, he dominated the conversation with philosophical ramblings, including his belief that there wasn't a damn thing wrong with being ripped, any time, any place. He didn't ask to come to our party, and we didn't invite. On the way back, I mentioned how I hoped I'd never have to depend on anybody as half-baked as him.

Topside of 1-3, we smoked a little, snacked, and listened to AFVN on Shukas's radio until the sandman worked his magic. It was only the second time I'd ever smoked, and I had to face the fact that I wasn't cut out to be a doper. The stuff made me dizzy and sleepy, and I swore off of it then and there.

Roberts was now a memory. He had swapped places on the resupply chopper with a baby-faced kid named Vernon Gibbs, an Okie from a town not far from mine. For the second time, I was now shorter than somebody, and I was beginning to see how fast the pecking order could change in combat. After only a month, the squad had changed faces. I tried not to think about the seniority a couple of good gunfights might bring.

I dropped off quick, hoping the night would pass without an artillery fire mission. But sometime later, I was jarred from my bunk by a succession of explosions that sprayed dust from the timbers and shook the slats beneath me. "Damn it!" somebody groaned. The cannon cockers were on another firing frenzy, and each salvo peeled off another layer of nerves. Finally, I sat up, amazed to find some of my squadmates still asleep. When it finally stopped, it got so quiet I wondered if I'd gone deaf. I settled back down, but the anticipation of new blasts kept me from sleeping. I was beginning to see the whole thing as a sadistic ritual. For once, they stayed shut, but there was no way of knowing that, and it was nearly dawn before I drifted off, fantasizing about one-room cabins on mountaintops.

I woke up hungry and for the first time actually looked forward to a breakfast of powdered eggs and elastic toast. Outside the wire, an unusual number of Go Dau Ha locals with wares to sell hung around like used car salesmen on an overstocked lot. Management wasn't happy about it, but chasing them off had about the same effect as swiping at gnats.

As soon as we filed through the gate to start hanging wire, they swarmed around us. A scraggy eight-year-old ignored the fact I already had a low-mileage Timex that had taken a licking but kept on ticking.

"Hey, GI, you buy watch. Five dolla."

"I don't need a watch," I said. "Beat it."

"Okie-dokie. You buy watch, I souvenir you ring."

"I don't want a ring or a watch. Scram."

"Come on, numba one GI man. I make you special, only three dolla."

"Di-di mau, you little fart, before I kick your butt."

At that, he scampered away with a parting shot. "Fuck you, man. Numba ten fucka."

Smitty was laughing.

"How come the little snots don't beg for candy and thank our asses like kids in other wars?"

"'Cause they're sharp enough to see the percentage in selling whatever they can lay their hands on," he said.

"Are they all that way?"

"The ones with any smarts."

"Helluva note."

"Hey, people have to adapt. Dinks have had to coexist with hostile armies for centuries. They live for today, man, and they're gonna take, take, take. You gotta understand that it's not personal."

"I'll try to remember that," I said. "Fuckers still ought to be polite, though."

At high noon, our crew came in off the wire to fill up and cool down. I scrounged something to eat, then planted my butt in the dirt next to Dave. He was scrunched up against his bunker in a shrinking fragment of shade, fanning himself with his bush hat.

"How long before monsoon?" My sleeves were soggy from brow wiping.

"Won't be any better then, amigo. We'll hate being wet at night and we'll roast the rest of the time."

I leaned back, trying to calculate the earliest date I could take R&R. McDonald scurried by, acting like a sneak thief and wearing an evil grin. We didn't have to ask to know something was up. We got up and followed him into 1-4's bunker, where a small crowd had gathered inside.

"Where is she?" Ridgeway asked.

"Inside 1-3 track," McDonald said. "And I'm next, baby."

"How much?"

"She wanted five, but I told her nobody around here had more'n a two dollar hard-on."

"How the hell did you sneak her in?"

"My secret."

"For two bills, she must look like dried up pizza."

"See for yourself." He pointed toward the door.

We looked outside, where Carl was standing with his face stuck to the side of the track, eyeballing the action through an old RPG hole.

A line formed fast.

"No telling what she's drippin' with," John said.

"Probably got razors up her snatch," Smitty observed.

When my turn came, I took a short peek. The whore was short and dumpy with crooked teeth and marred legs, but then I realized this wasn't Vegas and she wasn't out to win any beauty contests. I decided she was a cut above an eyesore, but it wouldn't cause me a problem if I missed out.

I was still gawking when Dewayne showed up and ruined the party with word that Captain Littlefield was on the prowl and we'd better get rid of the boom-boom girl quick or risk landing in a world of shit. Scouts went off in different directions to run interference while the girl pulled on her clothes. She slipped into the bunker and was turned over to the McDonald underground, then disappeared, clean as a whistle.

It was time to get back to work, but civilians congregating outside the perimeter had gotten thick enough to twist the dial on Littlefield's thermostat, and he was at the gate, surrounded by an entourage. He'd already ordered the Vietnamese back to town a time or two, but it hadn't had much effect, so he called the remaining workers back inside, thinking it would leave them no reason to stay.

They didn't fall for it, though, and within minutes, he was fussing at them again. I stood watching with Dave and John.

"He's really huffing and puffing. What do you think he'll do?"

John fired a smoke. "He's been known to shoot from the hip when he gets riled. Could be interesting."

For some reason, the Vietnamese had concentrated near the LZ's entrance in groups of twos and threes, reminding me of eager shoppers waiting for a store to open. They didn't look intimidated. In fact, they seemed as curious as we were to see what would happen next.

Five minutes later, a jeep pulled up. Mounted on the back was a big shiny aluminum box tilted toward the sky. I recognized it as a multi-tubed projectile launcher, designed to fire sixteen canisters at once.

"Bad news," I said. "He's gonna waste 'em."

"Worse," John said. "He's gonna gas 'em, and it's a good bet he hasn't checked wind direction."

There was a loud *whoosh*, and a cluster of vapor trails streaked out in a high arc over the crowd. The Vietnamese came to life and darted off like startled minnows as the canisters hit the dirt and released hissing clouds of gas.

"Time to wet down some towels." John said, and headed for the bunker.

The gas rose, shifted, drifted. I caught a whiff that burned my throat and made my eyes water. It quickly got worse.

With no place to run, we huddled in the bunker and endured, breathing through wet towels, wheezing and coughing.

"Fucking moron," McDonald said. "If he's gonna go off half-cocked like that, they oughta issue masks."

"I'm sure he has the only one," Smitty said.

We laid low until Carl stuck his head in the door twenty minutes later. "Good news and bad news," he said. "We don't have to work anymore today. That's good. But I heard a rumor about taking some tracks out to patrol all night."

Ridgeway stood up. "That's bad. But I'll trade the reality of no work for a rumor as dopey as that any day. Now I'm going to disappear."

I grabbed a warm soda to help wash the taste of gas out of my mouth and resumed resting. Later, I was alone in 1-4's bunker, trying to keep sweat drops off a half-written letter when Lieutenant Yearout darkened the doorway.

"I'm looking for volunteers," he said.

I looked at him suspiciously, unsure of his true intent or the actual weight of his announcement. I didn't like the con man's smile he wore.

"Uh, what for?"

"A mission tonight."

So Carl was right.

"A mission? What kind of mission? " I frowned. The tracks never went out after dark except as a reactionary force.

"The platoon's been detailed to police the highway—after hours." He said it as though we had won a raffle.

"Seriously?"

"Would I kid about something as strange as that?"

There was nowhere to run and I couldn't hide. All I could do was ask more questions. He told me that Battalion wanted to let the VC know that use of Route 1 during the wee hours would no longer go unpunished. The dinks knew we didn't patrol at night, and they had been getting away with using the highway carte blanche. Our objective was to rove the road from Devin to Cu Chi and back, all night—about fifteen miles one way.

"That's crazy."

"Maybe so, but the mission's still a go." He smiled that wily smile. "Now, are you in or not?"

I eyed him, still leery. "Why do I have a choice?"

"Because somebody has to stay here to cover our share of the perimeter."

I thought about it. It was loony-tunes, but then I hadn't been knocked in the head enough to want to miss anything, and whoever stayed behind was looking at beaucoup hours of extra watch. If I had to stay awake either way . . .

"Okay I'll go." The words jumped out without due deliberation— another hallmark of newbies who haven't learned to give such decisions adequate consideration. I felt an inner twitch at the realization that I couldn't take it back.

"Good man. We move at dusk." He left, and I sat there staring at the wall, thinking about what a moron I was.

With the exit of Roberts, Ridgeway became the new M60 gunner, but he was staying behind, so for tonight, I would fill in. The others on 1-4 were John, Mike, Spencer, McDonald, and Renfro the sniper, who insisted on going.

We eased onto the night pavement in numerical order, steel pots strapped down, chests smothered in bandoliers. Engine noise and the clatter of treads seemed amplified in the still, moonless night, and with head-lights off, we moved like a slinky—accelerating, braking, accelerating. It would take a while to smooth it out, so we hung on tight, hoping an early ambush wouldn't cause a four-track pile up. None of it made any sense. We could be heard a mile away and still stood out, lights or no lights. Keeping them off only made the drivers' jobs harder.

A half-klick outside Cu Chi, we turned about and stopped dead on the deserted blacktop for a breather. We were a scary distance from the security of Devin and the rest of the company, and it didn't take long for the intrigue I'd felt earlier to be replaced with a creeping sense of doom. We were four tracks in the middle of Vietnam in the middle of the night, daring the VC to take a swing at us, and as we sat staring into the dark landscape, I began to fidget. I felt like a kid who had just entered a haunted house on a double dare and was too far in to back out. I dug for a smoke.

"Spooky," Mike said. He sat across from me, on the left side of the track.

"Suicidal is more like it," John said. He had crawled out of the driver's hatch and sat hunched over, sucking hard on a Winston.

"There it is," Mike said. "The gooks have plenty of time between passes to arrange a very meaningful ambush."

John grunted.

"We might get lucky," I said. "Could be there aren't any dinks working this stretch of road tonight."

John spit. "Yeah, maybe," he said, playing along. "Maybe."

"Keep telling yourselves that," McDonald said. "In the meantime, you'd better get ready to stomp ass, 'cause that's where this joy ride's headed."

Spencer said nothing, but I wasn't sure anybody noticed.

Pass two proved me right so far. We pivoted outside Devin's shadowy perimeter, then gave it gas and rattled right back to Cu Chi. Wayne's pre-diction still hung there, but with less weight, and I was just about ready to proclaim myself the platoon's wise man. The challenge now was time. It had started to drag, and after another lap, the prospect of even one more trip seemed worse than the guard duty I had avoided to be here. On top of it, the drone of the APCs conspired with the late hour to lure most of us into a state of drowsy tranquility. It had reached the point of chins on chests and bobbing heads.

The tiny hamlet a few klicks northwest of Cu Chi was no more than a scattering of grass-and-mud huts silhouetted against the coal-black sky. The platoon was in numerical order and aimed at Devin when we entered the ville for the sixth time, where once again John had to slow at the slight curve there and then accelerate to catch up. We rounded the bend just as the disappearing outline of 1-3 drove through a brilliant white flash. The detonation slammed the blackness in a deafening crack that was momentarily blinding. This was followed by the bright light of flames jetting out from the rear of their track.

Dozing brains were slapped awake hard by the sudden jolt as John, ever alert, reflexively braked and swung hard left, bouncing off the hot-top and into a rice field next to the road. Blistering gunfire swept the highway, pushing us along, and as reality set in, the track swiveled back toward the road in what seemed like deadly slow motion.

Those with rifles lunged from the track, hitting the ground hard. The squad laid out lead and struggled to determine the source of the incoming. 1-4 had been lagging and now paid for it with isolation. 1-3 was a hundred yards up the road. The others, still farther ahead, were out of sight. I heard Spencer yell something at McDonald through the roar, but he was ignored as Wayne worked the .50 maniacally, pumping red darts of death across the highway. Hot brass tumbled in an arc onto the deck, bouncing like grease popping in a hot skillet. I stood inside the track and leaned into the M60, directing a stream of red lines into the hootches across the road, my only thought to beat them down.

A glance to the left explained a lot. The kill zone stretched up the roadway, and the incoming was strong enough to persuade us to stay put, even without cover. Through the web of tracer fire, I could see the profile of 1-3 beyond a wisp of trees, its rear deck still burning. Somebody fired flares that whooshed, popped, and pulsed, illuminating the nightscape. Small arms cracked from a new direction, and an RPG gone berserk skittered across the ground and blew out a hunk of dike behind us. The noise was overwhelming, making it hard to think straight.

Spencer climbed in through the rear door and stood next to me. "They're gonna chop us up if we don't move," he hollered.

"No place to go," Wayne shot back.

"We gotta—"

"Get me some ammo!"

Spencer shut up long enough to hoist up a box of .50 rounds, then crowded in next to me and jerked the trigger, an act that sent hot M16 brass bouncing off my head. The M60 was mounted, leaving me no wiggle room.

"Get out of the way," I shouted.

He shifted a couple inches and ripped off another twenty. More shell casings stung me like bees. I yelled louder. He scowled at me, then shifted and reached for the radio handset draped over the .50 turret. He ducked down to give the lieutenant his version of a sit-rep, then stood up. "LT says everybody get away from the track. Now."

"The hell you say," McDonald shot back. I got enough ammo on board to kill every fuckin' gook in the AO." He never let up, continuing to tattoo the huts in uneven rows.

"We need these guns," I shouted, wishing I was a hundred miles from the track but knowing McDonald was right.

"We're dead," Spencer insisted, "if we don't di-di. We're wide open and they're tossin' RPGs, man!"

"Bullshit!" Wayne wouldn't have it.

"You can't hit 'em anyway!" Spencer wailed. "They're dug in, man!"

We kept firing. Spencer hopped out through the rear door.

"Get off that track," he bawled. Now he was on the ground right below me. I started to tell him to shut up when another RPG whizzed by and harvested a few yards of somebody's rice field behind us. This convinced even McDonald that we should take cover, at least until they ran out of rockets. We were KIAs waiting to happen and wouldn't be much help in the form of human hash. Wayne reluctantly let go of the .50 and angrily snatched at his rifle. Nobody had to tell me to follow.

We fell to firing positions on the right side of the track next to Renfro and Abbott, our only salvation the slight incline where the paddy met the road. McDonald, swearing in gusts, commenced to expend magazines a pull at a time. Spencer scurried back to the track to grab a radio and toss out ammo. John had dismounted the other side, staying in position for a quick re-entry. Spent clips covered the ground.

Spencer scrambled back over, gesturing wildly, and flopped on the ground in the middle of our rag-tag firing line.

"Say it!" Wayne said. His patience was used up.

"It's Petrowski. The box of C-4 he was sitting on flamed up when the dinks blew the 'bush. Apparently, the Claymore blast blew him off the back of the track."

A quick mental calculation told me he would have hit the ground close to our position. He must have landed on the other side of the highway.

"That would put him across the road from us, right?" I couldn't see that there was any other explanation.

"I dunno," he said. "Maybe. Doc wanted to go after him, but he's way up on One-One and the lieutenant vetoed the idea. I told him we'd keep our eyes peeled in case Carl's alive and tries to move."

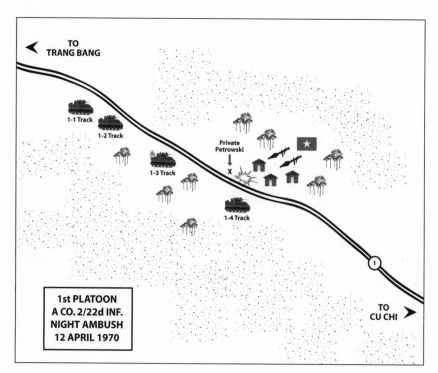

TO
TRANG BANG

1-1 Track

1-2 Track

Private
Petrowski

1-3 Track

X

1-4 Track

1

TO
CU CHI

1st PLATOON
A CO. 2/22d INF.
NIGHT AMBUSH
12 APRIL 1970

A voice in my head immediately said, *Nope, that won't do.* "I'm going after him," I said. Once again, the words tumbled out before I could stop them, like soup slopped over the edge of the bowl. There was no undoing it, but I wouldn't have taken it back anyway.

Spencer's eyes narrowed. "Listen up," he said. "I can't risk losing you or anybody else. They may try to overrun us any time. And even if you make it across, you'll never make it back. Look at that crossfire, man!"

I knew what he'd said, even though the noise drowned out half of it. But my mind was made up. I glanced around, figuring on getting some help. Renfro just happened to be closest, so I turned to him and said, "Are you gonna help me?"

He held his fire and stared at me in surprise, as if to say, "Surely you don't mean me." He looked at the others, but got no help. Then, with no way out and his reputation on the line, he put his war face back on and said, "Let's go, then."

"Don't do this, guys," Spencer said weakly.

"Shut up," Wayne said.

With a bewildered look, Spencer clammed up. I started out in a crouch, glancing back to make sure Renfro hadn't changed his mind. He hesitated slightly, then followed. The others laid out covering fire, not that it was any different than what they were already doing.

There was no easy way to go. We were in an open field on one side of the road, while the hamlet and Carl Petrowski were on the other side. I doubted that calling a timeout would fly, so we duck-walked around the back of the track, then low-crawled to the edge of the road and waited for flares to fade. Small-arms fire still cracked like bullwhips, but seemed less intense than before.

Spencer called after us one last time. I only caught bits of it. He may have accused us of disobeying orders, but it wouldn't have mattered and he knew it. Even he understood that once somebody loses their ability to reason, they can't be swayed.

On a silent signal, we vaulted forward and darted across the blacktop in a low stoop, emptying our rifles as we ran. We dived headlong down the opposite slope, rolled to stop, reloaded, and then scanned the smoky nightscape for Carl's carcass. A new flare popped overhead, sectioning the ground into a patchwork of pale yellow and angled shadows. Above our heads a scattering of misdirected and stray rounds slashed the air.

Carl was a big boy, and we spotted him at the same time. He was stretched out face-up in the dirt fifty feet away, looking as out of place as a crocodile on a Kansas prairie. He wasn't moving, but that didn't prove anything. He could be unconscious or even playing dead. No bullets had zeroed in on us yet, so either we hadn't been spotted or the VC were conducting a practice session for their worst marksmen. Either way, our chore wasn't one that could be rescheduled, so we moved out.

Under the pendulous light, we rolled and squiggled, inching along, heads down, wishing OD green could repel hot lead. We could have been elephants in somebody's living room and been less conspicuous. Our big hope was more lousy shooting and their preoccupation with taking out the APCs.

Carl was out cold, but alive, breathing in gasps. His chest was punctured and there was a fist-sized hole in his upper right leg that had leaked enough blood to drench his pants. I already had raw elbows to go with a mouthful of dirt, and when I saw how heavy he looked lying there limp, I started to have serious doubts about the outcome. I figured he'd go a good two hundred. Renfro and I were both around one-forty fully fed, and I knew the hundred-and-fifty-yard man-carry technique they'd taught us in Basic wasn't going to cut it.

"We'll never get him back," Renfro said, puffing.

"We have to now," I said, still staring at Carl's bulk.

That covered the subject, so we moved into position, squatting at each end of his lengthy frame. We slung our rifles. I took the top half, gripping him under the arms. Renfro cradled his legs.

We churned up out of the dirt fast, knees bent, and stomped up the embankment, hoping to outrun any daggers of fire sent to rip us apart. We were fully exposed, and just when I was convinced my war was about to abruptly end, the lone flare above blinked out and bestowed the blessing of darkness. The god of timing had given our wretched souls a small break. Short of divine providence, the rest was up to us and the laws of probability.

All bets were off, and with the deck reshuffled, we stumbled onto the road in a staggering frenzy. So far so good, but Carl's butt kept scraping the asphalt, and when I strained for more lift, my rifle slipped to my wrist and clattered against the pavement. I hauled in the reins enough so I could try and scoop it up, but only succeeded in tripping myself, a mishap that caused us all to tumble.

"Shit!" I snatched at the weapon, reslung it, and got a fresh grip on the cargo, but not before new flares poofed accusingly, spotlighting us in the act. The only thing missing was an evil voice proclaiming, "Advantage here!" We came off the deck all arms and legs, bobbing and weaving in a crouch-run, like stock-car drivers in traffic.

The track was now thirty yards away, but Carl had gained a thousand pounds during the trip and I could see my physical limitations coming into view. I was certain my shoulder sockets were about to come apart like popped hubcaps, and my hamstrings felt like they were latched to a safe headed for the sidewalk from the tenth floor. If we didn't get there quick, they were going to need extra stretchers.

We crashed again going down the slope, but I was too exhausted to care. I heard Carl groan. "Hang tough, buddy," I wheezed. "We're just about there."

We sucked in air, then cuffed an armpit apiece and dragged him on in, letting loose at the rear of the track. Spencer saw us coming and made his way over with two towels. He stuffed one under Carl's head and tied the other one around the mushy crater on his upper leg. I heard the sound of a helicopter about the time we crawled back to the firing line, but the LZ was too hot and he had to back off. I stuck my face in the dirt at the hiss of something big hurled our way, waited for the explosion, then slapped in a new magazine and jerked the trigger. Amazingly, the track hadn't yet been blasted to cinders.

After a couple more magazines, I noticed a slowdown in tracer fire and a minute later realized we were no longer pinned down. The VC were running low on either spirit or ammo, so McDonald and I raced each other to the track. John was already aboard. The back ramp came down as he imitated an auctioneer in his radio conversation with the lieutenant. "More tracks are comin' from Devin," he yelled at us. "LT says to mount up and get our asses over to their position!"

Spencer and Renfro drug Carl inside while Mike emptied his rifle on a backward run. John was coiled like a spring, set to jam gears, and once everybody was in and the ramp came up, Mike yelled, "GO!" and he stomped the accelerator.

We charged the road. Spencer hollered some unintelligible orders. The rest of us punished phantom targets with rifles and machine guns. Hovering nearby, the dustoff beat the air like a rug. The thought of what might happen when we hit the blacktop if the VC were half-smart interfered with rational acts—which is why we were on the highway before anybody noticed that the lumpy thing underfoot was Carl's maltreated body.

"Hey, get off him!" I yelled.

This had no effect.

"Move, goddammit!" By now, we were closing on 1-3, and the incoming had become sporadic. The message was finally heard and feet shifted. We linked with 3rd Squad, then scooted another fifty yards to rendezvous with the other tracks and circle the wagons in a deeper paddy with good dikes.

Yellow smoke popped and billowed, and the medevac dropped in for the pick-up as we got situated. John lowered the back ramp for the extraction while Doc jogged over with the lieutenant.

The LT motioned to Spencer. "Everybody but gunners and drivers spread out along this dike." He then stood on the treads and asked John if we had any other casualties.

"Just Carl, lieutenant."

He looked surprised. "No shit?"

"No shit, sir."

"Looks like you guys are in good shape, considering the heat you took. We've got a couple of minor wounded. The bad news is that Shukas was killed."

For a few seconds, I wasn't sure I had heard him right. Shukas was *killed?* Shukas was short. He was cool. Everybody liked Shukas. This couldn't be right. But I knew it was right. I could tell by the slight hitch in the lieutenant's voice when he'd said it.

"He was hit the same time as Carl when they blew the ambush." He paused and said, "Stay alert, and stay ready"—then abruptly walked off, leaving us to deal with it.

I fumbled for a Marlboro, torched it, and wished I was drunk but doubting that even a whiskey buzz could drown out the unwanted emotions rolling through me. I didn't know Jim that well, but at the moment, it felt like I'd just lost a brother. He was on-deck for a freedom bird. He had survived eleven months of this shit. Now he was dead. No freedom bird. No future. Nothing. It wasn't right. I was no longer a rookie and yet I still refused to believe the fact that nothing about combat was fair. It occurred to me that I would have to become much tougher mentally. I had no choice. It was also plain for all to see that 1-3, already known for having been hit more than any track in the company, had once again lived up to its name of "Blood, Sweat, and Tears."

The lieutenant ordered a mad minute into the now-burning hamlet. It brought no return fire. All contact was lost. The firefight was over.

A flare ship reported for duty and dropped jumbo globes of illumination so bright they stole darkness even from nooks and crannies. Plumes of smoke drifted lazily, filling our nostrils with the tangy stink of gunpowder and incinerated straw. Fatigue took over as I absently watched the fire gain momentum. Crackling flames flickered up from thatched roofs, blending eerily with the swaying flarelight, and from some secret place, a cache of munitions slowly cooked off.

I looked up at the sound of chopper blades thumping the air. A Cobra gunship eased in and stood by, hovering up high. In the distance, the clank and rumble of APCs announced the arrival of 3rd Platoon and Littlefield's command post. They stormed onto the crime scene like over-eager cops called to a disturbance already quelled.

The gunship re-killed the dead hamlet, then we headed back to Devin, having apparently completed our mission, at least in Littlefield's mind. Our reinforcements stayed behind to recon the rubble.

———•———

After breakfast, I huddled up outside 1-3's bunker with Dave to see if there was any news on Carl.

"The word from Sergeant Pitt is that he'll make it, but they don't know yet if he's keeping that leg. He also took a couple of Claymore pellets in the chest and collapsed a lung. At some point, he'll be transferred to Japan."

"So it was a Chicom Claymore?"

"Yep, and a big one. My ears are still ringing."

"Any word on the others?"

"The others should be back in a week or so."

"Except Shukas," I said.

He looked at the ground. "Right. Except Shukas."

We sat on a half-wall of sandbags, smoking. Dave seemed accepting, considering it was his track and his squadmates that took the whipping. 1-3 was getting a reputation, and I started to ask him if he was superstitious, then thought better of it.

"At least Carl made it," I said.

"He was damn lucky. You guys were lucky, too."

"What did the sweep turn up, any idea?"

"Hard to say how many there were. Maybe a company. Who knows? Everett in Third Platoon told me the bodies included six VC and nine civilians. The rest of the villagers boogied, probably before the fireworks."

"Hold it," I said. "Wait a minute." I leaned forward. "We wasted *nine* civilians?"

"That's assuming they were civilians. And who's to say it wasn't the VC that did the killing?"

There was a lesson in this, and I wanted to hear it.

He went on, "Basically, villagers have three choices when an ambush is set up in their living rooms. They can leave, join the fight, or lay low and hope they survive. A lot of them have hidey-holes under their hootches that they get into when this shit happens. But any way you cut it, some of 'em are gonna get caught in the crossfire, and the VC love it when it looks like we massacred a ville. The press eats it up."

I mulled it over while he struck a match to a Kool.

"Maybe you can explain something to me," I said. "I'm still learning, but common sense tells me they knew what the outcome would be when they jumped us. Right?"

"More or less."

"So in return for fuckin' up the health records of a few GIs, they lost fifteen of their own and a whole town. That about right?"

McDonald heard this as he strolled by and quipped, "Fuckin'-A. There wasn't enough left of that place to carry out a decent weenie roast." He continued on, not expecting a reply. I would have laughed if it hadn't been so serious. Dave just shook his head.

"That's about right," he said. "They do it all the time. Have since the beginning."

"I don't see the advantage in it, even if they do make us look bad. They alienate their own and create more refugees."

"Yeah, but they're not the ones out to win hearts and minds, my man. If they can drive us out, they'll reunite their country by force. These set-ups are tailor made for Uncle Ho's divide-and-conquer strategy. Headlines are what count. And you can bet that if the press gets wind of this, we'll look like a bunch of renegade psychos by the time it gets back to the World."

He drew on the smoke, wiped his brow. "If LBJ had gone the limit, we might not be here." He nervously flicked at the cigarette, trying to knock off ash that wasn't there. "We've spent years struttin' around the jungle, piling up bodies, and all the while Ho's been using it to work his propaganda magic."

Dave was more knowledgeable about all this than me. I had never given any real thought to the political side of it.

"Even so," I said, "the main idea is for the South to remain a democracy, right? And what about Vietnamization? Aren't we supposed to be turning this whole thing back over to them?"

"Right, but that only works when people are determined to be free. The South hasn't come up with a legitimate government yet. And why should they fight as long as we'll to do it for them? Between the protestors at home and the stupid strategies, it couldn't possibly be turning out any other way."

He ground the butt out on a sandbag. "We can't kill them all, and it's too late to shift the load. The funny thing is, the South Vietnamese don't really believe we'll bail out and leave them to the wolves. So far, they've been right."

He spit, squinted against the sun. "So," he said, "our job now is mostly keeping the bad guys in line."

"I guess I don't understand what our leaders really want."

Dave pondered. "They want us to keep stacking bodies and working with the South to take over, but it's a smokescreen and everybody knows it." He paused. "They don't want to lose, but they will never do what it takes to win."

"Which is . . . ?"

"Move the war into the country we're really fighting against."

He meant North Vietnam. I had to think on that one a minute.

"You're right," I said. "That will never happen."

He just smiled as if to say, "There it is."

There was a lull while we each rolled these truths around in our heads.

Finally, I said, "It doesn't seem possible that we could win all the battles and still lose the war."

He didn't hesitate. "Sure it is. Think about it. One day, the higher-ups will announce some kind of cease fire with the North and we'll withdraw. They'll make a big deal of it, but it won't fool anybody."

He stood up. "Ho's driving us out the smart way, with the help of our own people. He doesn't care how many of his own die. When we're gone, the NVA will be hoisting their flag over South Vietnam in short order. Wait and see."

My first thought was that I only hoped to live long enough. I looked up at him, shading my eyes from the rising sun. "So if what you say is right, the South is fucked any way you cut it."

"Roger that."

I stood up, searching for words that might help legitimize our mission. "Even so," I reasoned, "every VC we waste in the meantime will never kill another American or terrorize their own again, right? That's worth something, isn't it?"

He just shrugged.

"I mean, Jesus. I don't want to be in a phony war with real bullets. And I sure as hell don't want to die for nothing." I stared, waiting, but didn't really expect an answer.

We both gazed out at the wasteland beyond the wire. "It's a goddamn crazy war, Dave."

He just smiled. A thin, knowing smile.

12

Another Day Older and Deeper in Debt

*War . . . burned me out in some ways, so that now I feel
like an old man, but still sometimes act like a dumb kid.
It made me grow up too fast.*

—AUDIE MURPHY*

April 1970. 25th Infantry Division. LZ Devin.

"What's this? Everybody layin' around in the shade when it's just getting
warm enough to work." Lieutenant Yearout stood in the bunker's doorway.
We were on noon break.

"Funny," Mike said weakly. He was fanning himself with a towel.

"What do you really want, lieutenant?" John grumbled. He was
stretched out on one of the wooden berths with a wet T-shirt draped over
his face.

"I brought a replacement for you," he said, as if introducing a stage act.
"Henderson, meet your new buddies."

A skinny black-haired kid with thick glasses and a push-broom mustache stepped into the bunker. We greeted him with grunts and gestures,
too hot and tired to do more. His fatigues and the shade of his skin suggested he wasn't still nursing a stateside hangover, so I offered him a place
to sit and stuck a hand out, curious to find out more.

---

*Quoted in the *New York Journal-American*, 30 August 1955.

Dennis "Ranger" Henderson liked to talk, and he told me about getting orders to a Ranger unit, where he spent two months performing duties he hadn't been trained for. He learned a lot, but couldn't get along with his team leader, and was soon persuaded to find employment elsewhere.

"So here I am," he said. "No regrets."

He wanted to know about our area of operations and where we'd been, so I told him about the Filhol and what happened in the Renegades and on Highway 1 and that we'd been at Devin long enough that some of us would commit felonies for a change of scenery.

Doc, 1-3's Dewayne Russell, and his squad leader, Bucky Mayfield, came into the bunker. Bucky was blond, small, and built like a street fighter, with a chest full of sand-colored curls and a rugged look. He probably never made the football team but would have been handy for the postgame brawl. I could see him playing Aldo Ray's part in *The Green Berets*. Dewayne, on the other hand, was a quiet redhead whose hallmark was a Sherlock Holmes pipe clamped firmly between his teeth. He had the fatherly demeanor of a displaced college professor who somehow ended up in a grunt's uniform.

"Quepasa, Doc-a-roo," Mike said.

"Don't be cute, gringo, just give me your feet."

"Who's goin' on AP tonight?" Dewayne asked. He put a match to his pipe and smoothed his wavy hair, appearing far too civilized for combat.

"Me," I said, raising my hand uncertainly.

"Same here." Invisible Willie raised his, too.

"There's been movement out there lately," Bucky said, "Watch your step and keep your ears pricked."

From what I'd seen of Bucky, he wasn't one to give orders. He gave advice instead. He respected the fact that we knew our jobs, so he was more coach than boss, and it usually paid off to listen. I noticed Spencer staring at him with a sour expression, but he knew better than to sound off.

After checking us out, Doc advised Vernon, the FNG, that he could either get rid of his boxers or spend his tour with his crotch on fire and walking bow-legged, his choice. Then he moved on, followed by his entourage.

Our ambush patrol was sweaty-hot and bug-miserable, but uneventful, and when we straggled back in at sunrise, we found the company gearing up to rotate out of Devin. For how long we didn't know. I didn't care. Just getting away was enough.

We rolled through the gate mid-morning, drove to Trang Bang, and then headed south toward the Vam Co Dong River to secure a gang of Rome Plows on a clearing operation. It was easy duty. We even lucked out and got positioned where there was a dapple of shade. The lieutenant wandered over after lunch and without so much as an interview offered me the platoon demolitions job. I thought it was a joke. I had just turned twenty-one the day before and didn't think adding more risk to my repertoire would increase my life expectancy.

When I realized he was serious, I said, "What's my reward?"—not thinking for a second that I had a bargaining position.

"No APs," he said. "None, that is, unless we're super short."

That sounded reasonable. "That's it? All I have to do is blow up dud arty rounds and tunnels when we find them?"

"Some of those arty round might be boobytrapped. And you may have to recon some of the tunnels."

"Tunnel rat, too, huh?"

"That's right."

I considered the pluses and minuses. There were lots of minuses. I'd heard about the tunnels of Cu Chi district. I also knew there was a special school to train volunteer "rats," which I had not been to. I reasoned that one could get quickly wasted if he didn't know what he was doing. I was also on the claustrophobic side, which could certainly factor in on survivability.

"Well?"

I mulled it over, admittedly intrigued. I hated AP. Everyone did. I hadn't forgotten the cluster bombs that had tried to slice and dice me my first week in the field. It's hard to shake the feeling of being the boiled egg in the blender. Getting a pass on AP was worth a lot. In my slightly sun-stroked mind, the trade-off sounded good.

"Assuming I was interested, when would I start?"

"As soon as you collect the demo kit from Easley in First Squad." I didn't bother to ask why Easley was opting out. Maybe he was short, maybe he was tired of pushing the odds. I supposed it didn't really matter. Finally, I said okay. Easley gave me a short briefing and a canvas satchel stuffed with fuses, blasting caps, and related paraphernalia. That was it.

I got my first chance to play Bomb Squad during a RIF the next day when I set charges on a couple of unexploded artillery rounds. A spider hole was next, which I destroyed with three bricks of C-4 bound together. A couple of days later, a more suspicious tunnel entrance was discovered next to some brush. After checking for tripwires and other traps for suckers, I tossed in a concussion grenade to rearrange the brains of any occupants, then lowered myself into the entrance once the smoke had cleared. It turned out to be a short tunnel, maybe fifty feet, with a poorly concealed opening at the other end. A halo of light shone through the haze of dust from the other outlet, and as it settled, I could see that at best I had annihilated a few insects seeking refuge from the sun. Piece of cake. It looked like a job for Bangalore torpedoes, so I climbed out and went to round up a few, only to find that everybody was out of stock. I had to settle for a pair of twenty-five-pound shaped charges instead. Thinking it was no big deal, I lugged the cone-shaped directional explosives back over to the tunnel and linked them above-ground with detonating cord, spooling the white, flexible tubing from one to the other. I carefully set blasting caps into the receptacles on top of the charges, strung a one-minute fuse, and gently lowered them into their respective holes. When the LT gave me the signal to light up, I put my Zippo to the fuse and then trotted back over to 1-4 and crouched down to wait for the blast.

A minute passed. Nothing went boom. Then another. I unplugged my fingers from my ears and glanced at the lieutenant. He was staring at me. As silent seconds ticked off, I could feel the bottom of my stomach slowly start to sag. I knew what he was going to say before he opened his mouth.

"Looks like you've got a bad fuse or a dud blasting cap, Ross. Go fix it."

I tried to think of a response, but there was nothing to be said. I knew what had to be done, and nobody was going to do it for me. Even so, as my wits settled back into place I decided some persuasion was worth a try.

"What do you think I should do?"

Without hesitation, he said, "You'll have to put a new fuse on it. If that doesn't work, we'll talk about it."

Just what I expected. Then I played the wild card, hoping it might fly.

"How about I frag it instead?"

He shook his head. "That's a lot of dynamite. You might not have time to clear."

"I ran track in school. I'll risk it."

"No, you won't."

We stared at each other.

"Tell you what," he said. "Rig a fuse to a stick of C-4 and slip it down the hole. That should do the job."

Damn. He had me there. I wouldn't have to tinker with the shaped charge, but I would still have to go eyeball to eyeball with it.

"Uh, can't argue that, but a grenade—"

"That's the best I can do. And the company's waiting to move out, so I'm calling for a fire-in-the-hole in five minutes. That'll give you plenty of time." He reached for the radio and turned away. End of conversation.

When I looked toward the tunnel, my heart started thumping like a bongo. We weren't dealing with firecrackers on the Fourth of July here, and I was the chump who had to end the standoff. I looked at my demo bag, then back to the tunnel. It measured out to be the shortest and longest walk I might ever take. Shit.

I took a deep breath and put it in gear. My hands got clammy, and as I closed the gap, I found myself getting lower to the ground. Soon I was on hands and knees, and with about twenty feet to go, I went into a low-crawl, stick of C-4 in one hand, blasting cap and fuse in the other. That charge controlled its own destiny. If it didn't like my looks, it might just decide to turn my head into scraps of bone and meat. Maybe it was even waiting, ear cocked, knowing the dumb fuck that put it there would come slinking back, and when he reached in to fiddle around, well . . .

But I had to look. I couldn't risk the bar of C-4 bumping the shape charge when I lowered it down. As long as I didn't touch it, the thing would have no reason to knock me into orbit. I drew a long breath and gingerly peered over the edge, queasy at the thought of the earth under me erupting into a spray of dirt and gore.

The tip of the high-explosive cone leered at me like an evil eye, and I found myself fixated on it, locked on the thought that the final sixty-odd years of my life could be confiscated on a whim by a hard plastic object that looked a lot like a dunce cap.

After a few seconds, I snapped out of it and quickly but cautiously lowered the brick of C-4, heart pounding, then slid back and lit the fuse with an unsteady hand, now shaky at the realization that I might just get out of this if things kept going my way. The fuse caught and hissed, and I bounced up and dashed for the tracks in a stumbling run.

A minute later, a muffled *ka-rump* reverberated through the ground and ended the suspense. Mission accomplished, I mounted up, and by the time we got underway, I was feeling like some kind of expert.

We pulled into a nearby village that had been built on a dried-out rice field dotted with loosely clumped stands of withered trees. It was a security job that called for two-man foot patrols to walk the streets, like cops on a beat. I had no idea why, but I didn't mind. My stomach was growling, so I teamed with Ranger and we headed out to find a market, hoping to score some non-canned food. A few kids and a couple of dogs tagged along; otherwise, we were mostly ignored as we trudged down a hut-lined dirt road.

"Look at that." Ranger nudged me and pointed toward a hootch up ahead. A woman was standing next to a well, soaping down the black pajamas still hanging on her bony frame. "Is that called taking a bath or doing the laundry?"

"Beats me," I said. "I'm just glad I'm not the dude bunking with her."

A naked boy, about five, wandered out of the hootch under escort of two chickens and a piglet and made his way to the woman, who continued to suds up. He watched her for a minute, then squatted, and with a grimace squeezed out an impressive turd. A rickety old mama-san with betel-nut juice dribbling down her chin ambled by just then, but didn't take notice. I looked from her to the boy, then back again. Her mouth was a blackened orthodontic horror, and she had a flat, dead-ahead expression that suggested she was looking forward to her own funeral. I questioned whether she would even make it to the end of the street.

We moved on. Here and there, adults and kids alike squatted, most of them smoking.

"What a life," Ranger said. "I guess when you don't have furniture, squatting is the way to go."

"Makes you realize how bad it can be."

"Yeah, but it doesn't have to be that bad. They could improve it. I mean, they could get an attitude. Be more sanitary, for instance. Even that might help get 'em some respect, especially when you figure they aren't spending much time helping us waste their enemy."

"You can't expect people to change their way of life to suit foreigners," I said. "I have to admit, though, I'd be hard pressed to step in front of an RPG to save one of them."

We rounded a corner, figuring the marketplace had to be close, only to come face-to-face with a water buffalo standing in the middle of the road. He switched to red alert when he spotted us and assumed an aggressive stance, as if to let us know we had reached the end of the trail.

We held up. The bison pawed the dirt, eyeballing us, then snorted and shook his head in a double-dog dare.

"They don't like Americans, do they?" I said it out the side of my mouth.

"Hate 'em."

"Any reason?"

"No."

Onlookers began to gather, eager to see how we'd get out of it.

"What are we gonna do?"

"I have no idea."

Now we were the stars of a side show, with no graceful way out. We had to come up with something.

"We can't turn around and go back," I said. "The humiliation would be too much. Besides, we shouldn't have to."

Ranger glanced over his shoulder. "They're starting to snicker," he said. "They could end it any time, you know."

The buffalo took a couple of steps forward and scraped at the ground some more, maintaining his steely glare.

"Jesus, man, look at the size of that bastard."

"Keep your mind on pleasant thoughts," he said.

"That's hard to do at the moment."

"We just gotta show him we're not afraid, that's all. C'mon." Ranger started forward, a move that was interpreted by our adversary as an act of aggression, and he countered by lowering his head and swinging it back and forth, as if deciding which of us to kill first.

Ranger held up, and we were forced to look to our audience in hopes that a volunteer would step forward, but when we did, they became mannequins, hiding their smirks behind blank expressions. They weren't going to help us, and with only thirty feet left between matadors and bull, I decided I'd had my fill.

I brought my rifle to port arms. "I'm gonna shoot that mother if he gets any closer."

"Don't do it, man. They'll bill Uncle Sam a thousand dollars for it and Littlefield will have our heads."

"I don't care. He's getting ready to fuck us up."

The buffalo must have smelled the hostility. He stared coldly for a second, then pointed his snout at the dirt and stepped off.

I leveled my rifle for a head shot. "This is it. You die, fucker." I squinted down the sights and heard Ranger say, "Oh shit." I flipped the safety and steadied the barrel just as a squawking Vietnamese broke ranks and ran into the street, waving his arms. He collared the animal and steered him off to one side, then turned to us like a lord who had just rescued his kingdom from destruction. He wagged an arthritic finger and slung what must have been choice Asian curses at us. We just stood there, stone-faced, until he finished up and skulked off, bison in tow. The crowd broke up.

I looked at Ranger. He shrugged and started walking again, as if nothing had happened. I figured we'd saved face in spite of a few jeers that followed us down the street. We hadn't exactly bested the brute, but we hadn't backed down, either. *Let 'em snicker*, I thought.

We found the vendors, but by then, all the fresh food was gone, so we headed back to the tracks in a bad frame of mind, only to discover that our buddies had hogged up all the goodies in town.

The sun was sagging on the horizon when we pulled out in a swirl of dust and rumbled into the wilderness a couple of klicks away to spend the night. Once the tracks were situated and engines switched off, we stood up to stretch. A foul odor was quickly detected—a dead-animal stench so strong that it brought out the towels and prompted a quick search for its source. Willie spotted it first, a dead Viet Cong lying limb-stiff in the dying cockroach position next to some bushes about thirty feet to our front. He had turned black and puffed up bigger than the Pillsbury Doughboy, a real sight. His clothes had been rendered several sizes too small by trapped gas, and it looked like even money as to whether he would explode in the next five minutes.

"Somebody call the boss and see if we can move upwind a bit," Ridgeway said. His words were muffled by the towel pressed against his face.

"Won't do any good," John said. "No way Littlefield's gonna reposition the company to improve our sleeping position."

Then the lieutenant came up, holding his nose, and told us he didn't care how we did it, but to get rid of the carcass, ASAP. Then he left.

More towels were produced while we stood there, scratching our heads, each thinking of reasons why someone else should handle it. Then McDonald put on the face of one slapped with genius and said, "Hold up. Hold up." He looked at me. "You're the demo man, Ross. You could just blow him up!" He grinned big, palms up. Solution found.

"There it is," Mike said. Others quickly jumped in.

"Right on."

"Do it, man."

I'd been had, so I threw my hands up and headed for the ammo stash inside 1-4. I grabbed an armload of C-4, a blasting cap, and three feet of fuse, expecting the lieutenant to veto the plan anyway. In the least, it was going to make a hell of racket. But to my dismay, the LT thought it was a dandy idea and had no trouble getting clearance from the captain.

Drivers were advised of a fire-in-the-hole, and the platoon backed the tracks up for good measure, leaving me alone with the reeking stiff.

The stink wafted, fouling the air, and when I knelt next to the body, it came in a sickening wave, as if the corpse had been a week inside a sun-baked trash can and I'd just opened the lid. I tried to breathe shallow, wondering if I would keep my groceries or if I would be feeding the vermin a hot supper. I fanned at the flies so I could position the C-4, but the fat green ones took exception to me muscling in and refused to stay shooed for more than a second or two. The thickening odor soon beat a path from my nostrils to my belly and mingled with the contents, trying hard to send it north. I worked fast, figuring time was short. The pistol belt cinched around his waist was as tight as a knot in a balloon, and if I didn't snap things up, I might not get clear before the whole works blew without my help.

I laid three bricks of explosive along each side and lightly set two more on his chest. I strung a thirty-second fuse, fired it, and took off for fresh air. The blast shook the tracks, suggesting that eight bars might've been overkill, but I was hoping to avoid clean-up. We rolled back in and found only a shallow crater. There were no flies and only a hint of lingering odor. If chunks of body were about, they weren't evident, and we didn't look for them.

"Wonderful thing, C-4," Ridgeway said, drawing a deep breath. "You can heat food with it, destroy bunkers with it, even use it to deodorize your campsite."

"Next time, I'll let you do it," I said.

Over at the command post, a decision had been made to send 1st Platoon on a mission of its own for a couple of days, so in the morning, off we went, heading for a swamp. An Air Force spotter plane had crashed nose-first into a marsh southwest of Cu Chi, and our job was to provide security. When we got there, we were confronted with what looked like part of the Florida Everglades. Knee-high grass stood over an inch or two of concealed water for as far as the eye could see. A couple hundred yards from the dry ground, the tail section of aircraft stuck up out of the bog. Next to it, men stood motionless in a half-circle around the jutting steel, like pagans gathered to worship an object not fully understood. As they contemplated the wreckage and what to do about it, I got the distinct feeling that their efforts would eventually add up to a big waste of time.

Once the tracks were parked, eight of us slogged out for the first shift. At the crash site, we found pieces of broken airplane slung everywhere. Next to the protruding tail section was a big yellow backhoe, a caved-in ditch, and a bewildered recovery crew that had already spent two days attempting to exhume the muddy grave of the two airmen interred within. Reaching the cockpit looked hopeless. Every trench started had ended with a wall of shifting mud sliding in to fill the hole. Now they had to decide the best way to proceed.

Ranger looked from the hole to one of the engineers. "Why are you doing this?" He said it honestly, unable to come up with a sensible reason.

The guy frowned. "Higher-up doesn't want to give the dinks salvage rights."

I laughed out loud before I could stifle it, visualizing five years' worth of aircraft wreckage slung from one end of Vietnam to the other.

"Seriously?" I said.

"We hope to recover the bodies, too," he said, his tone now defensive.

At least that was a bona fide reason, but even us grunts could see that it wasn't going to happen, at least not the way they were going about it. Even so, they apparently expected to succeed. No ludicrous dredging going on here.

Infrequent rains had already begun, but I decided not to suggest waiting until the next dry season. "How long's it gonna take?" I was sizing up the terrain, scouting for a potential dry spot to park my butt.

"Hard to say." Then he said, "Well, gotta go now," with just a hint of a smirk, knowing we had been sentenced to spend the night in the soup.

Standing up all night wasn't an option, so we tried to create sleeping positions that would at least eliminate the chance of drowning. By dark, I was glad I had brought plenty of Marlboros and extra towels. The mosquitoes raged, and even with a poncho beneath me, it was impossible to keep the water out. So I sat hunched over, chain smoking, until my throat was raw and my back ached so badly I had to stretch out. I dozed off once and dreamed of floating on a choppy lake fully dressed and struggling to keep my leaky air mattress from taking on water. The dream ended when I jerked awake from swamp water trickling into my ear.

At sunrise, we stood up in the steamy grass and tried to get organized. The first order of business was to test-fire weapons to see if they still worked, all the while scanning the distant high ground for signs of life. We munched some canned breakfast and slowly dried out as the sun started to cook the land. After a while, something big and metallic appeared on the horizon. A close look revealed that it was moving, because whatever it was gradually got bigger.

"Comin' our way," Ranger said, squinting against the glare.

As it grew in size and took on shape, we could see that it was a massive land crane, rising up out of the horizon like a lost behemoth in search of a metropolis. It was the kind used to set bridge beams and stack short buildings, and soon it loomed large, inching along on its journey, its derrick nodding slightly as it moved forward.

"Are they for real?" I said. I stared, shading my eyes and straining for a better view.

"There's only one way to find out," Mike said. "Let's go check it out."

The crane had pulled to a stop a few hundred yards away. We cleared it with the lieutenant, then shouldered our M16s and sloshed our way over. By the time we got there, the crane was at the edge of the swamp, poised for entry. A dozen mud-caked men urged it on, guiding it onto sections of perforated steel planks they had laid out to serve as a roadbed. The thing hesitated, teetered a bit, then chuffed out some black smoke and proceeded to clank and squeal its way into the mire. It squared itself on the PSP, then clattered forward fifty feet to the end of the steel trail and stopped. The engineering crew then plucked the planks from the sucking mud at the rear of the beast and lugged them to the front so the process could be repeated, the plan being to leap-frog it out to the crash site.

It looked like one of those ideas that ought to work but never does. Thirty minutes into the excursion, the massive arrangement of iron and cables developed a slight list, and the walk boards on the affected side responded to the extra weight by sinking deeper into the goo. Anguished engineers watched in stunned silence as the thing gradually tilted more and more, like a torpedoed ship, until it bottomed out just shy of toppling. It was irreversibly stuck, marooned in the squishy sea of mud.

It was all over but the head-shaking and finger-pointing, so we waded back to the wreck, figuring to be released soon. I speculated that the crane would have to be abandoned, left to become a rusty permanent fixture in a hell of a strange setting. No one argued against that prediction. A head or two would likely roll somewhere up the line, but that didn't concern us. It was the price they paid for wearing uniforms stained with fruit salad and riding around in choppers looking to start fights that others had to finish.

We wrung out our gear and sat back to wait for the honchos to call it off. It took all day. We were finally relieved just in time to splash back to Alpha's camp before dark, tired, bitten, and cranky.

Dave followed me inside the track and fired us each a smoke while I dug for dry socks. While he finished up a letter, I leaned back, marveling at how good a pair of soft fuzzy socks could feel on wrinkled feet. He folded up the paper and lazily stuffed it into an envelope. He wrote "FREE" where the stamp goes, sealed it, and stuck it back in his shirt pocket. I gyrated my ankles and wiggled my toes.

"And I thought college was boring," I said, blowing smoke rings while I studied my feet. "Antsy to split after one year. I could be lounging in my dorm room now, watching *Laugh In* and figuring the odds of getting laid this weekend."

"Don't take it so hard, amigo. The war probably would've waited for you anyway."

"You got that right. I remember one guy, down the hall. A senior. Really worried about getting into graduate school so he wouldn't get drafted." I bummed another Kool, lit up. "Come to think of it, he's the only guy there I remember talking much about Nam."

Dave looked up. "What school did you go to, anyway?"

"A small one. East Central State College in Ada, Oklahoma. They average around three thousand students, and a lot of them come from hick towns you couldn't find on a map. They are seriously behind the times, no doubt about it. When I was there, politics on campus was mostly about dormitory rules or voting for the football queen. They heard stories of hippies and demonstrators at other schools, like OU, but where they came from, long hair was only found on rock stars and West Coast mental defectives. No offense."

He just smiled. "So how'd you end up on the hot seat?"

I took a long draw and blew smoke, nodding. "Good question. One I've been asking myself lately. I think mainly it had to do with how I was raised. I grew up in Midwest City. It's home to an Air Force base and as blue collar as they get. Most of my buddies either joined or got drafted. So far, four of them didn't come back. It's a bit of a rough town, with lots of local pride and little tolerance for non-hackers. By my sophomore year in college, I was feeling self-conscious about laying low in the classroom."

"What about your folks? Were they okay with you getting sent here?"

"It was never talked about. If my dad doesn't approve of the war, he has never said so. As far as I can tell, he's pretty neutral."

"Aren't you bugged by that?"

"Naw. My dad was an aircraft gunner in World War II. He works in civil service now. It was drilled into my head early on that healthy young men are indebted to their country to the tune of a military obligation. If you're called, you go. No questions asked. At the same time, he was determined that his kids would go to college. So he may be wrestling with it some. Anyway, after my freshman year, I got restless. I wasn't exactly eager to dive in, but I felt I should at least have my hat in the ring."

"You quit school?"

"Not at first. I just got lazy, dropped a few classes. I guess I was letting nature take its course. It didn't take long before my deferment was repossessed."

Dave didn't have to say anything for me to figure out what he thought about that.

"Wanna know the funny part? The first draft lottery came out three months after I was inducted. My number would have been three-forty-five."

His eyes widened at that. "So you had two ways to skate and came up empty?"

"Yeah, I guess so. I've never really thought about it that way."

"What about you?" I asked.

"Me? Simple. I had no money for college. End of story."

"So you got drafted, like me, only quicker. You must have studied up on the war ahead of time, though. You seem to know a lot."

"I don't know a lot, but I like history. Some of it is pretty interesting. Some of it is pretty scary, too."

"But you came anyway."

"Yep." He paused. "I didn't have any more choice than you, for a lot of the same reasons."

It started raining like a bastard and Dave bugged out. Soon the squad had crowded inside. I had first watch, so I climbed into the driver's chair and raised the deck hatch enough to see out. Staring into the blur, I couldn't help but think of the crane. I smiled to myself, groped for a sundry four-pack of Marlboros, freed one, and lit up. Within minutes, my back started to ache and I wondered how long this hour would really last. At least I wouldn't have to worry about bugs for awhile.

Bugs. I toyed with the idea of which was worse, the fear of getting wasted or the elements. Thinking about it reminded me of the last tunnel I had reconned, and I shuddered. It had been a simple unconcealed hole in the ground on land that was parched and naked. Armed with the lieu-tenant's .45 and a flashlight, I dropped into the tight, five-foot deep entrance and flipped the light on. I drew a deep breath, went to my knees, and lowered my head to peer into the dusty darkness. The passage was tight, extending about forty feet. At that point, it appeared to hook sharply left. So far so good. I started out, already sweating freely and hop-ing I could wrap it up at the point of the junction. I inched along on hands and knees, flashlight and pistol held awkwardly in each hand. The ceiling was low, and dirt crumbled and fell with each forward motion, pelting my hair and sticking to the back of my neck. I visualized a cave-in and felt a sudden urge to back out of there. For a minute, I held still, mentally forcing myself to steady up. When my nerves settled, I slowly continued to the turn, scanning carefully for hidden trapdoors or pressure-release detonators. I was sweating a river and sucking in equal parts of dirt and air. By now, my hands were so slippery I could barely keep a proper grip on the weighty .45. At the bend, I held the flashlight around the corner in an outstretched hand so that if shots were fired or a machete flashed, at least it wouldn't be my head. Nothing happened, so I scrunched forward for a look-see.

Thirty feet ahead was another sharp turn, highlighted by a dim glint of light filtering in from an apparent outlet. After a careful scan with the hazy beam of light, I continued my forward creep. Halfway along, I happened to glance up when my beam of light hit the ceiling and I found myself nose-to-nose with a monstrous centipede. I reflexively jerked back, smacking my head and showering myself with dirt. I gasped, sucking dust down my throat. Holy shit! I took a couple of breaths, then repositioned the light to make sure he hadn't advanced on me. I figured he'd go ten inches easy, and while he hadn't moved, all those squiggly legs were in motion, rising and falling in some bizarre firing order, as if warming up for the charge.

It was no contest. I couldn't shoot it, and I couldn't risk losing my light by taking a swing at it. The thought of having that thing end up in my hair or on my bare back sent goose bumps racing up both arms. I stared at it for a minute, then did the only sensible thing. I started backing up. It was a long way to go in reverse, but there was no choice. It took a good ten minutes to work my way out. I was shiny with sweat and caked with dirt. I told the LT I couldn't get through because the passage got too narrow, which from my point of view wasn't a total lie. From the look of me, he had no problem buying it. Once I caught my breath, I rounded up some Bangalores and blew both entrances, leaving the oversized insect with at least a headache and a few tons of earth to burrow through if he planned to ever see daylight again.

Lightning flashed, interrupting the reverie. The illumination revealed nothing sinister, only the density of the raindrops splashing into the soupy land. I was glad to be out of the swamp, inside the track, and mostly dry. I thought of the centipede again and shivered, but not like I had then. I remembered that at the end of that day, we had set up a night laager in the defoliated wasteland, and just before the sun met the earth, a cloud layer slipped in from the east and it started to rain. It was a moderate cloudburst, but heavy enough that the squad took refuge inside the track. Recognizing an opportunity, I grabbed a bar of soap, stripped, and had a shower so refreshing it was hard not to sing.

13

Here Today, Gone Today

War is hell, but actual combat is a motherfucker.
—COLONEL DAVID HACKWORTH

Late April 1970. 25th Infantry Division. Southwest of Cu Chi.

The platoon clanked out of the swamp to rejoin the company, but before we could link up, they got into it with a sizable force of well-armed Viet Cong in the vicinity of the Sugar Mill. We upped the pace but were too far away to get there in time to do any good. It was over when we arrived. With the help of artillery, the company was credited with seven enemy killed.

From there, we returned to LZ Devin, where we spent the afternoon cleaning weapons and equipment. I was hoping for a short layover, but it was to be another week of filling sandbags, standing guard, and suffering the incessant late-night arty fire missions. The big guns were apt to go off any time, and the holler of firing orders was the only warning we got. Sleep was spotty, and I was eager to get out of there when it was finally time to rotate with Charlie at the end of the month.

A bunch of us were in the squad's bunker cooling down when the lieutenant stepped through the door with mischief in his eyes. Ridgeway got to his feet and held his hands up. "I don't like this already." This was backed up by a small chorus of affirming noises. All eyes were on the LT.

"Take it easy, guys," he said, half-grinning.

It was not a trustworthy grin. Ranger said, "Unless you brought beer, women, or orders for the World, we're not interested."

The LT smiled. "You sure you don't want to know? Cause I can peddle this happy news elsewhere."

This time everybody spoke at once. He waved us off. "Calm down. Take it easy."

"Seriously, lieutenant," John said.

"Okay, okay. What we're really going do is RIF for a few days—he stood there beaming—and then hit Cu Chi Base Camp for a three-day stand-down."

With a slight look of wonder on his face, John finally sat up. "No shit?"

"No shit. I have it on good authority that beer and steaks await. Orders for the World aren't likely, and you'll have to find your own women, which I don't want to know about."

That afternoon, joined by a couple of flame tracks (known as "Zippos"), we saddled up and scooted into the outback to prowl for enemy and their hiding places near the Iron Triangle. McDonald was in the rear getting a tooth fixed and I had been left in charge of the .50. Some ARVNs we'd picked up at their compound in Go Da Hau were along for the ride. Two of them sat on the rear of 1-4, smoking and joking and for the most part keeping to themselves. We didn't like it, but so long as they stayed out of the way it would be easy enough to pretend they weren't there.

A couple hours of scorching tunnels by the flames called for a breather. The guys on the Zippos complained about the lack of "crispy critters," their name for roasted Viet Cong, and wanted to call the whole thing off. The riflemen dismounted and tried to capture slivers of shade next to the APCs. Then a lone VC materialized out of nowhere and walked up to our tracks, hands in the air. One of the flame troops hollered, "No fair!" but the lieutenant waved him off and took custody of the barefooted Cong.

He was the first live one I'd seen, and I stared down at him from the gun turret of 1-4. He was promptly handcuffed and quizzed by people from the CP and one of the South Vietnamese. It was easy to imagine the little turd setting Claymores along Highway 1 at night and lobbing rocket-propelled grenades at isolated tracks. It made me wonder what I might have done had he surrendered to me in a situation where I had choices concerning his future. After awhile a Huey swooped in to pick him up. Two ornery-looking Vietnamese commandos hopped out, hustled him aboard, and left in a rush. Judging by the worry on the VC's face, I didn't figure they had a problem in knowing what to do.

Just after operations resumed, one of the Zippos got lucky and lit up a couple of Viet Cong. Nine of their buddies tried to flee but were cut down by 2nd Platoon guns. 1st Platoon was in a holding position just out of range and missed out once again. All we could do was stand up and crane our necks.

It was a bad day for the VC, but the god of ill-fortune soon redirected his attention. Only a half-klick away, Littlefield had a lapse in map-reading ability and led the company straight into a minefield. At the discovery of this a halt was ordered and the lieutenant sent word: "Boobytraps in the area. Nobody un-asses their track."

"Too late," Ranger said.

Huh? The rest of us jerked around in time to see one of the Vietnamese hit the ground and step off toward 1-2. It was just like before.

"Shit!" Spencer yelled. "Hey, man, get back over here."

Everybody shouted, but it was a waste. The ARVN continued on, doing it his way, until he'd covered half the distance, about seventy-five feet. That's when he mashed a pressure-release detonator that sent a spray of shrapnel out of the earth with a jarring boom and enough velocity to shred flesh and amputate limbs.

The explosion stung our ears and pelted us with sand. The ARVN performed a short vertical climb, then did a half-twist and thudded limply back to earth face first.

"Goddamn," John said. Everybody knew what was coming.

Littlefield was on the horn. "What happened over there? Acknowledge. What happened?"

The lieutenant came back. "Got an ARVN casualty here, sir. Dismounted without permission."

"What do you mean an ARVN casualty? Whose track was he on?"

"One-Four, captain."

"One-Four!?" he bawled. "Why did you allow that man off your track?"

Spencer answered, "He hopped off before we could stop him, sir, and he wouldn't come back."

"What do you mean you couldn't stop him? Who's in charge, you or the ARVN?"

"I'm in charge, captain. But—"

"No buts, sergeant. Do you read me?" Then, not waiting for a reply, "Nobody moves. You copy that? NOBODY!"

"Copy clear, captain."

"What's the status of the casualty?"

The lieutenant took over. "Too bloody to tell for sure, but he's still sucking air, at least for the moment. Sir."

"Lieutenant, get your medic down there and call for a dustoff, and when we get laagered I want to see First Platoon leadership at the CP."

We watched wide-eyed as first Doc, then Smitty, ignoring Littlefield's order, lowered themselves from 1-3 and tippy-toed over to the ARVN—a thirty-foot trek that gave the rest of us a chance to practice the art of seat-squirming. Luckily, Littlefield's view was blocked by other tracks. Smitty and Doc were tight, so I couldn't blame him. I saw the LT on 1-1 throw up his hands, but he kept quiet. The last thing he wanted was more trouble with the CO.

The Vietnamese looked like he had lost his whole inventory of blood and then some. They tied off bleeders and stuffed gauze in holes with as much speed as they could muster, then waited for the medevac, which made the trip quick and floated in, but didn't land. Instead, it hovered a few feet off the ground, apparently not willing to risk touchdown.

Doc and Smitty waited, but no moves were made from the chopper. Finally, Doc hopped up and trotted another thirty feet across heart-stopping terrain to get a litter.

"Would you look at that?" John had stood up, shading his eyes. "God-damn ARVN gets blown up, puts us in a jam like this, and the only ones risking their ass are Doc and Smitty."

"They just figured the less people on the ground the better," Spencer allowed.

"Maybe the boobytrap was a fluke." I busily chewed a thumbnail while telling the lie. "Those guys have already moved around quite a bit."

"Don't mean nothin'," John said.

I had no response.

They flopped the slippery and gouged body onto the stretcher, hoisted it, and moved out. By now, I was gnawing my thumb like a hamster working an almond, and my heart had climbed into my throat where it could throb better. I was vaguely aware of my left knee bouncing to an nonexistent rhythm. *Come on*, I said to myself. *Just a few steps. Walk on air. Walk on air.*

They moved at a measured pace, hunched over, following the same path Doc had just cleared. The chopper's jet engine whined and its rotor smacked the air in defiance of gravity, dispensing grit in gusts and causing the litter-bearers to lean into the whipping wind it brewed.

They made the delivery and started back, Doc out front, Smitty a couple of steps back. The dustoff shifted around some, but didn't leave. It just hung there, waiting to make sure nobody else would need a lift.

All eyes were glued to Doc's footfalls. Wisely, they choose the nearest place of refuge relative to the chopper, which was 1-4, but they had to veer off-course to get there. They stepped lightly, squinting against the dust kicked up by the Huey. About forty feet out, I saw Doc glance back at Smitty just as he took the final step of his Vietnam war.

The blast lifted them both into the air at odd angles in a geyser of hot dirt. The platoon came to its feet and stood frozen in shock as they hit the deck in another grisly display of human demolition.

"Son of a bitch!" Before I knew it I was on the ground, running, completely oblivious to the possible consequences. I reached Doc first and dropped to my knees. He was struggling to draw air, and I had no idea what to do. I leaned over him and frantically tried to make sense of the blood-streaked mess he'd turned into. I couldn't tell a thing, so I looked up and called for help. The dustoff had settled, and I kept hollering until one of their medics dismounted and worked his way over. He nudged me aside and started digging in his aid bag. He rolled Doc over onto his back, stuck him with morphine, and then went to work on his legs. I pulled off my flak jacket and worked it under his head. From the corner of my eye I could see somebody next to Smitty, hands busy.

Doc groaned through tightly clenched teeth. "Can you hear me?" I said. His back was arched and he was trying to gyrate, but his legs wouldn't work. His face was blood-streaked and twisted up and his hands shook violently.

"Listen to me, Doc. You stepped on a toe-popper." This was a lie. A toe-popper didn't have the punch to take out two men with such force. I didn't know what it had been, but I didn't want Doc thinking the worst. "You took some shrapnel but you're still in one piece. Do you hear me, Doc?"

His eyes were clenched shut, his face a grimace. I got no answer. He was capable of nothing beyond struggling against the agony that had been inflicted. I leaned in close. "Listen to me if you can, Doc. You're cut up some, but you're gonna be okay. Smitty too." I patted his shoulder lightly, but he didn't know I existed. He was cooking in an oven of pain that kept his jaw clamped so tight it made the tendons on his neck stand out like thin ropes.

I watched while the medic worked. Doc's fatigues had been turned into a tossed salad of red and green. He was slashed from one end to the other, with the worst of it up the insides of his legs and around his knees, where fountains of blood oozed and bubbled.

Another medic muscled in, so I moved back while they got ready to move him. He was still quivering when they loaded him onto the chopper next to Smitty, and I just stood there and stared, wondering if he had heard a word. I didn't get a close look at Smitty, but I figured he wasn't in much better shape. I knew that I would never see either of them again.

The medevac set pitch, skimmed the ground nose-down, banked, and sailed away. I watched as it gained altitude, then for the first time became aware of my own predicament. I stood alone, flak jacket in hand, with forty feet of deadly ground between me and ROTTIN "8" NO. II. Inside my head, everything I'd just witnessed was replayed in Technicolor—a preview of wheat I might experience as the next loser. New sweat trickled while I tried to make myself take the first step. Everyone was watching.

The vest was my only protection, and it wouldn't do much good at the wrong end of a blast. That's when I did the first sensible thing. I wrapped it between my legs, got a good grip on it, and drew a long breath to steel my nerves. I took one more look at the expanse of earth I had to negotiate and the scuffed-up boots that for now still held my feet.

I stepped off, mustering all the positive energy I could, but each time one foot went in front of the other the suspense started all over again. I had it figured at about fifteen paces, stretching as far as I could without losing balance. Sweat stung my eyes, making it hard to see, and I had to use both hands to stay in the saddle. I didn't care how ridiculous I looked. That I could live with, given the opportunity. Five steps to go, now three, now only two. All I was conscious of was the pounding of my heart and how cruel it would be to go up in smoke this close to home.

At last, I reached out and swung myself up onto 1-4's treads, paused, and let out a long breath. I slung my flak jacket topside and pulled myself up. As I climbed in behind the .50 I noticed expressions of relief on a few faces. Mike gave me a little pat on the back and said, "Good work, my man." I couldn't think clearly enough to answer. I just nodded my head.

If Littlefield had imposed his wrath on the platoon over Smitty dismounting, or if he knew I had done the same, I didn't hear about it. Nor did I care. Once he got his directions straight he ordered an about-face and we proceeded to ease out of there. Nobody had to be told to keep all body parts away from the deck's edge.

Once we had cleared the area the company went back to work reconning the wasteland, as if the incident had been little more than a slight interruption. Spencer was the only one with much to say, and he was more worried over the meeting with the CO than he was Smitty or Doc, and he wouldn't shut up about it.

"I know those guys were your buddies, Ross," he droned, "but you're not supposed to leave that Fifty under any circumstances. When you're behind that machine gun, that's your only responsibility." Blah, blah, blah.

By now, my internal engine had dropped below redline, and I felt tired. Tired led to cranky, and Spencer's blather grated like sandpaper on sore ears. I was thinking how good it would feel to crack some bones in his face with a short butt stroke, never mind that he was right. I shouldn't have abandoned the .50, even though we could have seen attackers coming a klick away. I just didn't want to hear it. At least not now. Spencer's lack of reverence and non-stop mouth had reached the limits of my endurance.

I was still in a sour mood at dusk, sitting alone atop 1-4, when Dave climbed aboard and asked if he could share my space. Within minutes the talk turned to what had happened and from there to deeper subjects, like how war robs men of their future by confiscating their lives or leaving them crippled. The conversation was dark and depressing but we both needed to have it. I was in mid-sentence when Spencer walked up and interrupted.

"I need volunteers to uncrate the Bangalores dropped off earlier," he said, "and you're it."

His words scraped my mind like crushed glass dragged by a steel rake. I slowly turned my head and stared down at him, feeling the pressure rise up like an over-stoked boiler.

"Find somebody else," I said. "If you can't find somebody else, we'll do it later. We're talkin' here. Leave us alone." I turned back to Dave, confident my tone had helped him glimpse the undercurrent at work.

It didn't.

"Listen, Ross," he said snidely, "what happened today is over, and the rest of us, including you, are still here and still have to do what we're told."

It was how he said it more than anything. I turned back to him, searching for words.

"I don't know what your problem is," he went on, "but I'm your squad leader and I'm telling you to come with me. This work needs to be done and there's no sense putting it off."

He still didn't understand that he had picked the worst time to fuck with me, but I was beyond making allowances.

"Get the hell out of here," I said as evenly as possible. My self-control was all but gone.

"Who do you think you are?" he shot back. "You're a PFC, I'm a sergeant, and I'm telling you to come with me. Understand?"

I felt my face screw up and I jabbed a finger at him. "You listen to me," I seethed. "If you don't get out of here, now, I'm coming down there and rip your goddamn fucking throat out."

Now it was his face that contorted, but he just stood there, soaking up my glare. Either the murder in my eyes or the conviction in my voice had penetrated his reinforced skull, and after a long moment of deciding whether or not to call my bluff, he said, "You're crazy, you know that?"

"Goddamn straight," I said. It was the most intelligent thing I had heard him say yet.

"Don't think we won't take this up later," he said, and walked off, shaking his head.

———•———

Word circulated that Smitty and Doc would both survive but would not be back. There would be no good-byes, as they would be on their way to Japan before the company returned to Cu Chi. I dwelled on it for a day or two until I realized it was useless to stay down over things that couldn't be changed. At least they were alive. I made a promise to look them up when I got back to the World, even though realistically I knew it would probably never happen.

By the time we came in from the field, I was ready to get showered, get fed, and get loaded. Spencer had failed to deliver on his threat, not that I cared one way or another. We'd been promised three days of the good life, and I planned to get a full share. When I bellied up to the bar that night, I had a smile stretched from one side of my face to the other. Everything that had gone before had been stuffed into my mind's pantry, padlocked, and removed from conscious thought.

14

Strangers in
a Strange Land

Gentlemen, we are being killed on the beaches.
Let's go inland and be killed.

—GENERAL NORMAN COTA, D-DAY, JUNE 6, 1944

Early May 1970. 25th Infantry Division.
Cu Chi Base Camp.

The Enlisted Men's Club had a fresh shipment of Schlitz in stock, more than I could slurp down in one night. I lost count of the empties somewhere between the Pilipino band's version of "Little Bit 'O Soul" and the start of the Australian magic act. Then a shouting match broke out when somebody at the bar switched off a rerun of *Playboy After Dark* and cranked the volume on AFVN radio. I bought two more to go and wobbled off into the night.

Right around daybreak, I rolled over and felt the first spears of pain announcing my hangover stab through my left eye. Before I could suppress it and doze off, the CQ of the orderly room banged into our tin-roof barracks with a slam of the screen door and ordered everybody up pronto for a formation. He repeated himself, then tried to rip the hinges off on his way out.

When this information crawled down my ear canal and wormed its way into my brain, my aching eyes popped open wide. *Formation?* There

151

weren't supposed to be any formations! I sat up, groaned, and groped for my boots. It couldn't be a mistake, so it had to be bad news. No, it had to be worse than bad news. They were going to screw us out of our vacation. I could already see my three precious days evaporating, fading into thin air like dissipating swamp mist.

"What the fuck?" McDonald was hanging half off his bunk, sideways. His hair was a snarl and his eyes were puffy and bloodshot. He was digging earnestly for a booger.

John was already on his feet. "Hurry up," he said. "I wanna know what's goin' on."

"We're not gonna like it, I know that." I had my hands over my ears, trying to maintain noise discipline inside my skull.

"You got that right," McDonald allowed. He was struggling for balance while trying to right himself and ream his nose at the same time.

"Come on," John said, "let's go."

We tromped outside, a bedraggled, half-dressed bunch, and joined the gathering of other confused, bleary-eyed men. Littlefield and the lieutenants were clumped together next to the orderly room, staring at maps. Clerks were shuttling information between the powwow and ringing telephones inside.

"Nam sucks," a woozy voice announced.

"I don't think this has a damn thing to do with Nam," somebody answered.

I turned toward the voice and was about to ask what that meant when Littlefield came before the group and lowered the boom.

"The stand-down is canceled."

Moans and protests filled the air. "Nam SUCKS!" the same voice cried.

"As you were! In one hour, we will be moving out as part of a task force ordered to clear NVA base camps inside Cambodia. Your platoon leaders will brief you at the motor pool after you draw your weapons and top off your tracks. That's it. Let's move."

We just stood there, trying to get our heads around the sudden turn of events. But there was not a damn thing to be done about it, so we shuffled back to our racks, packed it up, and headed for the armory.

The LT told us it could be as long as sixty days but that penetration across the border was limited to fifteen miles. Some consolation. He also suggested that chasing NVA through the jungle was going to be a little bit different than RIFing the Filhol.

"Can you believe it?" McDonald bristled. We had geared up and were waiting in line for fuel at the motor pool.

"I believe it," John said. "They've been hankering to kick ass on Cambodia for years."

"They could've waited three more days." I rubbed my temples, hoping to cushion them from the rubber hammer beating them in time with my pulse.

"You got that wrong," Mike said. "We needed two more months. I would have been gone. Lord."

We headed north on Route 1 toward Tay Ninh. It was a long ride and allowed time for contemplation about what lay ahead. Around Cu Chi, we knew basically what to expect. Cambodia was a mystery, humming with main force NVA, and it could be a head-knocker. I had to consider the idea that some of us might not come back. I then had to remind myself that it was pointless to try to apply levels of risk. Getting uptight about a change of scenery didn't make a helluva lot of sense. Stand 'em up and we'll knock 'em down. Anyplace, anytime. That was the unspoken motto. Still, dark thoughts hung in the recesses, clinging to my mind like a snoozing bat.

We linked with Battalion HQ and the Scout Platoon along with Bravo and Charlie companies outside Tay Ninh City, where we pulled over for a breather. A column of over fifty APCs lined the roadside while the colonel and the captains huddled. Surveying the assemblage, I had to wonder what we might be pitted against that would require this much firepower. In the distance Nui Ba Dinh, the Black Virgin Mountain, stood as the sole matron of the land for as far as the eye could see.

We took advantage of the stop to scrounge for lunch.

"Anybody pack sodas?" McDonald was an admitted popaholic.

No one had.

"Damn! I can't believe that shit. Gotta do every damn thing myself, seems like." He sulked for a minute, then snapped out of it. "Who's gonna trade me C's, then?" The squad's latest policy was to bust only one case of rations per meal and take turns picking.

"Whatcha got?" Ridgeway peered at the cardboard box in McDonald's hands.

"Ham and motherfuckers."

"No."

"How about you, Mikey?" He stretched out so he could peer over Abbott's shoulder.

"You're outta your mind," Mike said. He hunched down, protecting his grub.

"Yeah? What are you hiding down there?"

"Beans and franks. Stay away."

McDonald's face went long. "Don't think I won't remember this, buttlick."

About the time the rest of us finished, a Vietnamese came along selling subs and McDonald had the last laugh. He bought two, and every few minutes hollered, "No bites!" He was still munching happily when we pulled out.

Chinook helicopters, high overhead, flew by one after the other, and farther north we passed some staging areas for the impending assault. Clusters of civilians along the roadway appeared puzzled, as if witnessing a parade that had arrived without prior billing.

Another aftershock of the night's boozing kicked in shortly after lunch, and I was dog-ass tired by the time the sun was halfway through its descent, but there was much ground yet to cover. With Nui Ba Dinh fading behind us, our tracks turned off the blacktop and picked up a rutty dirt road leading into a loosely-jungled outback. We snaked our way into the wilderness, bouncing along, until the sun sat orange and bulging on the treetops, forcing the brass to finally call it a day.

Alpha was directed into a vast clearing spotted with rotting logs and sun-bleached skeletons of standing dead trees. The jungle on three sides was a dense wall of triple canopy towering into the sky. There was no wind, and the curtains of poker-faced emerald stood as motionless as cliffs, casting hard shadows across the land. The whole picture had a don't-tread-on-me look to it, and I kept glancing over my shoulder, feeling like a sneak-thief whose cover had just been blown. Sitting atop the track, the sense of being watched became so strong I expected to see beady eyes staring back at me every time I scanned the boughs. It was the haunted house syndrome I'd felt that night on Highway 1 all over again. Internal sentries were on the move, pushing alert buttons at every turn. I blew out a deep breath and reached for a smoke.

The light was low when Littlefield dispatched patrols to recon the buffer zone and set out trip flares. Ranger and I got stuck with Spencer, tagged to cover our part of the perimeter. Unless we wanted to stumble around in the dark, it would have to be quick, so we set a fast pace. About forty yards out, we started finding empty artillery casings and other artifacts not worth further inspection, so we began scouting for a place to set the flares. That's when Spencer discovered two aluminum canisters half-buried in the sand that none of us could identify. With the light fading fast, Ranger and I voted to leave them alone and started off. But Spencer didn't follow. His curiosity was too great.

"Hold on a minute," he said. "I want to see what's in these tubes."

We both stopped and turned around.

"Leave them alone," I said. "They could be boobytrapped."

"Naw, there's nothin' hooked to these things," he said. "I already checked."

"Yeah?" Ranger said. "How long have you had X-Ray vision?"

Spencer knelt down, scrutinizing his find. "You guys worry too much. These babies have been here for ages."

"Do it alone, then," I said, and we walked off. I looked back in time to see him pull one of the containers loose and rattle it next to his ear, like a kid with a gift box. "What a fucking dullard," Ranger said. We agreed to always be near cover when Spencer tried to commit suicide.

The night air was thick and still. Littlefield ordered mad minutes twice, both after my watch, and by the time I finally hit a dead sleep, the first hint of light was on the horizon.

We moved out at sunup, still speculating on how bad it could get once we crossed over. It's one thing to swat hornets when occasionally encountered, but quite another to crawl inside their nest. Entering a bandit's hideout was sure to have consequences; the only question was whether the

NVA would choose offense or defense. Ridgeway was getting short, and decided he didn't want to be topside during contact. He offered the side-mounted M60 to me. Mike could have had it, but turned it down flat, so John cleared it with the LT and I took over the machine gun on the spot, not sure if I had been upgraded or suckered.

In a far corner of the clearing, a narrow corridor stabbed off into the jungle. It was a rugged path bulldozed by the engineers who had gone ahead to build a floating bridge across the Rach Cai Bach River separating Vietnam from Cambodia. As we entered onto the path, Littlefield decided there could be mines about, so he directed us just off-trail to traverse the debris field left by the dozers. We inched along over the sea of splintered tree limbs and bamboo stubble, rocking and bobbing along. For the first time I was bounced off the track, landing hard on my ass but without injury. Mike thought it was funny until he took a spill and let go with some choice words. I could have laughed, but decided the fall was payback enough. Getting to the border took all day.

The trail flared into a clearing near the river's edge, where the Rach Cai Bach's murky, pea-green water moved sluggishly through the jungle. The snaky waterway looked to be about a hundred feet wide. Along both sides, drooping branches swept the wet surface like drowsy brooms. Dead-center of the clearing, engineers toiled to finish a pontoon bridge stout enough to support a convoy of armored vehicles. On the opposite bank, a squiggly trail disappeared into the thickness through a mouse hole in the jungle. On all sides, dense foliage billowed up, leafy and dark, giving evil-doers good cover for dirty deeds.

Bravo Company had escorted the engineers. Charlie, Delta, and the Battalion HQ pulled in at twilight and spread out in the brush by a bend in the river. Straight-legs from 3/22d Infantry, neither seen nor heard, had choppered in earlier to secure the other side, positioned a safe distance inland. Just about dusk, as the construction crew put the finishing touches on the bridge, a column of tracks from 1/5th Mechanized rolled in to join the gathering.

Alpha's tracks fronted the riverbank, with the bridge to our immediate left. At midnight I climbed topside and snuggled in behind the .50 for watch. An occasional firefly blinked in the still, sultry air, and after awhile

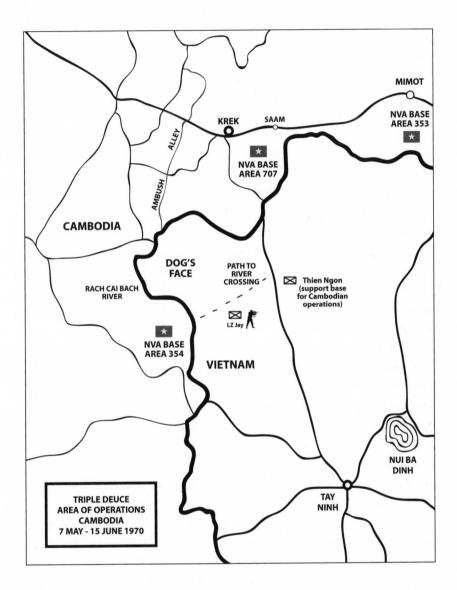

**TRIPLE DEUCE
AREA OF OPERATIONS
CAMBODIA
7 MAY - 15 JUNE 1970**

a rising moon, glinting pale yellow off the dingy water, made the boxy APCs appear in stronger silhouette. Unlike Cu Chi and the Filhol, there were no sounds of war bleeding through. It was as quiet as you might expect in such a primitive place, and except for wandering fireflies and the whine of mosquitoes, even the night creatures were laying low. The bridge was continuously watched by sentries from the HQ camp, who blooped

M79 grenade rounds into the near thickets on the opposite bank every so often. The flash and karump of their detonations split the stillness and resonated eerily along the river's curves.

I stared at the tangled branches dragging the current, thinking we were about to be fed a pill more bitter than your average Joes are used to swallowing. I was no longer a rookie. I considered myself combat-worthy. But this was an unchartered and unpredictable mission, and I was tensed up like an over-torqued mainspring. Such jitters would have to be snuffed if I expected to navigate Dracula's mansion without having my jugular drained. That much was certain, so I concentrated on beefing up my resolve. It worked, but took a lot of concentration, and by the time I woke Ranger for watch I had a headache mean enough to kill a small dog.

At dawn, diesel exhaust hung in the wet air as we revved up and rambled across the floating bridge into Cambodia. Our point of entry was just below the chin of what the maps called the Dog's Face. Sister companies and the other units headed west and north. We shadowed the river southward to rummage around an area tagged NVA Base Area 354, whatever that meant.

The triple canopy blocked enough light to keep the foliage thinned out down low, and our pace was quick. The jungle floor was flat, damp, smelly. At the first curve along the river we found a cluster of crude hootches and lean-tos that appeared to be a rest station of sorts for the NVA. A quick search turned up nothing, so we torched it and moved on. Pretty soon the radio got busy with reports that Charlie and Bravo Companies had already clashed with small pockets of NVA. Charlie killed three, then gave chase and drove two tracks over land mines, triggering the ambush they had just been conned into. We could hear machine-gun fire far off, and chatter on the box made it sound like they'd launched the next global war.

We held up briefly, waiting to see if they needed help, but things died down quicker than expected, so we kept moving. At some point we turned west, and as the day wore on it began to look like we were trolling in the wrong place when 2nd Platoon's lead tracks took small arms and automatic weapons fire from a feisty but small element of NVA. With only five tracks in front of us we joined in with return fire, aiming up-trail on the right flank. Occasional green tracers zipped by overhead, but they were either ricochets or horribly misguided rounds, because the core of the action was concentrated at the front of the column. It was over in a few minutes. There were no casualties or damage to the tracks, while four NVA gave it up for Ho Chi Minh. They were left where they fell to rot. After that things heated up, and by day's end we had been harassed by small arms fire four more times, on each occasion quickly knocking it down with machine guns and grenades before moving on.

We caught up with Delta, Bravo, and Battalion HQ at a night defensive position on open ground sparsely spiked with lofty trees. A pair of mobile 175mm howitzers served as the centerpiece of the camp, and we were barely settled in when the first fire mission dispensed brain-rattling shockwaves that echoed through the jungle. For the next several hours, sleep came at the discretion of artillery forward observers, further nourishing my hatred for loud noise.

Things got quiet late, and I soaked peacefully in the silence. I rotated my stiff joints and rolled my head in self-massage, settling in for blissful rest. Just as I dropped off a different kind of explosion jerked me upright. Mortar rounds were dropping in on Bravo's slice of the perimeter. Return fire lit up the blackness with a roar, but it was a quick hit-and-run and I was barely on board the track when it ended. Even so, by the time the Red Alert was downgraded to Yellow another hour had passed. I felt half dead when I finally stretched out, pledging to clobber the first person who disturbed me. It was an empty threat, but it had a calming effect and in a few seconds I was out.

—•—

Rockets are dropping inside the perimeter. Everything is hazy and sepia-toned, like dreams sometimes are. But this is too real to be a dream. I see men jerk up out of sleeping positions dazed and disoriented. They race in every direction, yelling. I climb for the M-60 and brace for a human wave attack. Weapons are going off in a roar. I hear screams and see a grunt from 2nd Platoon writhing on the ground. He's clutching his left knee and thrashing his head in agony. I can see that his right boot is gone, his foot blown off. I holler for a medic, but my cry is lost in another ear-splitting detonation. I have the trigger fully depressed and my machine gun recoils jerkily on its mount. The noise is overwhelming, but not so loud it drowns out the whistle of another incoming shell. I'm convinced it will be a direct hit, but with nowhere to go I remain frozen in place. Just before it hits my eyes pop open to silent blackness.

Sweat beads covered my forehead and my breath came in puffs. For several minutes I didn't move, afraid it was not really a dream, and that if I moved I might somehow get pulled back into that other reality.

Then a coarse voice whispered, "Hey, are you awake?"

It was John, rousting me for watch.

I sat up, looked around. "Yeah, okay," I said. "I got it." I climbed aboard the track wide-eyed, heart still thumping. I spent the next hour expecting the dream to resurrect itself for real.

———•——

A resupply chopper brought us a new medic, Carter Johnson. He was a big, round-faced black with a ready smile and the right attitude but no experience and too much anxiety. He would have to overcome these defects quick to avoid finding himself in a world of shit. Even so, it was good to have a new medicine man in the platoon, and an honest effort was made to welcome him aboard.

We had moved from the jungle into the open and traversed a treeline. The tracks were in column, two abreast, about a hundred yards off the woods. Staring at the mute wall of trees was giving me the willies for some reason. Something wasn't right, and I couldn't shake the feeling that we were about to get thumped. In fact, I was so sure of it I said something to McDonald. I kept my eyeballs glued to the greenery and sure enough, a faint *tunk* announced a launched mortar. I yelled "INCOMING!" long and loud while the first round made the trip. The sharp crack of the detonation stung eardrums and sent tremors through the ground. It hit way short, slinging dirt and shrapnel into the sky. Number two came closer, and by the time we put on the brakes and swiveled to return fire they had walked in a third.

We poured lead into the woods while drivers jammed gears and spread out to dodge rounds. 1-3 track avoided a direct hit by about three feet, and it sent a bucketful of shrapnel up the side of their track like a wave smacking a cliff. Luckily, it was the last round. As soon as a cease fire was called I noticed Doc Johnson dismount 1-1 and head for the opposite side of 1-3, out of view.

"I can't believe this shit," I said. "I knew this was gonna happen. I knew it." If anybody heard me they didn't let on.

Spencer was on the horn getting the lowdown.

"We've got one for dustoff," he finally said. "Joe Jensen had a boot parked over the edge of the track and lost a piece of his foot."

For a second, I didn't make the connection, then the dream I'd had the night before came rushing back. I looked at Spencer and started to say something, but held up. It was too off-beat. Nobody would believe it. So I kept quiet and prowled my pockets for a smoke. I didn't believe in premonitions myself, and finally decided it had just been a weird similarity. By the time I finished a second cigarette, I resolved the issue by simply stuffing it into my mind's basement on top of the growing heap to be reckoned with another day. The medevac came to haul Jensen and his million dollar wound to the hospital, and the company moved on.

On May 10, the company turned back east and headed for Vietnam. It was a quick run to Thien Ngon, one of the forward support bases, for new orders. Why we had to go to Thien Ngon to get that done was lost on me, but there it was. Along the way we found ourselves single file on a sandy trail that was almost against the treeline on our left. Trolling for mines and inviting point-blank ambush is what it amounted to, but then I was too far down the food chain to have a voice in the matter, so I just kept a grip on the machine gun and left my lip zipped. Littlefield must have had his reasons, because there was a wide-open field next to us nobody was using.

"Glad somebody else is point," McDonald said lazily. We chuffed along at walking speed, way back in line. Little puffs of sun-warmed dust rose up in gritty clouds, sticking to our skin and reducing visibility.

"You got that right." I tried to remember what it felt like to be in the shade of the jungle. I tried to think of cool objects, like blocks of ice and swimming pools, but it didn't help. In spite of the potential danger at hand, the heat soon had me fighting a tingle of drowsiness that blossomed behind my eyes. Then something went wrong. A horrendous clap slammed ice-pick sharp into my ears, and I had the sensation of becoming weightless. Sparkles danced around my eyes and a peppering of sand stung my face. But before I could yell about it I was clubbed on the hip by what felt like a bat swung at a homerun ball. That put me in a stupor until my butt crashed into something hard enough to jar my bones.

I was in a daze and, for a minute, confounded about where I was or what had happened. Then the pressure inside my head eased up and for the most part I got my senses back. I realized I had come down to earth. Feeling an urgency I didn't understand, I struggled to my feet and tried to find balance. I looked around. The world was moving in dizzy slow motion and my thoughts were fragmented. I had the dim idea that we'd hit a mine and gotten tossed from the track. That would explain the cloud of dust sifting down and the shrill ringing in the center of my head. I tried to put a sequence of thoughts together but ended up with a heap of incomplete sentences.

I saw Ranger through the haze. He was stooped over, fumbling for his glasses like a drunk. He began a staggered climb back onto the track. I had trouble seeing the point in it and just kept watching him until he was on the deck, when all at once the breakers inside my head reset and danger signals flashed like highly charged neon. It was like coming out from under anesthesia. Everything made sense.

"Get down!" I yelled at him. "It was command det!" It almost had to be. Too many other tracks ahead of us had passed over the same patch of ground. Ranger looked at me and frowned, as if waiting to hear something that added up. I awkwardly climbed topside and lunged for .50 turret, hollering like a maniac, completely dumb to the fact that nobody else was shooting. Ranger still looked dazed, but he was coherent enough to take my word for it. He half-climbed, half-fell inside the track. I swung the machine gun toward the trees and lowered my head, ready to get to it, amazed that we hadn't been shot to pieces already.

Seconds passed. Nothing happened. For some reason there wasn't going to be a firefight. What the hell? Why blow a mine by remote control if it's not part of an ambush? I mulled this over until I heard a voice. When I turned and looked down, I saw the lieutenant staring up at me. He was talking, but there were gaps in his words.

"Are you okay?" he yelled.

I stared at him stone-faced until I pieced it together. "I don't know. I think so."

"You can come down now."

"What?"

"I said you can . . . never mind."

I figured I would have to climb down to get to the meat of the conversation and find out what he wanted. I gave the woods another close look, then dismounted, still trying to shake the cobwebs loose inside my head.

The rest of the squad stood silently around the track, like a collection of groggy zombies. Some looked up, some down, but nobody was talking. Each seemed lost in the same fuzzy world I'd been in.

Doc Johnson checked us out while the LT went to inform Littlefield that 1-4 track was beyond repair. My thinking cleared up, but a high-pitched guitar note with the amp at full blow continued to scream inside my head, making it difficult to understand words that were already muffled to begin with. I also had a knot on my hip where I'd glanced off the track on my way to the ground. Doc suspected most of us had ruptured eardrums and recommended that we all go to Cu Chi for proper evaluation. After talking it over with the captain, we were each given the option of staying or going.

My first thought was, *You've got to be kidding. I can choose whether to stay or go? Huh.* I was damned if that made sense. I wasn't qualified to make the diagnosis and in no shape to make such a decision, for that matter. I reasoned that rational people jumped at such opportunities, but given my nature I balked at the idea of bailing this early in the mission. Nobody else seemed to have a problem with it. Maybe they were in worse shape. How was I to know? When the dustoffs landed I was the only dimwit still hedging, and the lieutenant wanted an answer. I couldn't hear shit and I didn't have a track, but I wasn't bleeding. By my own standards, I wasn't injured. There was also a voice in my head telling me that if I chickened out now I could never lay claim to enduring Cambodia for the duration. Not a mature justification, but it won the argument. No quitter here.

I told the lieutenant I wasn't going. Time passed while a Sky Crane came and lugged 1-4 to the bone yard. With my meager belongings in hand, I shuffled over to 1-3, figuring my head would get back to normal in a day or two. Meanwhile I would have to adapt. My squad was gone, my machine gun was gone. The guys in 1-3 were buddies, but I was a loaner and would have no privileges and no place in the pecking order.

The company made Thien Ngon before dark, whereupon we were put under the operational control of the 2nd Brigade. At first light we fueled up and charged back into Cambodia, this time heading to the top of the Dog's Face, the suspected location of the southern headquarters for all NVA operations, known as COSVN, the so-called Central Office for South Vietnam. The dog whistle blowing inside my head hadn't eased a lick, and it occurred to me that Cambodia wasn't the best place for the hearing impaired. I thought of that old saying about never hearing the shot that kills you and had to suppress a laugh, as un-funny as it was.

By the time we squirmed deeply into the Cambodian wilderness, Cu Chi loomed in my mind as brightly as the Land of Oz.

15

The Body Farm

The bastards have never been bombed like they're going to be bombed this time.

—RICHARD NIXON

May 1970. 25th Infantry Division. NVA Base Area 707, near Krek, Cambodia.

The hiss of a projectile streaked through the night sky like chalk scarring a blackboard. But instead of fading as it spun on, it got louder, and when it turned to a low whistle conversation stopped dead. Dave and Bucky looked up. The rest of us froze in place, knowing what it meant but not believing. We had heard no tubes announcing the launch of mortars, and the dinks didn't have artillery this far south, even in Cambodia. The whistle changed pitch as the shell arced downward, until finally somebody snapped out of it and hollered, "INCOMING!"

We lunged from the top of the track, but the spinning shell was quicker. It smacked the earth and detonated thirty feet behind 1-3. From somewhere in mid-air, I watched time stop in the grip of a blinding silver flash that spread across the night canvas like a kicked bucket of paint. As I drifted downward the light swallowed me up, announcing the afterlife in mesmerizing visual fanfare. I felt no pain, no emotion, only the sensation of tumbling across the cosmos through a sea of platinum silence.

Black specks began to appear in the metallic white. The spots grew larger, becoming holes that stretched and pulled, struggling against rubbery resistance. The white became taffy pulled too far and strung itself out until it all became dripping iridescent globs. Then it vanished and everything went dark. I felt a pain in my knee and heard screams. The world I had taken a detour from gradually constricted into focus. It was as if no time had passed.

I was on hands and knees. My lower back ached. I took a few breaths to make sure my lungs worked, then hauled myself up out of the dirt. People were running. Some of them were spattered with glowing white goo, and I noticed little pools of the stuff all over the ground. Some of the APCs were decorated with it, and I saw men hopping around and tearing at their clothes.

The lieutenants and the medics directed traffic and hollered at the men, trying to restore order. I watched it all dumbly, waiting for the fog inside my head to burn off. I heard somebody say something about white phosphorous. Someone else said it was a 105mm location marking round that was supposed to pop in the sky near Bravo's laager down the road. *Well, son of a bitch*, I thought. *Another friendly fire incident. First cluster bombs, now fucking Willie Peter splashed on us. What the fuck will they come up with next?*

A dustoff was called to cart off the burn victims. The rest of the platoon was dazed but okay, and it didn't take long for the anger to boil up. Threats were made against the canon cockers who had tried to kill us, and Renfro demanded official action from everyone within earshot. Being the second time for some of us, chits of forgiveness were all used up.

Lieutenant Yearout, always the voice of reason, assured us that it would be investigated, then calmly suggested that we not let it ruin an otherwise enjoyable evening. It was such a disarming understatement I couldn't help but laugh, and I wasn't alone. Once everybody had calmed down Bucky called the squad together to personally make sure none of us had burns. We then climbed topside again and picked up where we'd left off.

It was late by the time our section of the perimeter returned to normal. I should have been as riled as everyone else, but I just couldn't see the percentage in it. I snuffed a final butt and closed my eyes on the world,

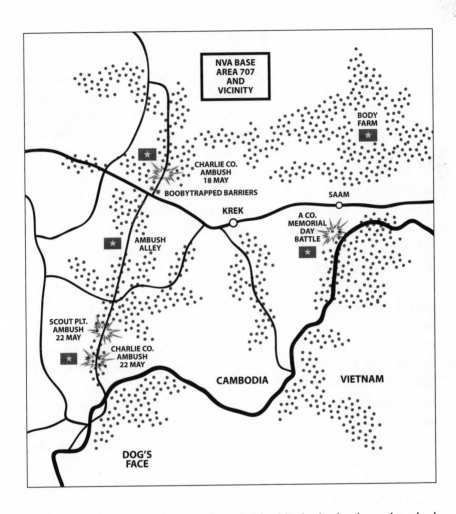

feeling a strange sense of peace, though I had little doubt that others had racked out with scowls on their faces.

—•—

Alpha Company left its bivouac near the village of Krek under a new sun and clanked into the outback. We wiggled down a vegetated hillside, swung to the right around a finger of woods poking out of the jungle, and came into a grassy peninsula bordered with double canopy, where we set up a blocking position. We weren't told what we were blocking for, but it didn't matter. Thanks to the heat and the pace we had kept, nerves were edgy, and sitting in the open like stationary targets didn't help.

After a couple of hours, attention shifted more toward the swelter factor than the treeline, which explains why a lone man carrying a rifle walked into the open two hundred yards downfield and was well into the clearing before he was noticed. Somebody in 3rd Platoon finally stood up and pointed: "Hey! There's a goddamn gook! Look!"

Heads turned and weapons drew down. The little man trooped along, seemingly oblivious to our presence, maybe even whistling a tune. Otherwise, he had to know that the odds of surviving another five seconds at this point was about the same as a crippled antelope cornered by jackals. 1st Platoon was out of position to join in, so we settled for being spectators.

An instant before the first volley flew, he stopped and looked our way. Even then he could have dived for cover and had a chance, but instead he stood motionless until the first rounds knocked dirt in his face, at which point he jumped straight up in the air and then proceeded to run and dodge in a wild dash of death. Hunks of earth and leafy ground cover followed his every step, but to his credit he covered a good hundred feet without the blizzard of fire catching even a leg or a shoulder. Either he was somehow absorbing bullets like a man-size block of soft cheese or he was the luckiest Asian on the planet. I watched all this in disbelief, as if the whole thing was some kind of elaborate gag that everybody laughs at later.

He had just about doubled his yardage when he finally went airborne and then hit the deck flat, out of view. The roar stopped. The captain broke squelch to order out a search party, but before the cleanup crew even got underway the little he-man vaulted out of the ground like a launched missile and twisted the throttle full open.

"Look at that sucker go!" Dewayne yelled, and the avalanche of lead resumed. It was hard to tell if he was trying to check out in a blaze of glory or actually thought he could make it to the treeline. Either way, his odds of success were on the south side of zero. Yet he kept on. He bounced and darted and ducked and sidestepped in a decadent dance that defied the laws of physics and cost the taxpayers serious money for the ammo that made up the music.

It was a hell of a performance, but he finally went horizontal and sailed behind a stump. He was finished. Or was he? We waited. After a couple of minutes Littlefield dispatched a recovery team to drag in the corpse while gun barrels cooled. They moved out cautious, rifles ready, not convinced it was over. As they approached the stump they fanned out, soft and easy, leery of the mystery man's magical powers.

They edged in close, and as I stretched my neck to see, my brow wrinkled and my jaw sagged as I watched a figure gingerly rise from the earth, ghost-like, hands in the air. One of the patrol flinched at this and I expected the ghost man to be cut down, but the startled troop held his fire. They must have been as dumbfounded as I was. I strained for a better look at this mighty-mite, but by now they had huddled around him.

They started back, and when they got closer it was plain to see that the man was carrying a long stick or a crude garden tool, not a rifle. He was dressed in ragged brown clothing and was easily on the wrong side of fifty. Miraculously, he was unwounded. He was also shaking uncontrollably, like he might be just a . . .

"Cambodian dirt farmer," Bucky said. He looked like a retriever on point, leaning so far forward I thought he might topple off the track. "He's a goddamn farmer. Probably on his way to the south-fuckin' forty. Kee-ryst."

We gawked, caught up in the wonder of it.

The little hunched-back man trembled as he was marched into the lion's den. His eyes flicked back and forth, as if trying to assess whether he would survive the next thirty seconds. One of his escorts stood the confiscated hand-made hoe against the command track, then presented the prisoner to the captain. Littlefield extended a hand and smiled, proof that no malice had been intended, that the whole thing was just a little mistake. An assistant offered up a smoke and a soda, compensation for nearly turning him into chipped beef. Another hand held out a box of Cs. The shaking man stared at it like it was time bomb.

A conference ensued, and by the time the Cambodian had huffed the complimentary cigarette to the filter and lit a new one, an interpreter had convinced him that he wasn't being conned. Together they munched rations and slurped Pepsi, and soon enough, the Cambodian allowed some smiles and nods, no doubt promising to remember that he now lived in a free-fire zone, never mind that he didn't own a map or have an inkling as to why the fuck our army was in his country.

Meanwhile, Littlefield must have decided that a hidden agenda could be at play, so to be safe he called for a chopper to pick up the old geezer, and he was soon whisked away by interrogators. Mama-san was never going to believe why he was late for dinner, assuming he was ever heard from again. We returned to our standoff with the treeline, and interest in the tragic comedy that had just played out soon faded. We held fast all day, waiting for something to be chased our way, but all we got for our trouble was a deeper tan. The elusive COSVN, the prey we'd been dispatched to lasso, had either slipped away like quicksilver or was never there in the first place. When the sun got low we repositioned on higher ground and dug in for the night.

At sunrise, word circulated that an emaciated and delirious North Vietnamese had wandered into Battalion HQ with a tale to tell. The story was that he had crawled out of an underground hospital in a base camp that had been B-52'd a couple of days before in the same area we'd been blocking and our new orders were to conduct a thorough recon. Evidently higher-up had already planned the recon in the wake of the arc-light strike. The NVA just helped confirm what they already suspected. The LT gave us the lowdown while we ate breakfast.

"We'll talk while we eat," he said. "Anybody got any applesauce?" He looked around hopefully, knowing somebody would give it up.

"Trade you mine for your B-2 Unit, lieutenant," Dave said.

"Deal."

Dewayne, pipe between his teeth, drew a tobacco pouch from a pocket. "What's all this about a base camp, LT?" he asked.

"Well, it's not COSVN, but significant. There could be a couple hundred bodies in there if the intel is accurate."

Chewing slowed.

"That's a lot of dead gooks, sir," Bucky said. His right cheek bulged with canned meat and he had a plastic spoon wedged in his mouth. "We gonna have any backup or prep in case it's a trick? Hell, they could draw us in and slap the sauce out of us."

Joe's expression never changed. "Let's don't get our imaginations revved up. So far the story checks out. We go in today. No air strikes, no arty, no backup, no tricks."

Dave waved a held-up a finger and opened his mouth to speak, but the lieutenant cut him off.

"Let me finish," he said, then paused. "I'm not saying we go in lackadaisical. In fact, we're going to assume there's still some cranky live ones in there hoping for payback, okay?"

"No air strikes, no arty," Bucky said. "I don't like this shit. Not even a little bit."

Joe stood up and smiled. "We don't have to like it. We just have to do it." Then he walked off, leaving Bucky with only the choir to preach to.

———•———

The sun was high by the time we moved out and it took most of the morning to worm down the hill, cross the valley, and squeeze into the woods. At first the trees were so thick we couldn't enjoy the shade. The platoons were side by side in columns of two, and the foliage thrashed us every inch of the way. Staying topside was a chore.

"Wait a minute! Hold it!" The track stopped. Bucky swiveled around. "Somebody get raked off?" He cranked his neck to count heads. "That you, Ned? Christ a'mighty."

"Yeah," Ned scowled. He was struggling against a snarled bough. "Another second and these fuckin' vines would've lynched my ass."

Ned Shelton and I came to the platoon about the same time. He was generally reliable but made sure nobody confused him with someone who gave a shit. It was no secret that he would pounce on any chance to get out of the field. He had a handlebar mustache that reminded me of David Crosby.

Littlefield followed somewhere behind on an already-blazed trail, and was irritated by the lack of progress. "First Platoon," he scolded, "nobody told you to stop. Get those tracks moving and keep them moving."

"Point got caught in some vines, captain," Joe answered.

"Vines!" Littlefield hollered. "They're driving a thirteen-ton war machine, and they're stymied by vines? One-Three, you get that track moving and keep it moving. Do you copy that?"

1-3's driver, Terry Pilcher, answered. "Loud and clear. Sir." Pilcher broke the connection and then said to the radio, "Now why don't you come up here bite my ass, you pinheaded cocksucker?" Pilcher was a big wide boy with a flat face and a jaw shaped a lot like a back-hoe bucket. He was a good driver but didn't make friends easily and didn't like being told what to do. He gunned the track and ripped into the greenery, causing Ned to nearly flip off backwards. I reckoned that both Pilcher and Ned would be hard to live with the rest of the day.

We worked our way through the tangle into a humid triple canopy where hardly anything grew at ground level. There were no signs of enemy about. Nothing. Shadows were deep, and there was an odor in the air. The stink intensified the farther we went. Nobody had to be told that the stench was generated by decomposing corpses. Soon enough wet towels adorned faces.

A bomb crater we clanked by suggested that we were getting close. It was surrounded by fallen trees that had splintered from the blast. Here and there rays of weak light poked through the hole-filled canopy like amber-colored spotlights. Dust particles swirled lazily in the beams.

Littlefield called a halt so we could take chow before getting down to business. "Best to eat now while we still can," Bucky proclaimed. He reached for a case of rations. "Whose turn to pick first?"

"Mine," said Snake. He was the squad's full-blooded Hawaiian, and was known by no other name. He went about six feet and was broomstick-thin with thatchy black hair and posture that made it look like he was always leaning forward. From what I'd seen, Snake kept his attitude on the upside but was virtually without sensibilities. He grinned, exposing crooked teeth. "Gimme the beenie-weenies."

I still struggled to mask the nauseating odor that hung over us like a wet blanket, and it was hard to think of eating. Plus I figured that going hungry might be the best way I'd get through the afternoon without chucking up my insides. My stomach growled in spite of it, though, so I forced down some crackers and pound cake, and actually felt better for it.

Drivers and gunners stayed with the tracks, which hung back, watching our flanks. Everybody else dismounted and moved out on foot. Fifty yards along a few bunkers came into view—what was left of them, anyway. They looked like they'd been hit with a ten-ton wrecking ball. In places only fifty feet separated one bomb crater from another. So many trees were down it looked like a logging operation gone wrong. At a silent signal we spread out even more, eyes wide, ears perked, and stepped lightly over the felled timber, scanning for tripwires or anything else that might draw blood. A little farther on we entered the heart of the killing zone. Bodies were slung across the turned earth like wind-driven debris from a sultry summer tornado. We sure as hell weren't in Kansas, I knew that much. It was a smorgasbord of carnage, and for a minute all I could do was stand there while the scene burned itself into my memory like an obscene painting.

Some of the NVA had been crushed by falling trees, others buried by rubble, with only a leg or hand poking out of the turned earth. Those who were still whole had died from concussion or shrapnel. Ripe innards— some animated by squirming larvae—hung from torn torsos. The stench was so concentrated that each breath brought a new urge to run. Only once before had I smelled something so sickeningly powerful, when my adolescent buddy and me decided it would be a good idea to drive a hunting knife into the belly of a bloated dead cow floating in a creek. The nausea induced by the putrid hissing gas plagued me for months afterward every time I thought about it. Here in this jungle, it was as if I had been handed the knife and told to work the whole herd.

After the general area was cautiously swept for bushwhackers and booby traps, Littlefield ordered the tracks in closer for tighter security. The rest of us prepared to do what had to be done—fleece the dead of their booty. Just the thought of it fueled the sour churning in my gut.

The corpse closest to me was splayed out on his back like a dead frog. His blackened skin had stretched over his bloated body like an overinflated innertube and flies feasted from head to toe. Bayonet in hand, I knelt down and attempted to saw off his pistol belt. I worked mostly with my head turned and breath held, which made it more difficult. But if I slipped and punched through to trapped gas he could pop, and I didn't want to get splashed in the face with whatever was trying to bust out. At the same time, I had to repeatedly shoo the flies.

The fouled air worked hard to lure stomach juices toward my throat, and I was forced to stand up and regroup once the pistol belt and rucksack straps were cut. I drew a couple of long breaths and thought about the best way to get the pack out from under him. Using my feet instead of my hands made the most sense.

I sat down and positioned myself with a boot against his shoulder, then rocked him back and forth until his ruck peeled loose from the mulch and he flopped over like a mildewed log stuck to the forest floor. Nesting insects panicked at the exposure and scurried for cover. I stood up and waited for the exodus to end before kneeling again to check out the rucksack.

Whatever killed him had knocked out a hunk of his head. Inside the jagged hole, clotted blood and decaying brains had morphed into what looked like a moldy jar of blood bait. I thought I saw the goop on the surface quiver, and the idea of something rooting around in there caused my gag reflex to twitch. I snatched up the pack and moved back a good distance. I had no desire to witness whatever might chew its way to daylight.

Inside the NVA's worn canvas carry-along was a small tangle of filthy clothes, an empty spare ammo pouch, a small bag of rice, and the mandatory snapshot of Ho Chi Minh. Nothing else. I tossed it aside and moved on.

Several more bodies yielded nothing of value. Most of the dead were lowly schmucks like us. Snake took my photo standing over a body, as if the Vietnamese had met his end by my hand. I was only vaguely aware that my sense of morality had just slipped another notch. The stiff was stretched out face-up with the left half of his body pinned beneath a tree trunk. His right arm was bent at the elbow, both legs were bent at the knee. His tongue had stiffened to a sharp point in his open mouth, reminding me of a just-hatched chick straining for nourishment. A few feet of intestine had squirted out from a tear in his trousers and sat coiled on his hip in a pale wad. Flies circled lazily, as if they'd feasted their limit but were unwilling to abandon their find. After a couple of snaps we traded places, and Snake became the conquering hero.

Goods were stockpiled, including two trucks, a large cache of rice, some tools, documents, commo equipment, and two mangled survivors extricated from a collapsed bunker. Gradually the smell got more tolerable, making the task at hand less repulsive, and before long we were old hands at shaking down the dead, with interest in the bodies shifting more to souvenir potential than anything. I kept a pistol belt and laid claim to an old Russian CKC carbine, my first spoils of war.

I noticed a small group hovering around one of the dead and wandered over. They were debating what had killed him. I saw right away why he was a topic of conversation. A circular piece of scalp had been cut away from the crown of his head. A cleaver lopping off a slice of firm fruit couldn't have been cleaner. There were no other apparent injuries. I decided to look around while they speculated and head-scratched.

After surveying the surrounding area for a minute, something on a nearby tree drew my attention. From a distance it looked like a Portobello mushroom, but I knew it wasn't. The thing pasted to the tree turned out to be the hairy, blood-matted patty of missing scalp. A bomb blast had bounced the poor boy off the tree like a hard-served racquetball. Odds are his neck was broken, too, but I doubted anyone had wiggled his head to see. When I reported my find the more curious of the bunch traipsed over for a look-see and the case was closed.

The underground hospital had collapsed and permanently changed the prognosis of the patients. At the only part still propped up, a minor excavation uncovered one half-crushed but breathing NVA. He was convulsive and delirious with fever, and bugs had made his exposed skin look like a pizza doubled up on sauce. He was dug free of the rubble and laid out on a dry bare spot, where the CP's medic stuck him with morphine, then reported the man's condition by way of shaking his head. A few bets were made as to whether he'd even see the inside of a dustoff helicopter. He did, but looked so dead when hoisted up through the trees it invoked arguments over who owed who.

With the day getting on, bounty was tallied and loaded into slings lowered by Chinooks. After firebombing the trucks, we mounted up and pulled out, leaving the carcasses to the elements and flesh eaters. By dusk we were back at Krek, bivouacked along the blacktop a mile outside the village.

I shared guard with Dave. Neither of us talked at first, but it was obvious what was on both our minds. Finally, Dave said, "I've seen some shit, man, but nothin' like that, and I never got off the track." He fished for a Kool, lit up, and blew a plume of smoke at the stars.

"Right on," I said.

By now, the slaughterhouse in the jungle had soaked in and activated one of those shadowy circuits designed to pit the physical against the spiritual just long enough to punch a new hole in your faith. I wasn't sure how to talk about it, or if I should. So I took a detour.

"The dinks have lost a lot of shit thanks to this mission, for what that's worth," I added. "Back in Nam, they're gonna be low on bullets and food for quite a while."

"I don't know," he said. "I don't know."

It seemed neither of us wanted to dig any deeper, and so we passed the time talking about home.

Sleep did not come easy. My poncho liner trapped the smell of death absorbed by my fatigues earlier. I doubted that even a change of clothes would get rid of it, though. It seemed to sift from my pores, and it made me toss and turn. At some point a vulgar dream jerked me awake and I lay there wide-eyed, fighting an urge to sneak outside the perimeter in search of water. If I could find a well, I could wash away the dirt and for a few minutes even the world around me.

4th Squad's new track after arrival in Cambodia.

The Memorial Day battle south of Saam, Cambodia left Alpha's 1-3 track demolished and Dave Santa-Cruz KIA.

3rd Squad's destroyed track is retrieved from the jungle near Saam, Cambodia, on May 31. 1-4 track is in the foreground.

Nui Ba Dinh, the Black Virgin Mountain, from LZ Rawlins near Tay Ninh, Vietnam.

Alpha Company troops enjoy a cookout at Cu Chi following the Cambodian mission.

Alpha Company's CO conducts an awards ceremony at Cu Chi following the Cambodian incursion.

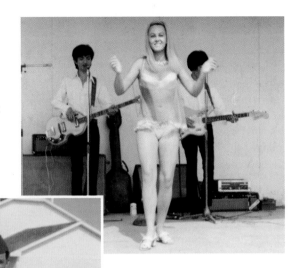

An Australian dancer
backed up by Filipino
musicians entertains at
Cu Chi.

The author in Norman,
Oklahoma, while on emergency
leave in August 1970.

A CH-47 "Chinook" helicopter hauls cargo near Dau Tieng.

4th Squad's nearly new ROTTIN "8" NO. III takes a land mine hit soon after Cambodia.

Eye for an eye: Viet Cong killed by a boobytrapped Claymore mine left in a garbage dump by Alpha Company troops.

1/8th Cavalry's area of operations as seen from the air southeast of Song Be.

LZ Dragonhead, 1/8th Cavalry's fire support base and operations center.

"Mob 1" at LZ Rash.

Following a ridgeline somewhere in the jungle.

"Mob 1" moves out after taking a breather.

The platoon's community hootch at LZ Dragonhead.

Resting with rucksacks off before
re-entering the thickets.

Mob 1's Steve Farber at LZ Rash.

Engineers work to push back the treeline at LZ Rash using Bangalore
torpedoes.

A hot meal at LZ Rash. Andy Brenn smiles at the camera, with Steve Farber on his left.

Denny and Paul of Mob 1 pose for a snapshot while in break in the jungle.

The sun sets on another long day at Dragonhead.

16

Street without Joy

We were cut off from the comprehension of our surroundings; we glided past like phantoms, wondering and secretly appalled, as sane men would be before an enthusiastic outbreak in a madhouse.

—JOSEPH CONRAD, *HEART OF DARKNESS*

May 1970. 25th Infantry Division. Southwest of Krek, Cambodia on Ambush Alley.

Our tracks moved fast down a dirt road through thick jungle, kicking up telltale plumes that reduced visibility and restricted breathing. Soiled towels covering faces made us look like desperados on the run. We had been in NVA Base Area 707 only a matter of days, and the road we followed was already known as Ambush Alley, so named because each time our sister companies ventured along its reaches they got pounded by NVA attackers. A two-man RPG team could wreck an APC and then vanish like some hellish demon, striking terror into the hearts of men in a matter of seconds. A larger force could do much more before having to answer for it. Riding point was a fact of life. When your number came up you just hoped that when the day ended you'd still be around to spin the cylinder and pass the pistol. Speed helped.

Somewhere ahead of us a short burst of machine-gun fire cracked in a long echo and without warning Pilcher hit the brakes hard to avoid rear-ending 1-2, causing all aboard to lurch. My butt took leave of the ammo box I was on like a sack of groceries off the back seat and I smacked the .50 turret hard enough to hurt.

"Christ!" Bucky was all sideways, hanging on with one hand. "They oughta give us some goddamn tie-down straps if they're gonna play stop-'n'-go like that!"

We waited to see what the holdup was while he listened to his headset.

"Second Platoon's point nailed an NVA caught crossing the road. There's a good chance he was part of an ambush at some hootches nearby where Charlie got jumped earlier this morning. We'll be going through easy, so be ready."

Trees crowded the road so close it was like crawling through a tunnel. Overhang blocked out everything but thin rods of grainy sunlight that hit the ground at odd angles. There was no wind to rustle leaves or do more than swirl dust as we crept along.

1-3 track was seventh back in line overall. As we eased around the dead NVA I moved my thumb to my rifle's safety and scrutinized the brush as intently as a child watches a jack-in-the-box while cranking the handle. Sweat coated my palms. We were working a real hotbed, and I'd known for days that it was a question of when, not if. The idea of tippy-toeing through didn't help. It wasn't as if they'd back off just because it looked like we were waiting for it. The only advantage would be a quicker dismount, assuming we got the chance.

Up ahead, a small, grass-roofed hut came into view where the trees thinned. Not to be distracted, I stared stonily at the brush silently sliding by. Gradually the jungle receded as more hootches appeared. As we moved through, there were no signs of life, not a chicken or a pig or even a dog. The place was deserted, out to lunch. The chores would have to wait.

It was too quiet and too pat. Strained eyes searched for movement. .50 barrels were pointed in opposite directions all the way down the line, herringbone style. I mentally practiced dismounting, trying not to think about well-positioned mines waiting for anyone who hit the dirt in a rush to find cover. There was enough tension in the air to keep a movie audience spellbound, except that here there was no background music, the bullets were real, and—unlike Hollywood—I was pretty sure no hero would save the day.

Sweat tickled my cheeks as we moved through in a slow drift past one dwelling after another, scanning, waiting, twitching at any sound or movement, real or imagined. Some distance up the road I could hear tracks pick up speed as they pulled away from the hamlet. "Come on," I whispered through a clamped jaw. But the ghostly huts just stared back, deadpan.

1-2 cleared the kill zone and hit the gas. In a few seconds we did the same. As we picked up speed and closed the distance with our sister squad, their track hit the brakes hard again and swiveled left. Explosions and small arms fire echoed through the dust from somewhere up ahead. I was airborne by the time the track swung right and jerked to a stop. I hit the dirt hard and rolled to a stop against the thick brush at the edge of the road. Nearby branches popped and snapped, telling me the fire was working its way through. I opened up, flinching as errant tracers skipped about. Through the racket, I heard shouts for help and glanced up the road.

"Medic!" a voice squalled.

I looked again but couldn't see anything through the dust and smoke except the outline of 1-2 track. The cry for help was ahead of them, likely at 1-1's location. When I looked to my right, there was Carter Johnson, our medic, only a few yards away. He had been riding with 1-3 for a couple of days. He was stretched out low and looking up-trail with an expression that explained why he hadn't moved.

"Medic!"

Louder this time. Johnson squirmed in the dust, then came to a crouch. He looked at the length of road before him the way a condemned man might stare at the electric chair.

"They need you up there, man. Get going."

He looked at me, wide-eyed, like a rabbit in the high-beams. He was stiff as stone, and I realized the chances of him going it alone were about the same as the North Vietnamese Army surrendering in the next five minutes. So I got to my knees and scrambled over. "Come on, Doc. We'll both go." I prompted him with a pat and motioned to move out. That finally did the trick. Once he got moving, I had trouble keeping up.

I emptied my rifle while we darted up the road like startled deer. We passed one track, then zeroed in on a hand signal from a cluster of grunts huddled around a bloodied squadmate in front of 1-1. Johnson dived in like a runner stealing home. With my part done, I pulled up short, spun around, and sprinted back to my own turf.

I slid feet first into my old position and went back to work on the woods, thankful for all the running they'd made us do in training. I went through a couple more magazines and thought about changing positions to see if I could get a better fix on things when the firing slacked off. Somebody yelled out a cease fire and everything got quiet. I jabbed in a fresh clip, then rose to my knees and gulped some dirty air. Through the drapery of dust and gunsmoke I saw others nearby getting to their feet. To be on the safe side I waited another minute and then stood up.

A dustoff came and carted off the wounded while the mechanics strained their backs replacing busted treads on 2nd Platoon's point track. A couple of hours passed before we got underway. Doc gave me a hint of a smile when he climbed aboard. It was his way of letting me know the ice was broken and that he'd handle it on his own from now on. I had no doubt of it.

The radio came alive once we were up to speed. While Bucky talked Dave listened on his handset. "Charlie got hit again up ahead," he hollered. "A track got wasted and they've got a bunch of wounded."

Even at a good clip, it took fifteen minutes to get there, and by then the NVA had escaped. Once again, we rolled in slow. Charlie's APCs were scattered along the roadside. Weary men stood in shadowy groups around their tracks. The downed APC was a sight. Exploding ammo had melted steel on the insides and charred the outer skin, making it look like a scorched tin can just raked out of an incinerator. The sides had bulged to the point it split at the seams.

"Jesus," I said to no one. The sight of a track reduced to rubble was not an easy thing to swallow. My biggest worry so far was having an RPG splatter me like a pumpkin smacked with a mallet. Now I had to factor in the potential for being roasted alive, too.

"Hard luck," Dave said. "Just pure hard luck."

"Hard luck Charlie," Bucky echoed.

A few heads nodded.

"Let's don't make it bigger than it is," Pilcher said. "It's a bad idea to put a jinx on 'em. A goddamn bad idea."

He was slouched back, drawing easy on a Camel. I wondered what it would take for him to really get pulled out of joint. If I was a driver, I would be tight-assed all day just thinking about a land mine punching through the floor and changing me into a hot beef casserole from the waist down. Pilcher never seemed worried. In fact, he had a habit of leaving his flak jacket off, as if he were somehow bulletproof. Not smart, at least in my view.

Hard luck Charlie. In spite of Pilcher's warning, I had a feeling the name would stick. Once the area was secure we moved on, leaving behind the bewildered men of Charlie and another scar on the earth. Littlefield ordered a halt when the sun go low, but it wasn't to circle the wagons for the night. It was to take custody of a disabled 105 wheeled howitzer from an artillery unit in a hurry to get somewhere. They promised to come back for it tomorrow.

Lieutenant Yearout walked back to 1-3 with the order. "The company's laager site is about two miles up the road. The CO wants to leave four men here to secure this gun."

Four men? I couldn't have heard that right.

I saw Bucky frown. "Come again, sir?"

"Look, the towing hitch broke and they had to leave it. We can't let the NVA steal it. Is that clear enough?"

"I know this probably won't do any good, lieutenant," Dave said, "but—"

"You're right, it won't."

"We could blow it, or hook a chain to it and drag it along," Bucky said.

"We could boobytrap it!" Snake's face lit up, certain he had the solution.

Joe ignored them. "I got Culver from 1-1, Briscoe from 1-2, and I want Russell and Ross with them. Culver's got a Sixty; Brisco has a radio. You guys bring some Claymores and an M-79."

I knew it was a waste, but since we had already been on the chopping block a couple times today, I had to say it: "Why not leave the platoon here?"

"Because the captain said four men." At the moment, he was fresh out of humor. "And he's waiting, so let's get a move on."

End of discussion. I looked at Dewayne. He was tamping tobacco into the bowl of his pipe, a ritual with him whenever we stopped. He hadn't said a word. He was the only one smart enough to save his breath.

The four of us stood in silence and watched the tracks disappear, the dust they kicked up gathering in pale golden light that filtered through the canopy. It was light that would be lost soon, so we slipped into the brush and huddled up for a conference. There was a lot to consider.

All of us had been on APs before, but those were in close proximity to the company and involved more firepower. This was closer to being tossed into the shark tank and asked to guard a slab of bleeding meat. We had to plan a strategy before it got dark.

We took stock. First, we acknowledged that basically we had been abandoned in the jungle, and the options if the bad guys came and the odds weren't right consisted of 1) suicide or 2) letting them walk off with the prize, which was preferable to getting killed and then having them walk off with the prize along with four M-16s and maybe some Claymores to boot. We couldn't rely on our buddies riding to the rescue in time to help us, and trying to evade through the night jungle to the company's location would likely get us lost or captured.

With the situation sized up, we agreed that option number two was the only sensible choice. We didn't know why Littlefield expected four men to hold off whatever force might come along and lay claim to this bit of booty, but we did know the howitzer probably cost less than the ammo Alpha used up on a busy day, and we put a slightly higher value on our lives. There wasn't time or the right tools to boobytrap it, so we decided to put the monkey on Littlefield's back, where it belonged. If we were seriously out-numbered, we'd radio the CP, tell them it was an overwhelming force, and that they would have to come on the run if they wanted to save it.

That settled, we agreed on a three hour watch schedule and burrowed in for the long pull. Mine started at 1:00 A.M., and by the wee hours all that kept me awake were buzzing bloodsuckers and thoughts of stealthy NVA. My joints ached mightily, but I had to stay in a sitting position to stay conscious. It helped to imagine Littlefield in serious pain.

It was a hard way to spend the night, but living to tell about it and avoiding a showdown with the CO was the important thing. By daylight we were more like cadavers than warriors, with dazed eyes drooping and minds as vacant as the dead. Eventually two tracks arrived, escorting some arty guys in a truck. While they hooked up the howitzer we crawled atop the tracks, exhaustion giving way to the demands of a new day. Back at Alpha's perimeter, Littlefield was waiting to move out. There was no time to rest, so I hurriedly scrounged a box of C-rations, determined to at least sneak in a quick breakfast.

I was still chewing a mile downtrail when 3rd Platoon's point track rounded a bend and got walloped by an RPG. We heard it from our position in the middle of the column, but for the moment were told to sit tight. That changed only seconds later when we were drawn into it by small arms fire that cracked through the woods close by. My unstrapped steel pot went flying when I hit the ground, but at first I made no move to fetch it. The incoming persuaded me to scoot up against the brush and get busy putting out rounds instead. There was no real cover, and that didn't help. A hot AK round snapped a twig over my head like a cheap pencil, making me jam my face in the dirt. I rolled over and flipped the selector to rock 'n' roll, thinking this might somehow make up for having a bare head.

I felt naked without my helmet, so I risked a quick low-crawl to retrieve it and slapped it back on my head, all the while looking for something that offered real protection. A couple of clips later I let up for a second to gauge incoming and check my surroundings. To my left I saw Snake and Ned about thirty feet away, and others beyond them. Ten feet to my right was a new guy from 2nd Squad. His nearest squadmates were another forty feet away. I noticed he wasn't firing. He didn't look shot, but his head was down, his M-16 held by the forward stock in his right hand. I thought maybe his weapon had jammed, but he wasn't working on it. He couldn't be out of ammo already. Damned if it didn't look like he was playing possum.

I finished a clip and then turned his way while reloading. "Hey, are you hit?"

He lifted his head. "Nothing wrong here," he yelled back.

I let that soak in for a second.

"Your weapon jammed, or what?"

"Nope. I'm just stayin' low till it's over."

Say What? I couldn't believe what I'd just heard.

"Say again?" I felt my eyes narrow and a frown spread across my face.

"Layin' low, bro. If I don't shoot, they don't know where I'm at."

I turned away long enough to send more red lead toward the NVA and try to swallow what he was telling me. Incoming was now sporadic but hadn't dried up by a long shot. When I looked again he hadn't moved a muscle. His squadmates were either too far away or too busy to notice.

"Hey!"

He looked my way.

"What the hell's wrong with you?" I hollered. "Start putting out some rounds and give me a hand here. Do it now!"

He shook his head like a rebellious child. "No way, man. Uh-uh. As long as I pretend not to be here I got a good chance of stayin' alive." He scrunched down even lower in reinforcement of that belief.

Anger flamed its way up my throat. "Listen, dickhead. Every second your face is in the dirt, somebody else, namely me, has to cover your goddamned piece of the pie. So get busy!"

"Not a chance!" His face was screwed up with fear and defiance. "They can make me do a year in the jungle, but nobody can make me pull this trigger, man. I'll be layin' low every time we get fired up. That's a fact."

"You sorry piece of shit!" I wasn't close enough to take a swing, and the impulse to force him at gunpoint was pushed back before I could act on it. So I turned to the other enemy and raked the brush, then glared at him again. He stared back.

"Get the hell away from me," I yelled. "There's no room here for cowards, asshole."

He didn't budge.

"Move it!" I yelled. "Get away from me before I open up your skull motherfucker!" By now, I didn't know if I was bluffing or not.

His eyes got wide and he looked around for a witness, but the squad was spread out and everybody preoccupied. He looked back at me, then initiated an awkward sideways scoot down the edge of the road.

"More," I yelled. Keep moving, shithead." I emptied another clip into the woods. By now he was about twenty feet away, curled halfway around a tangle of vines. I refocused on the jungle, all the while trying to will enemy rounds his way.

Contact was broken by a pair of screaming F-4s that freight-trained in and jettisoned packaged fire, converting the jungle into hell on earth. Anger still burned like a dull blade, and while we waited for medevacs and repairs I made it my business to corner the lieutenant and demand satisfaction.

"I'll talk to him," he said. "But don't be so quick to jump on your high horse. The guy's new. He's probably just scared. If you really try you might remember what's that's like."

"Sir—"

"I said I'd talk to him." He started to turn away, but I wasn't done.

"Lieutenant, this guy's dead weight. He's not gonna change. Only cares about himself. He—"

Joe continued to walk away, leaving me without a soundboard. For a while, I just stood there, looking after him, frustrated that he hadn't taken it seriously. It was well after dark before I lost the hot head.

————

The first shell hissed through the night air like a Bob Gibson fastball, but my sleep was deep, and I never heard the call of incoming. Even the detonation only jerked me into a sitting position, my muddled mind stumped as to exactly what had rousted me. When another hiss cut the air I had no trouble making the interpretation. The impact jarred the cobwebs loose and I rolled over, snatching up my M-16 and steel pot in the same move. In seconds the .50 cals started up, puncturing the blackness with spears of red that tore open the jungle wall. The third shell whistled in closer yet, slinging shrapnel against 2nd Platoon's tracks. So far it was only a mortar attack and M-16s would be ineffective, so those of us on the ground low-crawled to positions between the APCs and waited. Bucky threw out flak jackets that had been left on board. "If you need more ammo, get it now and get if fast," he hollered. "It's all we'll have if the track takes a hit."

I saw Snake leap into the back of 1-3 and bounce back out with a full can of M-16 rounds. Another shell slammed the soft earth roughly thirty yards out, spraying dirt and hot steel into the sky. "Keep those pots on," Bucky yelled. "And be ready for a ground assault."

Rounds from our own mortar track flashed out as another incoming shell rocked the night. A fretful Ned was on my left. "They better get a fix on those fuckers fast," he said, "or they're gonna need a lot of plastic bags."

"Shut up with that shit," Bucky said. He was kneeling behind us. "We'll have 'em shut down soon enough. Just pay attention to the treeline."

I liked Bucky's confidence. But with mortars, where the next one lands nobody knows, and just thinking about that made me squirm harder against the ground.

I heard a successive *tunk—tunk—tunk!* from our own perimeter, followed shortly by their detonations deep in the forest. After two more volleys with no response, everything got quiet. Apparently it was effective. Either that or the NVA had simply used up a meager ration of rounds and strolled away. There had been no human wave attack. Still, I knew Littlefield would keep us on alert for an hour or two, so I climbed topside, where I found Dave slouched back in the .50 turret.

"Nice work, dude," I said. "Not many gunners can knock 'em down on their way in. You get my vote for trick shooter of Triple Deuce."

"Right," he said. "Who needs a mortar track with me around?"

He offered up a smoke. I put the Zippo to it, took a drag, and contemplated the cigarette.

"You know, when I got drafted I made up my mind to quit smoking. I might've, too, if they'd taken away the privilege, but they didn't. Instead, it was 'Smoke 'em if you got 'em' every time we took a break."

"Cancer should be the least of your worries," he said.

"You got that right. I just figured it would be a good opportunity to give it up. You know, when I didn't have a choice."

"Those little fuckers out there will help you give it up," he said. "No problem."

I took a draw. "Now that you put it that way . . ."

"Being a rolling target every day is getting old," he said after a pause. He puffed his Kool the way agitated people do. The wear on everybody's nerves was showing, so I wasn't surprised at the chink in Dave's armor. At least some of us had the advantage of dismounting when we got hit. Gunners didn't, and that made them the top target in the NVA shooting gallery.

"I'll grant you that, amigo," I said. "But we both know there ain't no safe way to go. We gotta do our time. In my case, a whole lotta time."

"Time," he said, staring into the night. He sucked smoke into his lungs and blew it out in a hard gust. Then he turned to me. "I don't even know what day of the week it is, and neither do you. We're in a place where time has fallen down some goddamn bottomless Vietnamese well. We're in the Twilight Zone, man, only we're not watching it on TV." He took another drag. I waited, knowing there was more.

"We're like those little plastic army guys we played with as kids," he went on, "blowing up this group or that one over there with no rhyme or reason behind it. We're getting jumped almost every day, man. And assuming we get back to Vietnam, they'll reward us by letting us do more of the same shit there until none of us are left."

I had no idea what to say. I couldn't argue with it. "Well, you got me there," was all I could manage. We sat in silence.

"Some of us aren't getting out of here," he said after awhile. It was a gut check, and I understood it, but I didn't buy into it and didn't reply. It was the same admonition delivered by drill sergeants to help fortify their recruits' will to live, to get tough, and in doing so maximize chances of survival. I took such warnings no more seriously than when my dad used to prep me for college by warning me that I'd flunk out if I didn't really buckle down. The underlying message was that flunking out would bring dishonor to myself and the family. I had learned not to buy off on such sermons as early as the sixth grade, when Mrs. Curtis, that big gray battle axe of a woman who displayed (and used) a cherrywood paddle named "Cherry Pie," repeatedly warned us that when we got to Junior High we would have at least one hour of homework per day, per subject. I was pretty good at math, and I knew that expecting six hours of homework a day was a crock of shit. Flunking out of college if I didn't devote my entire existence to the books was also a load. True enough, some would flunk out, just as in war some don't come back. But I knew that using fear as a motivation for success was likely to backfire as often as not. College had proven to be a more advanced extension of high school, nothing more. Nobody had lied to me about war. It was worse than I ever imagined. But using "some of you won't come back" to imply that the survivors will be those most determined to live was a pile of dung. Except for the potato heads who clumsily offered themselves up or those tagged as plastic army guys by higher-ups to be sacrificed for dubious objectives, death played no favorites here.

Minutes passed. I stretched and yawned. I was tired but feeling pretty good in spite of Dave's mood. A breeze had come up and the bugs were AWOL. For some reason, I felt a grin growing from the inside. I had no idea where it was coming from or why, but I couldn't stop it. Dave looked my way just as it started to spread on my face. His expression turned quizzical, and that was enough to tell me some of the gloom had lifted.

"There's a booger on your lip, Dave," I said.

It took a minute, but he couldn't help himself, and soon we were both chuckling. "Fucker," he said. Then he sat up straight, took a deep breath, and let it out.

We lit up again and just stared at the black wall of trees to our front.

"It's a bitch, ain't it?" I said.

"It's a bitch," he agreed.

17

Street without Joy, Part II

*Goddamn it, you'll never get the Purple Heart
hiding in a foxhole! Follow me!*

—CAPTAIN HENRY P. "JIM" CROWE, GUADALCANAL, 1943

May 1970. 25th Infantry Division.
NVA Base Area 707, Krek, Cambodia.

Charlie Company got hammered again. It was an hour before sunset and
we had just set up a night defensive position in a field near Krek a few
klicks from where the blacktop intersected Ambush Alley.

Charlie had been coming down the Alley fast, running late, and was
about to close on the main road from the north when the NVA stopped
them as dead as a train wreck with a fury of small arms fire and unleashed
RPGs. They had rationed plenty of bodies and bullets, and quickly had
Charlie's lead element isolated, firing at them from both sides of the road.
Our sister company had to holler for help.

I was halfway through writing a letter when the order to saddle up
came. We dismantled camp in a scramble and the tracks roared to life. As
we moved out Bucky passed the news. "The gooks are dug in and Charlie's
pinned down!"

The company hit the blacktop and raced down the highway full throttle for about three klicks and then split up. 1st and 2nd Platoons hopped
off the highway into the rice paddy on our right and veered across the

flatland toward the distant jungle. The rest of the company stuck with the main road toward the junction with the Alley. It was a hammer and anvil maneuver. All we had to do was be in the right position. Maybe it would work, maybe not. Maybe the NVA would chose to shift position and suck us in while 3rd Platoon and the CP twiddled their thumbs back on the highway.

I didn't give a shit one way or the other. Adrenaline rushed through me like a flash flood. I couldn't wait to engage the bastards after taking pot-shots from them day after day while rarely making them ante up. This time they would pay. I could tell that the other guys felt the same.

After a few hundred yards Pilcher swung hard left and the tracks came on line to advance on the jungle, now about five hundred yards to our front. Ricochets could be seen dancing wildly across the treetops. Dull ka-rumps of detonating grenades and other heavy weapons echoed long in the musty undergrowth. Lazy drifts of white smoke had seeped up through the greenery and lay across the canopy. From the air it must have looked like morning fog on a lake.

We had advanced a couple of hundred yards when there was some noise on the radio about 3rd and the CP. Bucky pulled off his headset and swung around. "They've been held up by earthen berms across the road where there's a creek too deep to cross. The barriers appear to be booby-trapped. It's gonna take some time to overcome it."

Somehow the NVA had known Charlie would come along and from which direction. They also had known that reinforcements would be called in. It was a smart play, but the fuckers had not counted on us dividing our forces, and for that mistake they were going to suffer greatly. Up ahead, tracers hopped and swirled atop the jungle like insects bouncing around a street lamp. We were only minutes away.

This inspired the lieutenants to quicken the pace. Pilcher now ignored the dikes we had been slowing to crawl over, hitting them so hard it was a challenge to hold on. If helmets had not been strapped down they would have flipped off heads in every direction. After we slammed the second one, the thought occurred to me that if I survived the night my back would never be the same.

Dave looked my way. "They knew, man. They frickin' knew."

"They just thought they knew," Bucky yelled. "Now we're gonna bust their balls."

We closed on the jungle wall, which was only two hundred yards ahead. We were about to rescue the underdog from the neighborhood bully and nothing could stop us. Not the enemy, not the terrain, not acts of God or demons from hell.

Just then all eight tracks ground to a halt. The one thing that could in fact stop us was the radio. And it started squawking for us to stop. To stop now.

"What the fuck?" Pilcher growled. He stood up in the drivers hatch and looked around in disbelief.

Bucky waved him off, listening intently to his headset.

I was too dumbfounded to say anything. All the energy I'd built up was at a lather, aching to be unleashed. Now it looked as if we'd reached the end of our advance.

Bucky pulled the headset off. "Charlie broke free. They're fightin' their way to daylight and air support's on the way."

"Then why the fuck are we sittin' here?" Pilcher said. As usual, he wore no flak jacket. Lately it had become a sore point with Bucky. "How come we don't sandwich the cocksuckers and pound their ass?" he continued.

"Because the lieutenant says Littlefield wants us here in a blocking position, that's why. And get your damn flak jacket on." He went back to the radio, not waiting for a response, which was just as well, because Pilcher ignored him.

He took the headset off, looking as exasperated as the rest of us. "Littlefield thinks they may get flushed into the open when the sky starts fallin' on 'em."

"Bullshit!" Pilcher's face was a mix of anger and frustration.

Dave, typically calm, said, "He's right, Bucky. They'll scatter deeper into the bush. No way they'll run this way." He fished out a smoke, lit up, and then slouched back in the machine gun turret, knowing further discussion was pointless.

"This is fucked up," Pilcher said, but by now he knew it was a waste, too.

Bucky just shrugged. "What can I say?"

Morale flattened like a punctured tire. Pilcher sulked. Everybody else smoked and fidgeted, watching the jungle pop and smolder, itching for a chance to crack some heads. The idea of the NVA escaping into the jungle and making no move to stop it was stuck in a lot of craws. So we sat there, ratcheted up, and watched the sun disappear behind the treetops.

The first set of F-4 Phantoms screamed in low on a dry run. They swung wide, climbed, and came back, dropping sharply before leveling off over their chosen target. Released bombs tumbled from their bellies like fumbled footballs and detonated in thunder-claps that resonated across the land and spewed earth and vegetation skyward. Black smoke billowed from the charred earth, and as the roar of their engines faded, two more rumbled in, this time releasing canisters of napalm that sizzled their way through wide swaths of jungle. Others came on their heels, alternating high explosives with packaged infernos, rattling gear on the tracks and knocking ashes from dangling cigarettes.

"Bad news for somebody," Snake said nonchalantly. He sat next to me, absently chewing gum, but spoke to no one in particular.

"Just hope they got the coordinates right," Bucky observed. To this there were no comments. We didn't care about the air strikes. The focus was still channeled on the NVA and the fact we had been ordered not to chase them down. I had a clue now what a dog on a chain felt like when taunted by a mailman just out of reach. The air of frustration was thick enough to cut. It started to rain.

The last disappearing jet left what seemed like silence in its wake, with only the chatter of diesel engines and the slow cooking sounds of the hot jungle filling the void. There would be little chance of action now. Illumination rounds lit up the sky, and then artillery arced in, pinpointing areas not covered by the airstrikes. More detonations. More waiting. The arty action was followed by two Cobras that swooped in, led by a Loach. The light observation helicopter buzzed the treetops— stopping, moving, stopping, then circling, like a dragonfly in search of bugs. He failed to draw fire, but dropped smoke to mark spots on the ground for further annihilation. The gunships then uncorked fountains of minigun red, interspersed with the white flash of hissing rockets that blistered the forest floor.

When it was done, darkness and drizzle had settled on the land, the wall of green to our front concealing the cinders and smoke within. Charlie Company, minus a disabled APC, had rescued survivors and made it to the highway. They linked up there with the rest of Alpha, which had finally managed to debug and destroy the obstacles. Bucky held his hand up, a signal that he was getting more news. I continued to stare in the direction of the kill zone, convinced we could have made a difference if the plug hadn't been pulled. Now that could never be known. I tried to chalk it up to things not in my control, but it was hard. I lit a cigarette and rubbed my eyes, feeling the fatigue that came with falling from such a high to such a low.

"They got hit hard," Bucky said, "but they don't have any numbers yet." Again, there was no response. Visions of demolished tracks hung in my head like devils dispatched to follow me the rest of my life, however long that might be. In the distance, the jungle smoked and crackled. Medevacs came on station and circled for a landing out near the highway.

"Hard luck Charlie," somebody said. Pilcher, who had been staring at the jungle, turned his head. Even he had become a believer. "Yeah, hard luck Charlie," he repeated.

Bucky had more news. "Bravo's en route. They'll link up with Charlie and relieve us. As soon as they're on station we'll move out."

That was the end of it. Behind the rain-streaked glow of headlights, we formed a column and rumbled back to our original night defensive position, where we set up and sacked out, dog-ass beat. Later, on watch, I did some calculating and determined it was May 18. We had been in Cambodia for twelve days.

It came down in the morning that Charlie had lost one APC, had three killed, and a half-dozen wounded. Well-sourced rumors laid most of the blame on their CO, an apparently hated, overweight, belligerent fool who had ordered the entire column to dismount, gunners included, when the first rounds stopped them dead on the road. Fire came from both left and right, but the worst of it originated from a canebreak on the left side that stood a couple of hundred yards across an open paddy. Charlie's captain, known as "Fat Al," ordered a dismounted assault toward the canebreak rather than demolish the NVA positions with his heavy machine guns and M79s. So an entire platoon marched into the great wide open where RPG and small arms fire screamed across the clearing into them, killing and wounding them like carnival pop-ups. The surviving GIs quickly scrambled back to cover, dragging their wounded with them while ignoring Fat Al's orders. It was a miracle that the outcome hadn't been more tragic. It was also beginning to look like Charlie's "hard luck" was rooted more in their leadership than anything.

Hearing all this did nothing to buoy morale.

Meanwhile, the bosses were still unhappy with the level of action, so they ordered more junkets down Ambush Alley. Maybe we could stir up something major if we really put our minds to it. For the next several days the hit-and-runs and the killing and wounding continued. The alley was somewhere around nine miles long traveling south from the blacktop and about half that distance to the north of the highway, providing an ample playing field. It continued to rain at night.

———•———

On the morning of May 22, 3rd Squad, 1st Platoon, was once again up to ride point. By the time we left our encampment at the extreme southern end of Ambush Alley and began working our way back toward Krek, the sun was high enough for the sweat to flow and give the dust a place to stick. The uniform of the day, the same as every other day, didn't help—steel pots and flak jackets smothered in bandoliers, the exception being Pilcher and his flak jacket. Bucky had given up, deciding Pilcher knew the consequences and would have to pay them if need be.

The road was long and generally straight, with slight curves every so often. A curtain of trees lined both sides, interrupted by thin spots here and there and periodic clearings. The one consolation to riding point was having to eat less dust. Visibility was good, too, for what that was worth. We motored north.

There was little talk. Bucky sat next to the .50 turret, headset on. He was on the company net. The track's intercom speaker was damaged and wasn't much good beyond earshot of Pilcher, so we relied mainly on Bucky for what bits of information were passed down. With less than a mile of road under our treads we got word that Charlie, ahead of us, was taking fire. Hearing this and remembering the aborted rescue triggered a sick twinge in my stomach, but it was quickly replaced by the need to get even. But, once again, it was not to be, as we were too far to the rear. This time it was much worse than before.

"Looks like another bad day for Charlie," Bucky reported. "Gooks jumped 'em hard, then scooted. They've got six dead, nine wounded, and lost three tracks."

For a while nobody said a word, and I knew why. It was taking some time to wrap our heads around such an outcome in such a short encounter. The silence was finally broken by Ned. "Could've been us," he said. "Probably shoulda been us."

The fact that we had avoided Charlie's fate until now had to be on everyone's weary mind. The ever-moody Ned had finally said it.

Phantoms streaked by overhead and unloaded their wares somewhere in the distance, though it was way too late. Muffled detonations reverberated back through the jungle as we pressed on. By the time we made the scene the surrounding jungle was hot and silent, like a dying fire. Stands of small trees were broken and splintered from the exchange of fire, and clumps of singed brush still belched smoke. The demolished APCs had been left on the roadside, presumably to be retrieved later. The smoldering tracks were a sobering sight, and the fear that Charlie's misfortune was due to be passed around nagged at me.

We rolled by, all eyes riveted on the undergrowth. Sweat stung my eyes. The same fate could be waiting for us just ahead. I kept a white-knuckle grip on my M16 and scrutinized the roadside like a cornered animal, straining to catch a hint of movement or the glint of steel. All it would take was a snapping twig to unleash chaos. Ahead, a hunk of jungle had been gouged out—evidence of some other scuffle. We glided by, all the while itching to either get out of there or get it on. If the NVA were up for round two, it might be only seconds away.

That's when Littlefield ordered a rolling mad minute. The preemptive storm of fire eliminated the threat of ambush. It also went unanswered. The North Vietnamese had either long since departed or beat a retreat at the onslaught.

The relief was like steam coming off a pressure cooker.

"Damn, that felt better than the last blowjob I had," Snake quipped.

"Hard to believe you can remember that far back," Dave said.

Even Ned laughed at that one.

We'd been lucky again, or at least believed we had. The road ahead could be just as bad for our health as it had for Charlie, but at the moment that's not how it felt. It wasn't that Charlie got ambushed that much more, it was the losses they took. It was hard to understand how they kept getting the worst of it, but there it was.

We came to an eroded creek bed made worse by the earlier crossing of our sister companies and the battalion's command post. Several tracks tried it but promptly got stuck. While we waited for a portable bridge to be brought from the forward element we dismounted and found some shade in which to kill time.

Once underway, the radio got busy again. The battalion's Scout Platoon, bringing up the rear, had driven into an ambush so intense that within minutes their lieutenant was yelling for help. In the first few seconds, they suffered two KIAs and eight wounded. The NVA were so close that it looked as if they might try to capture some APCs.

We had passed the same spot only half an hour before and I was sure we would be sent back to help, but once again we were too far away. Instead we got the play-by-play from Bucky. A pair of Cobras escorting the battalion's command helicopter nearby got there quick, and it was a good thing. The NVA had swarmed around the isolated platoon, which survived only because the battalion commander, Lt. Colonel Parks, ordered the gunships to stick their rockets within fifty feet of the tracks. It worked, and the surviving North Vietnamese scattered.

Once again, we had dodged the bullet. I should have felt like a guardian angel was on board. Instead I felt like we had just played our last chip.

The day ended at a night laager back near the relative safety of Krek. The two contacts had put nerves back on edge, reminding us that we weren't dealing with poorly organized Viet Cong like in the good old days. Prowling the Alley day after day had become a game lethal roulette, and our number for a hard hit, whether there or somewhere else, was coming. It had to. I dwelled on that late into the night.

18

Eye of the Storm

*It appears we have appointed our worst generals to command forces,
and our most gifted and brilliant to edit newspapers. In fact,
I discovered by reading newspapers that these editor-geniuses plainly
saw all my strategic defects from the start, yet failed to inform me until
it was too late. Accordingly, I am readily willing to yield my command
to these obviously superior intellects, and I will, in turn, do my best
for the Cause by writing editorials—after the fact.*

—ROBERT E. LEE, 1863

May 1970. 25th Infantry Division. NVA Base Area 707, Cambodia.

But our luck would hold, at least for another day. We were taken off Ambush
Alley and sent back into the fields and jungle again, looking for new bounty.
In the afternoon, we found a food cache containing thirty-six tons of rice in
burlap bags. 1st Platoon was on flank security and never actually saw it, but
we did see the choppers that hauled it away. When it was done we returned
to Krek to occupy a rice paddy near the blacktop outside the village.

There was a water well next to some thatched huts a short walk from
our perimeter, and the LT sent us over in pairs so we could sanitize our
grimy skin. I had been filthy for so long it was hard to believe that the layers of crusty dirt could be washed away or that my matted hair would ever
again accommodate a comb. After almost three weeks, standing naked in
public was a small price to pay for a cleansing rebirth of body and mind.
The mama-sans hauling up the buckets only giggled as we worked GI soap
into our pores and welcomed the cascades of cooling life they obligingly
poured over us.

Afterward, I climbed atop 1-3 to smoke cigarettes with Dave and fantasize about the World. It felt like a good-sized chunk of the past couple of weeks had been rinsed away, carried to a quiet memory pond somewhere downstream. The dark forces eroding my insides had been neutralized, at least for the moment, and out here even a moment was worth a lot.

A Chinook dropped in at twilight with sundries, mail, and clean fatigues. One letter was from my brother, a senior at OU who had regressed in two short years from being clean-cut Joe College to drugged-out free spirit. Even in his spacey world, he had remained supportive, given that I had been drafted and was his brother. But no more. His letter was a cold lecture on the illegality of the war and the shooting of the students at Kent State, which he blamed on Nixon for sending us into Cambodia. That announcement had ignited a rash of campus uprisings, and naturally, journalists didn't bother to mention that hitting the North's Cambodian supply centers would subsequently save American lives and possibly shorten the war. Instead, the message was that Nixon was expanding the war. To hear my brother tell it, we were as guilty as the decision makers. He bragged about joining a protest on campus where some students had carried North Vietnamese flags.

My hands were shaking by the time I finished it. I had been labeled a criminal by my own brother, and my spirits went into a free-fall. At the same time, his words made me blaze with anger, both at him and the fools he ran with, none of whom had ever marched a step in my boots. I put a match to the letter, eager to write back and let it fly, but the energy wasn't there. I was too hurt and too distressed to act, and I realized that there was no point to it anyway. I tried the rest of the evening to buck up, but got nowhere.

In the morning, the order of the day was reconnaissance in force. The mission was to break brush all day along the flanks of Ambush Alley. The terrain was a flat patchwork of fields and thickets, where intermittent dapples of shade offered momentary relief from the sun. Except for getting switched by low branches and putting up with the dust, it was a day without action. Evidently the NVA were in no mood to take a swing at us, but they didn't see fit to share that information, so we remained vigilant while scouring the bushes. By dusk we had worked our way back to the familiar terrain near Krek.

It was pitch dark by the time the company was set up and secure, and the previous day's washing had been undone. New layers of dirt and tired faces were once again standard fare. Our APCs formed a ragged circle on the crest of a lightly vegetated hillside only a few hundred yards from the paved highway. Downslope, a treeline snaked across a valley like a black serpent, providing cover for the NVA. The moon was high and bright, and I had just plopped my butt on an ammo box behind 1-3 track when Sergeant Pitt appeared and told Bucky to pick two men for a platoon AP.

This was met with looks of disbelief. At first, even Bucky didn't respond. We hadn't sent out APs since crossing the Rach Cai Bach River into Cambodia. Sending them out after dark in any case was rarely done. It seemed especially unreasonable now, considering it was Littlefield's fault that we had worked overtime and didn't get in position until the light was lost. Bucky voiced that opinion but still had to acknowledge the order. Pitt then wandered off. We all just stood there, stone-faced. Bucky simply shrugged, as if to say he wasn't to blame.

I was selected along with Snake to suit up for the overnighter, and once we had collected our gear we linked up with the other four lucky grunts. Some things were said about the risk, and it was quickly decided that a more private conference was needed, so we huddled up behind 1-3 before reporting to the LT. There was talk about trip flares and Claymores already being set and what could happen if just one man on guard failed to get the word before we walked out. Beyond that, there was the peril of wandering into the night virtually blind. The consensus was that it wasn't worth what it could cost.

When the lieutenant checked us out, we laid it on the line.

"Sir," Snake said, "we don't like putting you on the spot, but this is a crock of shit."

The lieutenant's eyes narrowed, but he seemed only slightly surprised. "I'm not sure I get your meaning," he said.

"We're not going, lieutenant." 2nd Squad's Jay Phillips had even less tact than Snake, but there it was. The words were out, naked and unretrievable. Phillips just stood there, expressionless. Nobody jumped in to elaborate, and a stare-down ensued, with the lieutenant looking from Snake to Phillips and back again, then at the rest of us.

Finally, I broke the silence, more to end the suspense than anything. "The thing is, lieutenant"—but he waved me off. If Joe Yearout was good at anything, he was good at sizing things up quick. He also understood limits. Additional words were not necessary. More talk only ran the risk of one side or the other getting backed too far into a corner.

He studied our tired, dirty faces, deliberating. The result of the confrontation could be positive or destructive. If he chose the military tradition of unquestioned authority, we would have a choice to make. All of us understood the need for that authority. We also understood that our own need to avoid taking unnecessary chances had a legitimate place in the equation, the key word being *unnecessary*. We could only hope he did, too. It was a delicate balance, and tipping too far in either direction had to somehow be avoided. Everyone in that circle knew that if he stood by us, it would elevate our respect for him rather than diminish it. None of us were hard cases. He knew that as well. He knew that this was a serious stand, one not decided on a whim. Nerves were raw. If we went humping down that hill in silhouette under a rising moon, a lot of things could happen and none of them would be good.

"Get over here," he said, motioning us to a place between the tracks. We reassembled, like players in a huddle, all eyes on the quarterback.

"I'm only going to say this once." He looked at each of us, making sure he had everyone's attention. "Number one, you're going to walk your butts outside that perimeter, as ordered. Twenty minutes later you're going to call in a sit-rep and tell the CP that you've taken up a position a half-klick down that hill. If you take it upon yourselves to circle back in, I'd better not know it."

"No problem, sir," Phillips said solemnly.

Joe ignored this. "Number two, don't ever back me up against a wall like this again. You just used the only chit you'll ever have." He paused to let this sink in. "And number three, this conversation never took place. If you get caught I'll lead the lynch party. Now get going." With that he turned and left.

Snake radioed the CP for clearance to exit the perimeter. We wandered out only as far as the Claymores, following a designated path, and then quickly crept back in. We told a frowning Bucky about our meeting with the lieutenant. He said that as far as he was concerned, we didn't exist until daylight. That left mainly Sergeant Pitt to avoid. He was a lifer and would have our asses if he found out. He was bunking in 1-1, so we hunkered down on the far side of 1-3 next to 2nd Platoon's section of the perimeter and laid low the rest of the night. As far as the CP was concerned our sit-reps came from somewhere near the black wall of jungle. Just before first light we quietly dispersed to our own squads. Luckily, nobody important asked why we weren't seen coming back in.

The day brought more recon, this time scouting a flatland marbled with discontinuous single canopy. Littlefield must have been in a foul mood because he badgered the lieutenants every time he decided they weren't following directions. To make matters worse, somehow we got hemmed in by a winding stream. After playing rats-in-a-maze for a half-hour, the company was called to a halt by a now-frazzled Captain Little-field. After a short meeting at the CP, Joe put together a patrol and we set out on foot to find a crossing.

A thin belt of trees and brush lined the streambed and the bank was loose and steep, like a gully. With the LT in the lead, we soon put enough distance between us and the safety of the tracks to cause the needle on the vulnerability gauge to twitch. We moved quiet and slow, now watching as much for likely ambush sites as anything. After another fifty yards the lieutenant called a halt while he slipped down a low point on the bank to study the angle and check water depth. It was a no-go, so we moved on, spread apart and loosely on line, one abreast the other. We were navigating through a tangle of brush when Joe found another potential crossing site and waved us to a stop.

No sooner had we come to a halt than I heard distinct movement behind me. My blood iced up and in a single motion I whirled, dropped to one knee, thumbed the selector to full auto, and brought the muzzle of my M16 on level, adding pressure to the trigger as I went. I had it half squeezed before my eyes caught up with my reflexes and I recognized the wide-eyed newbie standing in front of me, the color drained from his face. For a minute we remained in freeze-frame. My trigger finger must have been a thousandth of an inch from spinning a burst of rounds through his belly, and the fact that somehow that had not happened left me dumbstruck.

When I looked around, I found the rest of the patrol staring in stunned silence at what almost happened. The newbie had lagged dangerously behind without anyone noticing as we worked our way along the bank.

The lieutenant let out a long breath and then stepped around me for a close-quarters talk with the rookie, who was so green you could still smell the World on him. I stood up but said nothing. He still had his life and I had been spared the guilt of killing one of our own. That was all that mattered. By the time we resumed stalking the creek bank, my heart rate was back to normal, but my stomach churned from thinking about it. In my mind, stopping that trigger squeeze was nothing short of divine intervention.

A crossing point was found where the bank tapered to near level with the water, and soon enough the company was on its way. The afternoon was spent advancing through a series of hedgerows, occasionally softening them up first with .50-caliber fire. Exercising the guns served as a reminder of just how much we could bring to bear in spite of our exposure and that was always good for the spirit. By sunset, the company was back at Krek, set up next to the blacktop. Word was passed after chow that 4th Squad's new track, already christened ROTTIN "8" NO. III, would arrive the next day.

———————

It was mid-morning when 1-4 rolled in, escorted by a contingent of tracks from 3/4th Cav. The refreshed crew included the usual suspects and a newbie, Jeff Longacre from the bayou country. Ranger and McDonald were still healing. Word was that McDonald probably wouldn't be back.

As soon as I rejoined the squad, John pulled me aside. "I can get you the Fifty gunner's job if you want it."

I wasn't sure I'd heard him right. But then he wasn't one to mumble or dispense bullshit, so I overcame my surprise and said, "Sure, I want it. But why me?" I was still a few notches down in the pecking order within the squad, never mind the platoon.

"We know Ridgeway's not interested, and neither is Abbott, so it's either you or Mosier in 1-2, and I don't like the son-of-a-bitch."

"You have that kind of pull?"

"Damn straight. Drivers have a say in who the TC is. I already talked to Joe, and he said it was my call if I'm satisfied you can handle it. I'm thinkin' about Gibbs for the side Sixty."

"Man, I don't know. Mosier might get really pissed."

"Don't mean nothin'," he said. "What counts is that I have somebody up there I can rely on and get along with."

"Thanks," I said. I just hope nobody comes gunnin' for me."

"Don't worry about it," he said. "I'll head off any heat."

So I earned a bunk inside the track and a smidgen of status as 1-4's TC, or Track Commander, a glorified title that simply meant I was in charge of the biggest gun. The risk level went up, but I still had too much calendar left to let that get in the way.

The rest of the day was consumed cleaning weapons and standing by as a reactionary force. Shortly after dark, I joined a bull session behind the new APC. There was a decent breeze and no sounds of war anywhere in the distance. Figuring the new guy wasn't already nervous enough, Ridgeway decided to have a little fun.

"You know how the VC overrun LZs?" he asked in a low, solemn voice.

"I heard they use dope," Longacre said. He looked around expectantly, hoping he was in the ballpark.

"That's right, newbie. They get doped up—weed, acid, uppers, skag, cocaine, whatever they can get their dirty little hands on. Makes 'em almost impossible to kill."

"You got that right," Snake confirmed.

Longacre had his brows up, soaking in every word. I had to wonder how long it would take before he realized his chain was being yanked.

"Dig it," Mike said. "They get whipped into a frenzy and then they attack like crazed lunatics. You can shoot 'em, blow 'em up with Claymores and Fougasse, but they just get up and keep comin', guts draggin' in the dirt. Before you know it half of 'em are inside the perimeter, howling like animals and throwin' satchel charges and slingin' grenades all over the place." He paused. "Then the hand-to-hand combat starts." He ended with that, as if there was nothing left to say.

Pilcher took the cue. Striking fire to a Camel, he said, "Heard tell of a dink at LZ Jay that got an arm blown off, picked it up with the one he still had and whupped a GI almost to death with it." He slowly shook his head in wonder.

"Doesn't work for us, though," Mike said. "Somehow our guys don't turn bulletproof even when they're ripped. Must have something to do with the raw fish those fuckers eat."

Gibbs worked a P-38 around the rim of a green can. Without looking up he said, "Best to be ready for hand-to-hand all the time."

Longacre now looked like he knew he was being fucked with but had to play along. From the looks of everyone else, it seemed we had spooked ourselves as much as our intended mark. Everybody knew that human wave suicide attacks were bona fide real. All they'd really done is fudge a little on the enemy's dope-induced immunity to death.

Spencer started a tale about Bamboo Vipers, but few paid attention. I'd heard too many times how every form of animal life in Vietnam is bigger, faster, meaner, and uglier than their CONUS kin. Here, cockroaches can jump rivers, rats are so big that hawks won't take them on, and some of the mosquitoes can siphon a man dry in one hard pull. Most of it was myth and exaggeration, but it made for good conversation, especially around those who didn't know better.

"This looks like an unauthorized gathering." Joe stepped out of the shadows. He advised the new guy not to swallow everything whole, then briefed us on tomorrow's RIF before we split up and racked.

We spent another day busting hedgerows and reconning with fire in a wide expanse of terrain northeast of Krek. We found evidence of recent NVA activity in a small deserted village and in a makeshift camp that had been recently abandoned. We didn't get shot at all day and tripped no mines or boobytraps, so all was well that ended well. The company laagered early, still in the outback. The reason for this became evident when a pair of Hueys drifted in for a landing.

"Hope they brought some ice and sodas," I said hopefully.

"Not likely," John answered. We had finished dusting off the track's deck and setting up the RPG screen. The sun hung low in the hazy sky like a defiant bully, getting in its last licks. I was topside oiling down the .50. John sat perched on the driver's hatch, a Winston hanging loosely from his mouth. The rest of the squad was busy setting out Claymores and trip flares.

A small entourage emerged from the choppers and marched smartly toward Littlefield's command post. The front man was a lieutenant colonel in starched fatigues and embroidered baseball cap. His left fist fiercely choked a roll of laminated maps, as if they might otherwise break free and run.

We saw the LT dust himself off and head that way, and that told us some kind of powwow was underway that involved the whole company. This put the speculators in action, and soon enough word circulated that the big shot was the new battalion commander, a hard ass named Nathan Stiles. By now we were on the ground, loitering with others who had also witnessed Stiles's George Patton impersonation.

"How did they get John Wayne to come to a real war?" Mike asked.

"A Hun for a commander could be dangerous to our health," Gibbs suggested.

"I'm too short for this shit," Ridgeway said. "That, fellas, is a man in search of fruit salad for the dress greens, and he will have no problem spending some of us to get it."

"Then again," I said optimistically, "maybe he just dropped by to tell Littlefield to stop doing stupid shit."

Dave shook his head. "Nope. This guy is here for a reason, and we're probably not gonna like it."

By the time the lieutenant emerged from the CP, most of us were convinced that some kind of suicide mission was about to be shoved down our dusty throats. Then the choppers left without Stiles, meaning we were stuck with him as a tag-along.

"Looks like he wants to play leader-for-a-day," John said.

"There it is," Dewayne said. "The question is, lead us to where, and for what?"

There was no briefing from the lieutenant, so it was a matter of wait and see.

We moved out just after sunrise. Stiles, firmly in command, constantly barked orders to the lieutenants, but it was the NVA instead of the colonel who pissed us off. The little bastards sniped at us with small arms a couple of times and lobbed one horribly off-target mortar round that somehow nicked a 3rd Platoon troop. It was just enough to keep everybody ginned

up and give Stiles an opportunity to play war, each time having us hurl a lot of ammo at ghosts. Also wounded enough for a trip to the rear was Mosier, who was hit in the leg with bullet fragments that ricocheted off his track. I figured that he was either doubly pissed at not getting my .50 slot or happy as hell at being hauled to the rear.

The night's bivouac was on a bald spot near the blacktop, east of Krek near the hamlet of Phum Saam. Only privileged characters with maps knew exactly where we were in relation to where we'd been. I tried keeping a journal, but locations were guesswork. For the most part those of us whose only concern was to stay healthy didn't care anyway. Other than the hardtop road and Ambush Alley, it was all a blur. To our good fortune the colonel had moved out, switching to Bravo company at a brief rendezvous late in the afternoon.

Once we'd settled in, Cambodians from the nearby huts wandered over, carrying pineapples and coconuts. Unlike war-jaded Vietnamese, they hadn't come to sell or to con, only to satisfy their curiosity. The kids were mesmerized by the massive steel machines. To them they must have seemed like something from another world. The fruit was juicy and sweet. We returned their offerings by passing out C-ration B-2 units to the kids. The desserts in cans caused a lot of eyes to light up and brought grins from the grown-ups. There was plenty of heart-felt smiling and bowing, which Littlefield allowed until the light started to fade. It was an uplifting end to another miserable day.

Shortly after dark, the lieutenant called a platoon meeting. He had just come from a huddle-up at the CP. "First thing is, I need to ask an important question, so listen up," he said.

Immediately, John said, "What's that?" He was in no mood for suspense, and by the look on his face, he was suspicious of what was coming.

The lieutenant paused for effect, then said, "All right. Here it is. I need to know if anybody speaks Laotian?" His face gave away nothing.

For a few seconds, there was silence. Then Snake said, "You're bullshittin', LT."

Joe said, "Yes I am," then grinned and waited. There were a few nervous chuckles, that's all. The joke bombed.

"Come on, guys," he said. "Why so serious all the time?"

"Funny, lieutenant," Bucky said. He was lighting a cigarette with the hot-boxed butt of one he had just finished.

"Okay. Here's the real deal. I know you guys are getting tired of cruisin' Ambush Alley and bustin' brush all day, so you'll be glad to know that tomorrow we have a real target to go after."

Spencer, unusually antsy, interrupted. "What kind of target, sir?"

"I'm getting there. Gimme a second," he said. Now everybody was interested. "A sizable base camp has been located a few klicks from here. Battalion believes it may contain beaucoup weapons and other goodies. The trick is that they also think there is a fortified security force positioned around it."

This time it was Ned, the resident pessimist. "They *think* there's a security force," he said. "And getting ambushed would be the best way to find out, right?"

"Give it a rest, Shelton. You can ask questions when I'm finished."

The LT took a breath. "Look, we've all been pushed hard ever since we got here. The fact is that not much is going to change until we get orders to vacate. Until then we have missions to carry out. So just listen and then make your preparations. Try to remember that we're all in this together."

Ned stayed shut but sulked. The need for vengeance had ebbed some since the incidents with Charlie, but in my mind going after a stationary target was better than cruisin' for a bruisin', and I thought others felt the same way. I didn't like Ned's attitude, so to rub it in, I said, "We're with you, lieutenant." There was some mumbled agreement to this and the meeting got more relaxed.

Pilcher yawned. "Anything else?" He was apparently bored by it all, even though the platoon was on deck to ride point for the company.

"Yeah. As much as I'd like to say that this objective is made to order for mechanized infantry, conditions are rarely ideal, and this is no exception. Assuming the camp is where it's supposed to be, it's in heavy jungle and could be a tight fit for the tracks."

Dave held a finger up. "That means restricted movement going in, is that right?" Unlike Pilcher, he wanted all the information he could get.

"You got it. Likely it will be a single file situation. The good news is that dismounts from Bravo Company will be involved, too. Their tracks and gunners will be held in reserve outside the treeline nearby, part blocking force, part flank security."

Bucky, who had just fired his third smoke, didn't like it. "Uh, not to question the wisdom of the battle plan, sir, but doesn't that create a situation where we won't know who we're shooting at when the dung hits the fan?"

"I didn't say it was a perfect plan. We've got to have grunts on the ground to help make up for the lack of maneuverability. If they make contact, they're likely going to need us close at hand. The bad guys may let them pass and take us on first. That's why it's important that our fire be directed squarely at the source of the incoming. Officers in both companies will be in constant commo. Any other questions?"

He waited, but was met with mostly blank faces. The subject had been covered.

"Our platoon leads the pack. Once we close on the objective, the order of battle will be One-Three, One-Four, One-One, and One-Two. That's it."

As night gained a foothold the air grew thick and the mosquitoes sucked greedily. I sat behind 1-4 smoking with a mixed group from our squad and 1-3.

"Fuckin' bugs," Snake said, slapping at his face. "I'd eat a plateful of dog turds just to keep what blood I have left."

"Bugs don't make deals," Bucky said. "Gimme a light, will ya? My Zippo's outta juice."

"All the dogs around here have probably been eaten anyway," I said. "Be realistic."

Bucky stood up. "Well boys, I'm off to clean my weapon. I'd recommend the rest of you do the same before lights out. Tomorrow could be a long day." He wandered off, and soon others followed. The stage was set, and there was little left to talk about.

I had just crawled under my poncho liner inside 1-4 when some dude from the CP came by passing out Kotex-sized bandages. He handed me one, then moved on before I could say anything. For a minute, I just stared at the thing in my hand, wondering how much they knew and weren't telling. I decided to go outside and smoke another cigarette. Somewhere artillery rumbled faintly, and on the distant horizon, I saw flares wink and fade, illuminating somebody else's fight. For some reason it seemed light years away, as if the flarelight originated from weak stars in a distant galaxy, and I couldn't sum up a shred of emotion over it. I was bone tired, but no longer sleepy, so I boarded 1-3 to shoot the shit with Dave, who was on early watch.

I couldn't get the bit about the jumbo bandage off my mind. It hung in my head like a warning, and I finally brought it up.

"I'd like to know what they have in mind when they deputize everybody as a medic," I said.

Dave just shrugged. "I'd say it means they're definitely expecting a rumble."

"And you're on point."

He took a long pull on a Kool, then looked at the sky. "Luck of the draw," he said. "It won't be the first time."

His sense of calm was no surprise. He knew he wasn't bulletproof, and he had his despairing moments, but he wasn't one to live in a state of pending doom. Even so, it didn't take a crystal ball to know he was feeling the same vibes as everybody else.

"Yeah, luck of the draw," I said.

19

Memorial Day

I hate it when they say, "He gave his life for his country."
Nobody gives their life for anything. We steal the lives of these kids.
We take it away from them. They don't die for the honor
and glory of their country. We kill them.

—ADMIRAL GENE LAROCQUE

30 May 1970. 25th Infantry Division. NVA Base Area 707, near Saam, Cambodia.

The morning air refused to move as Alpha's tracks eased onto the blacktop under a sun that promised a full ration of suffering, shade or no shade. It was May 30, and at the nearby village of Saam, Cambodian children played in the dirt. Far afield, the shriveled figure of a farmer directed a team of oxen across a dusty paddy, straining his bony back in hopes of squeezing another meager crop from the worn earth. The cluster of thatched huts along the roadside, most of them on stilts, would have been in high demand on a South Pacific beach. Here, they were rudimentary shelter for a poverty-ravaged people who slept on bamboo mats and shared space with livestock. In spite of it, their occupants smiled and waved as we rolled by. Other than the clatter of treads on pavement, the crackling of transmissions over the track's radio speaker was the only sound.

After a short distance, Pilcher pivoted 1-3 and slipped down the embankment into a paddy where the treeline pushed in close. He was followed by John, who did likewise. Within minutes, like a string of marching ants, the company left the hardtop and what had served as civilization behind. Soon the cultivated farmland gave way to rougher terrain, and we worked our way through a patchwork of hedgerows and clearings, now in columns of two. We crossed an open space where we had to navigate around a finger of woods reaching across our front. We followed 1-3 around it, but when 1-1 behind us made the same move they detonated a large mine that exploded in an ear-piercing geyser of smoke and debris and sent most of their squad skyward. Grunts along the column lunged to the ground as machine guns swung toward the woodline and opened fire, but no ambush materialized. Littlefield's voice squawked over the horn from somewhere back down the line, but there was no answer from the lieutenant's track.

Spencer keyed his handset and advised the captain that 1-1 had apparently hit a mine. The thinning dust revealed a bucket-sized crater under mangled roadwheels on the track's port side. Their driver, Wally, looked woozy but was still in the driver's hatch. Most of the others got slowly to their feet and worked to regain their bearings. Four were wounded, including the lieutenant. He didn't get up. He was flat on his back in serious pain.

Doc Johnson hustled over and was soon joined by the medic from 2nd Platoon.

"Not a good start," John said. The rest of us had nothing to add. We just watched and waited. John turned the speaker up and we cocked an ear. The next voice over the radio was Bucky's, who told the CP to get a dustoff on the way. "The medics think the LT tore some muscles in his back, he said. He can't get up."

A radio was brought to our fallen leader, and after a short conversation with Littlefield, he summoned 1-2's squad leader, Bill Dickson, who had just been promoted to E-6. Sergeant Pitt had taken the last resupply chopper out and Bill was pegged to be his replacement. Dickson was a bone-skinny, soft-spoken mid-westerner with black hair and a thin mustache, as unassuming as they come. He kneeled at the lieutenant's side, only to be motioned closer. He came down on his other knee, and with some effort the LT removed the radio codes and laminated map that hung around his neck. These he handed to a surprised Dickson as he lowered his head back onto a folded flak jacket. "You're it," he said with a strained grin.

Dickson stared at the lanyard in his hand like it was det cord set to blow.

"Ah, hell," he said. He glanced around, as if looking for an avenue of escape, then reluctantly accepted the fact that he was now acting lieutenant.

"You can handle it, Bill," Joe said. I have no doubt of it."

The look on Dickson's face was not one of total agreement, but the deal was done and he knew it.

"Whatdaya know about that shit," John said. He lit a Winston and blew smoke at the sky.

"There it is," Ridgeway added. "What do you think, Mikey?"

"Better him than others I can think of," Mike allowed.

"You got that right," I added.

This was lost on Spencer, who sat gazing into space as if he were somewhere else.

Yellow smoke was popped, followed by the sound of a Huey. Minutes later, the lieutenant and the others were whisked away to 12th Evac Hospital at Cu Chi. All we could do was wave good-bye, knowing that Joe Yearout's days of leading an infantry platoon were over. I liked Dickson and believed he would fare well for as long as it took. It was hard to imagine Joe's eventual replacement filling his shoes, but with casualties, rotations, and all the rest of it, the complexion of the company changed so fast that just trying to keep up was a waste. With officers, the musical chairs moved even faster, given that their field assignments were only six months at the outset. Joe was a natural leader, but we knew that most platoon leaders and a lot of company commanders came to the field green, replacing those who were just as green six months before. A lot of grunts thought that using their blood to train new officers was a poor way to run a railroad.

"Better Bill than some lily-skinned snot-nose fresh out of Palookaville," Bucky observed. Nothing else needed to be said.

—•—

An hour was lost while mechanics put the "Age of Aquarius" back together, time used mainly to dob sweat with dirty towels. The wind was still on strike and the shade of the foliage was just out of reach. The recent rains helped keep the dust down, but padded the humidity. I was relieved to hear some radio chatter, which indicated it was time to go. John draped his towel around his neck, lit a cigarette, and cranked the ignition. Once again, we moved out in columns. Dickson had returned to his original squad on 1-2 rather than take the lieutenant's seat on the repaired 1-1, in my view a smart move.

For a while, we chugged from one clearing to another, always shadowed by a wall of jungle. The earth had become softer and more grassy, giving us an opportunity to breathe air that didn't resemble brown fog. Finally we stopped in a big field where a perimeter was formed and a lunch break called. I huddled up with others in a thin slice of shade between 1-3 and 1-4 to get a bite and wait for the CP to fine-tune our destiny. I dug for my P-38 and managed to swallow just enough salty meat to calm my growling stomach, washing it down with long pulls of warm water.

"It's too stinkin' hot to even eat," Ned said. "When do they have winter around here, anyway?"

"This *is* winter, my man," Dewayne answered. He wiped his brow and ran a hand through his thick red hair, then retrieved a Zippo and reached for his pipe.

"It may be summer all the time here," Vernon said, "but I'll take this over freezing to death any day."

I gave Gibbs a thumbs-up. "Ten-four on that," I said. There's nothing worse than being cold." That brought nods of agreement from Willie and Jeff.

"Heat, cold, it all sucks," Ned said. "I'm thinkin' about takin' that six year re-up offer to get out of here."

I'd seen the re-up poster at Cu Chi. It was enough to make your mouth water. Fifteen grand cash bonus, thirty-day paid leave, and choice of duty station after that. Talk about immediate gratification. A guy could get out of Nam with his life, choose a stateside assignment, buy a new GTO or Z-28—and barely put a dent in that bonus. Tantalizing as it was, it wasn't for me. I knew that I could never adapt to the spit and polish of stateside duty again, not after this. Being nagged by lifers over the shine on my shoes and other meaningless bullshit just wouldn't fly. I was committed to staying in country until I could check out as a free man.

"Not me, brother," I said. "I'll take my chances on another eight months right here and be done with it."

"Ditto on that," Snake said. "That program's just a carrot on a string, man. Who's to say they won't bounce your ass right back here if this war is still on come rotation time from wherever you end up? It's a con, dude."

"Maybe I have my own reasons," Ned said sullenly. He didn't elaborate, but his expression suggested he didn't like having judgment passed or being seen as a non-hacker, for that matter.

"I spent some time at Fort Benning in December, and it got so damn cold they had fire barrels at the field training sites," I said, thinking it best to get back on topic. "Every day our hands and feet went numb in the morning and stayed that way. And that's in Georgia, for Christ's sake."

"There it is," Vernon said. "Fightin' a war in the snow, like in World War Two and Korea would have been a lot worse than this shit."

"Hard to believe anything is worse than this," Longacre said. He had a towel draped over his head.

"It can always be worse," Bucky said. He had just walked up. "Bravo's tracks are parked in the next clearing over. Their troops are gearing up to go in, so be mindful of that and try not to waste any of them if we end up in close quarters."

"So this is the place." Dave said. He looked at the distant treeline.

"Roger that. We're about ready to move out, so eat up."

I ran through a mental checklist to reassure myself that both the .50 and my rifle were ready and that I was well stocked with ammo. It was a helpful exercise, but it was no secret that a .50 gunner's turret wouldn't stop anything bigger than small arms or light machine guns, and the butterflies in my stomach stirred fretfully. I had my flak jacket zipped and snapped, and my steel pot in place. These were protections I couldn't afford to do without, no matter what the weather.

Spencer called us together to remind us of the obvious—that we would be the second track in a single column and what that implied. "Bravo's dismounts will be to our front flanks. They should be far enough out to avoid crossfire if their elements and ours become engaged at the same time. The plan is that we will be reactionary, depending on what they run into."

It sounded reasonable, but the old saw about the battle plan going out the window with the firing of the first shot hung in the dead air like a sure bet. Single file movement in thick jungle was so limiting I had to believe that Colonel Stiles wanted action no matter how far he had to push it. We had enough grunts to advance on the target without tracks. He must have thought the presence of APCs would scare them or that a few .50 rounds would send them running. Who knows.

Drivers cranked ignitions and on signal 1-3 moved out. Dave looked back at me and we traded a thumbs-up. John maneuvered 1-4 in behind Pilcher and crept toward the jungle wall two hundred meters distant. Behind us, acting lieutenant Dickson radioed directions from 1-2, with 1-1 bringing up the platoon rear, having earned the privilege for being hit once today already.

No sooner had 1-3 squeezed through a crack in the overhang that it became a struggle to avoid the sweep of stiff branches and cope with the lack of visibility. The going was dangerously slow, and lateral movement of any degree was all but removed from the equation. Mechanized infantry was never intended for such a battlefield, but then I'd learned early that few things done here had much resemblance to how they were supposed to happen.

We wormed our way in, ducking switches, and crunched along until intersecting a narrow pathway, presumably the same one followed by the Bravo grunts. I had to assume that they cleared the trail going in, but if they did the information wasn't passed down. We stopped long enough at this point for everyone but gunners and drivers to dismount and fall in behind their respective tracks. I saw Bucky and Pilcher exchange a few words as Bucky climbed down, no doubt over Pilcher's missing flak jacket. To his credit, he did have his steel pot on top of his thick skull.

I kept a tight grip on the .50 handles and studied the tangled brush as we resumed moving at a creepy-crawl and snaked our way deeper into the woods. The layered canopy blanketed out the day, allowing only angled shards of yellowed light to poke through. I figured that if the NVA wanted a secluded site for a base camp, this setup would do nicely.

It was anybody's guess as to how far forward Bravo's people were, but if they hoped to catch the enemy by surprise, they wouldn't get any help from us. Branches popped under the treads along the trail's edges and the trees on both flanks stood so close that getting even two tracks abreast was all but impossible. If there was a perimeter guard or blocking force for the camp, they would have plenty of warning that things weren't copacetic. Hopefully Bravo would get there before the sounds of our ruckus.

Dave's .50 was pointed left at eleven o'clock, mine to the right at one o'clock. Roughly fifty feet separated our tracks. The rest of the platoon was spread out between the APCs. 1-3 pivoted slightly right into a turn on the footpath. John swiveled likewise. At this point I had no idea of our true direction or how far we might go. I scanned the woods ahead but couldn't see beyond the leafy boughs almost within reach. So far not a shot fired and no indications of trouble up ahead. Dave must have been thinking the same, figuring the dead-still jungle was just that—dead. If this turned out to be another red herring, I had to admit I wouldn't be disappointed. I freed my right hand from the .50 and squeegeed sweat from my brow with the heel of my palm, then reached for a flattened Marlboro. I glanced sideways at the jungle. I was about to light up when I heard the unmistakable whoosh of an RPG as it flashed from the shadows on the right and slammed the stagnant air in an ear-splitting crack. The unlit cigarette fell as I swung the .50 barrel into position and jabbed the gun's trigger. A storm of fire raged from the undergrowth as I raked the trees like a madman, keeping the tracers just high enough off the ground to avoid our own troops. All of my arm strength was channeled through my thumbs and onto the butterfly trigger. I had a vague sense that something was wrong with 1-3 but I was too intent on beating back the incoming to risk a look. One thing I did know was that we were immobilized. There simply was nowhere to go. Given a chance to fire more RPGs, the NVA stood a good chance of taking us out.

Screams and other sounds occasionally slipped through the noise, but the snap of splintering trees and the hail of fire had my full attention. A second RPG detonated in a bone-rattling blast behind me, but in the chaos there was no way of telling where it originated. Hoping to have more effect, I swung the gun's barrel more to the right and sent a new stream of thumb-sized slugs into the dense underbrush.

My aim was measured but hadn't slowed the incoming. The bastards were dug in, and good. If anybody was directing our side of the drama, it

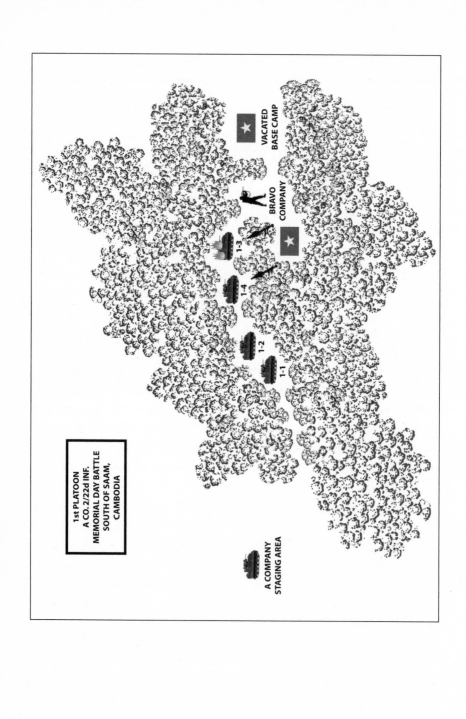

1st PLATOON
A CO. 2/22d INF.
MEMORIAL DAY BATTLE
SOUTH OF SAAM,
CAMBODIA

VACATED
BASE CAMP

BRAVO
COMPANY

1-3

1-4

1-2

1-1

A COMPANY
STAGING AREA

was lost on me. I was isolated within the noise and intensity of the firefight. I had no idea how many of our tracks were engaged, but knew it couldn't be more than four, and maybe only two. I could've looked but there wasn't time. Either way, we may as well have been cast in concrete. Now I sensed that 1-3 was burning, but there wasn't time to think about it. I was fixated on suppressing the incoming with as many rounds as I could push down the barrel of my machine gun.

Small arms popped like and endless string of firecrackers, bouncing off wood and steel. Twigs and leaves rained down from the overhang, and drifting smoke shrouded the whole mess. I knew the rest of my life was equal only to the length of time we could keep the RPG man's head down. I could hear the M60, so Gibbs was still at it, but with the density of the brush John couldn't use his grenade launcher. All he had was his M16. To the rear I could hear 1-2's .50 pummeling the woods. It was reassuring, but I didn't hear anything coming from 1-3. I swung the gun left to help fill the void and saw that Dave's track was on fire.

I renewed my attack on the jungle, determined not to be distracted. Don't mean nothing anyway, I thought, everybody's clear. The last of the .50 rounds snaked out of the hopper and I let go long enough to reach over the turret and grab a new can. In a matter of seconds I was back at it, wondering if the one can I had left would be enough. I chanced a look to the right. 1-2 stood solid. The others were around the bend and out of sight. I had no way to see the men on the ground without standing up but I could hear their rifles and assumed they were in prone firing positions along the trail's edges. The whereabouts of Bravo's straight-legs or whether they were also engaged may have been known to others, but it was lost on me. I had no headset and damned if I was going to pick up the handset and have a chat.

Fear turned to mechanical numbness. Occasional bullets pinged the track, but I was barely aware of it. The roar overpowered everything. I stayed hunched over and kept the pressure on with a steady onslaught of rounds. I had no idea whether I had hit anything other than plant life, but the RPG man was still in check. That was something. The barrel started to smoke and I had to ease up, an adjustment that took all the willpower I could muster. It was either that or let the barrel burn up, and there was no way I could change it out until this was over. If the riflings melted, it would cause rounds to bloop out in haphazard directions, making the gun totally ineffective. Luckily, after a minute or so the NVA lowered the volume as well. From there firing dwindled to little more than errant potshots and nervous short bursts. Soon this too fizzled.

It appeared to be over. I reloaded. There was chatter on the squawk box but I paid no attention. I loosened my grip on the machine gun and elevated myself enough to peer over the side of the track. Men on the ground had come to their knees; some were getting up. John hoisted himself out of the driver's hatch and we acknowledged each other as being okay. Gibbs signaled with a nod of the head. The deck was covered with empty shell casings. 1-3 was in flames, its storehouse of rounds starting to cook off. There was no way to go after the NVA. Maybe they stumbled into Bravo's dismounts during their withdrawal, but from where I sat even that seemed unlikely.

Snake, Dewayne, and a couple others from 1-3 drifted back toward 1-4, then stopped to stare at the inferno that had been their home on wheels. I didn't see Dave or Pilcher, but I didn't see any bodies on the ground, either, so I assumed they had escaped. The RPG must have hit the side of the track and burned through, starting the fire. Bucky and Doc Johnson appeared from the shadows in front of 1-3 and walked briskly in my direction. As they came alongside 1-4, I leaned over the turret and called down to them, eager to get a report. Either they didn't hear me or they were in a rush to connect with Dickson on 1-2. Ned had fallen in behind them. He apparently heard me and slowed, looking up. His face was strained and pale. "Dave's dead," he said.

His words came at me like an unexpected punch in the mouth. In spite of everything I'd just seen, I hadn't given such a possibility an inkling of thought. I was totally unprepared. Now here Ned had barged in, shoving aside my shield of denial and clubbing me with cold reality. It had to be a mistake, but I knew it wasn't.

"It was a direct hit from an RPG. Pilcher took a lot of shrapnel in the back. He's pretty fucked up."

He held my gaze, but I was unable to speak.

I couldn't hack up this bitter medicine any more than I could shove expended rounds back up the barrel of my gun. Even so, my mind raced to find words that would nullify what I'd just heard. Getting no response, Ned lowered his head and shuffled off, leaving me still speechless.

I slumped back. The inside of my head felt like it had been freeze-dried. Somebody else walked by and said, "Sorry about Dave, man." I didn't reply or even look down to see who it was. I just went on staring stupidly at nothing. Whoever it was knew that Dave was more than just a platoon-mate to me. I'd tried to keep that fact tucked safely away from conscious thought, but was only fooling myself. It was a bad idea to get too close to anyone, but when men who depend on each other to stay alive spend every day together it's hard to avoid.

I couldn't feel anything for Pilcher. He had offered himself up one too many times. If he fucking died, it would be mainly his own fault. In fact it almost seemed unfair that he might survive when David hadn't.

Bravo's troops began filtering out of the woods. They moved in slow silence, apparition-like, as if emerging from another dimension. There was no chatter as they made their way past our APCs, shuffling along in single file. Whatever they encountered had put the thousand-yard stare on their faces.

Two men materialized from the undergrowth. They were at opposite ends of a litter gripped tightly by soiled hands. Their sweat-streaked faces were grim. The soldier they carried was dead. A plastic poncho had been draped over the corpse, covering his face and most of his body. As they maneuvered past the track, his lower left foot slipped off the edge of the stretcher, exposing a few inches of pale flesh above the boot where his fatigue pants had ridden up. With each step taken by his pallbearers, the lifeless leg jiggled. I couldn't take my eyes off that limp, bouncing foot, and followed it until they were out of sight.

I was still in a trance when I overheard a Bravo troop say that the KIA had been hit by a .50 round. My head jerked around at this, and I almost called out to them, but then stopped myself. Instead, I just looked after them as they kept moving. I didn't want to think about whose gun might have done the killing. It was too much to take on, so I lit a cigarette and escaped into the numbness again.

Some of the squad climbed topside but said nothing. I acknowledged them but that's all. The sound of arriving medevacs filtered into the jungle.

With no LZ and no openings in the snarled overhang, jungle penetrators were lowered for the extractions. Pilcher was already strapped to a litter when the sling came down. What was left of him was quickly tethered and reeled in, followed by two other wounded. 1-3's rebellious driver then departed Cambodia, leaving his flak jacket and the never-ending war behind.

Engines started up as soon as the Bravo KIA was extracted and I was forced to pull myself together. The mission wasn't over. I tried to stuff everything that just happened into a mental cage so I could stay focused, but it was tough. Numbness had been replaced with anguish and fury. My mind burned with it. I felt like I did when I was eight years old and a bully had whaled on me outside the YMCA one day after swimming lessons. The more I fought back the more he pounded me. I was at his mercy, and when he was through, I was in tears, but the bawling had more to do with humiliation and anger than anything. He had acted with impunity, and being powerless to do anything about it had made me crazy. The NVA had killed Dave and gotten away with it. There was no way to rectify it. The identity of the enemy soldier who fired the RPG would never be known. The only consolation was imagining that some of my slugs had ripped him apart.

John helped distract me from it by handing me a smoke and saying, "Let's get the fuck out of here." I took the Winston and reached for my lighter. There was more talk on the ground and chatter on the radio. Spencer climbed topside and counted heads. I could hear tracks to our rear maneuvering in the thickets.

I looked again at 1-3. Flames licked up through the open cargo hatch. The .50 turret had slumped as the deck gave way from melting steel. Leaving it behind with Dave's body trapped inside wasn't right, but that would have to be swallowed, too, given the circumstances. So I directed my attention to the withdrawal as we finally began to move. After a couple of hundred feet, John was able to execute a multi-point turnabout where the others had, and we wormed our way back to open ground.

The company formed a perimeter back at the original staging area, and I busied myself helping John brush debris off the track's deck. When that was done, I restocked .50 ammo and used the canteen filled with motor oil to lube the gun's receiver and now-cool barrel. I was starting to get antsy about running out of diversions when Spencer and Mike climbed topside. Ned and Bucky followed them up.

"What's up?" John asked. A trademark cigarette dangled from the corner of his mouth and wormy trickles of sweat navigated the heavy stubble on his dusty face. He stared at Spencer in a way that suggested he'd better not offer up any bullshit.

"Now we wait for air support," he said.

"Which is where we should've started," Mike said.

"They had to have a good target," he answered. "Otherwise they're just wasting bombs."

I knew he would go stupid on us, I just didn't know how quick.

"Right," I said. "Why waste bombs when you can waste GIs instead. After all, bombs cost money. Draftees are free."

"Look," he said, "none of this was my doing, okay? Like it or not, what happened in there is what we're here to make happen."

"We're supposed to make our own guys get wasted? You're a dumb fuck, Stan." I glared at him, ready for it escalate as far as he wanted to take it. But he ignored the remark, maybe because he sensed the undercurrent of rage probing for an outlet. He wasn't smart enough to drop the whole subject, though. Instead he averted eye contact and softened his voice. "We can't pick the time, the place, or the situation, that's all I'm sayin'."

He was seeking an out, and I was too emotionally exhausted to continue, so I turned my back on him and worked on suppressing the cauldron of fire festering inside. Being left alone for the moment was the best medicine.

The sound of low-flying jets filled the air. We watched as they roared over our position and jettisoned their loads into the canopy, using the flames from 1-3 as a marker.

"Vengeance is mine, sayeth the Air Force," Bucky said.

High-explosive bombs tumbled into the NVA positions, sending plumes of fire-laced smoke belching up through the treetops. The F-4 Phantoms circled away in an arc, followed by two more that flashed in seconds later to unleash packaged death into the greenery below. The concussions sent tremors across the jungle floor that could be felt beneath our tracks. Brown puffs of smoke mushroomed up, leaving a smog-like haze hanging in the motionless air. Blacker, thicker smoke spires climbed slowly skyward, in no hurry to get anywhere. The jets came in pairs for the next ten minutes, offering a live demonstration of the term "scorched earth." We watched all this in silence, shading our eyes against the glare. Waiting.

When the last of the F-4s vanished into the blue, I reached for my smokes and a canteen, knowing what the next move would be. I gulped some warm water and lit up.

"Could've wiped Wisconsin off the map by now," Ned said.

"Air strikes don't mean nothin'," John answered. He was looking toward the treeline. Time in country had taught him that the safe play was to trust nothing.

Bucky drew on a freshly lit Kool and looked at John. "Glad we've got you to calm our nerves, Keinroth," he said.

John just shrugged. "What can I say?" he replied. "You know it and I know it."

Squelch broke on the track's intercom and Littlefield's voice bled through, telling drivers to crank their engines. With the order of battle already set, the next thing we heard was "Move out, One-Four." Since Bucky no longer had a track, he, Ned, and Snake rode with us. The rest of his squad had dispersed to the other tracks. I was glad to have Bucky on board, knowing he could shut Spencer down in a heartbeat if need be.

1-4 lurched and clattered toward the treeline. The plan was an exact repeat, with the idea of maneuvering around 1-3 to enter the base area. There, theoretically, we would collect booty, count bodies, and maybe even corral a few prisoners. Never mind that by now the NVA'd had plenty of time to gather their riches and blow town. Evidently, at this point, the outcome was less important than the act of completing the mission. I was too whipped up to think about their ideas for keeping score, though, so I dismissed the how and why of it and concentrated on the business of staying alive and the remote possibility of reprisal.

The jungle gobbled our track in one bite and we moved onto the heavily shadowed trail. Since everybody was mounted, I chambered a round and aimed the gun's barrel up-trail and slightly to the right, just as before. This time there were no straight-legs scouting ahead, which left nothing between me and the NVA except the veil of vegetation.

Sweat flowed as I gazed down the throat of the trail, but I paid little attention. I was too distracted by the thud of my heart trying to bust through my ribcage. The airstrikes should have been reassuring, but John's admonition along with a return to the scene revived the just-quelled grip of terror that goes with being pinned down under withering fire. Conflicting thoughts ran rampant behind my constantly shifting eyes. With no track in front of me to give ambushers a choice, I was ripe for taking, and visualizing what befell Dave kept my heartbeat at a dangerous level. Anger and the need for revenge had become secondary to fear. I felt more afraid of dying here that I had that night on Highway 1, or in the Renegade Woods, or on the day in the mine field when Smitty and Doc earned an exit ride the hard way. The fear clustered inside pushed for an exit, for some physical act. But there was nowhere to run, no way to hide, and no opportunity for even throwing the first punch. All I could do was react, and that left me with the same chance that Dave was given. My life now depended on the mettle and accuracy of the RPG man, and I had to bear it.

We snailed along. Time ground to a halt, as if to purposely stretch the suspense to the fullest measure. It was included in my fate, no extra charge. I tried but failed to deflect an image of a slow-motion rocket twisting out of the boughs on a trajectory that would intercept my gun turret an instant before I realized I was a dead man. I shuddered, knowing that just thinking such thoughts could seal the deal. I had to believe that I had the upper hand, even if it was a lie.

At the bend in the trail, we held up long enough to shuck the riflemen. Once dismounted, they spread out as before and followed along on foot as we eased around the slight elbow to enter the kill zone. I left the chambered round in the .50's breach but moved my thumbs into a hover over the trigger.

Ahead, 1-3 smoldered and spit flames. The top deck had caved in. Ammo continued to cook off. The barrel of the .50 jutted skyward from the wreckage at a skewed angle. Somewhere within this crematory, Dave's remains were slowly converting to ash.

I wiped my clammy palms one at a time on the knees of my fatigue pants and focused again on the woods crowding our path as we inched on. With everything else stimulating my hyped-up mind, I failed to notice the absence of bomb craters or fallen trees along the trail. Nothing had changed. Just as I realized this, I sensed a disturbance in the foliage and I swung my head to the right. At the same instant, wind blew across my face in the wake of a launched RPG that soared past and punctured the loose foliage beyond, exploding with a sharp crack and resonating boom. My insides locked up all the way to the skull, freezing any attempt to process what had just happened. All that sneaked through was instinct and training, and that was enough to swivel the .50 to the right and jam my thumbs down hard on the trigger.

We had jumped back in time—same spot, same cast of characters, same everything. It was as if the air strikes had done nothing other than provide R&R time for the NVA while awaiting our return, the one thing they could bank on.

.50-caliber tracers drilled holes in the brush and stripped branches from trees at about 200 rounds per minute—all the gun could handle without roasting the bore. It would have to be enough. If the rocket man got another chance, my odds had to be pretty weak. I stood out like a clown on a dunking board, a stationary target pigeon-holed into a hundred-foot kill zone. One hot rifle round or line-drive RPG was all it would take to turn me into a memory to everyone I'd ever known. 1-2, stopped halfway around the elbow in the trail behind me, was in the same boat. Between us we had to either conquer this moldy tangle of jungle or die trying.

Gibbs tore at the underbrush with the M60. Twigs and ricochets flew about in a loud popping of debris. If incoming rounds were bouncing off the track, I couldn't distinguish them, which was just as well. Grunts on the ground helped keep the pressure up. When the noise slackened a bit, I caught fragments of a voice in-between bursts, no doubt Littlefield's, yelling through the track's intercom. Since I wasn't the driver or the squad leader, it didn't make a flip to me what he might be squawking about, and I wasn't about to pick up the handset to find out. He was somewhere to the rear. I was on point fighting for my life. Sweat stung my eyes, but I couldn't wipe. An exploding grenade nearby stabbed my ears, telling me it was much too close. To make matters worse, the full belt of ammo I started with was getting short. All this interfered with concentration, but tending to any distraction could be the last itch I ever scratched.

The distressing and unanswered question was not knowing if the rounds I pumped out were having any effect. I covered a sector from roughly one o'clock to three o'clock. Incoming fire came intermittently from several directions along the trail. They hadn't been beaten back yet, but the RPG man's head was still down, so I decided to stay pat, hoping it wasn't all a waste.

The last of the ammo belt danced its way into the breach and banged through. Shit! I reached for another box and clearly heard Dickson's voice on the radio hollering "Cease fire! Cease fire!" Only then did I notice that firing had sharply tapered off, suggesting the NVA might have high-tailed it once again. But considering the misjudgments we'd already paid a price for, I thought it better safe than sorry, so I loaded up and pumped a few more bursts into the woods for good measure, orders be damned. Even after letting up, I stared intently at the jungle, thumbs resting lightly on the trigger. Everybody else held fast as well.

Dead calm now, as if God himself had called for a break. Smoke hung in the air. The jungle groaned and twitched in the aftermath of the firestorm. The only other sounds were idling diesels and the popping of ammo inside the broiling belly of 1-3's carcass. Nothing moved. I was arm-weary and my back ached dully, but I didn't dare move. I fully expected something in the narrow space between them and us to flinch and trigger another round. I mentally took stock. I wasn't dead and I wasn't bleeding. I wanted very much to finish this up with all body parts in place and a full ration of blood. But there was work left to do, so that probability remained iffy.

The standoff ended a few minutes later when Littlefield's voice blared through the track's speaker. "Back 'em out, platoon leaders. Get moving. Now." So once again, we began the slow process of extracting the bulky tracks from the confining space of the woods, squirming and twisting until we could get turned around and wiggle our way out. Why the hell we didn't press on was beyond me, but even bringing it up wasn't worth the breath it would take.

To everyone's amazement, the only injuries involved minor shrapnel wounds and other nicks that were treated by Doc Johnson once we reached sunlight and circled the wagons. There were only two that required additional treatment, and they were soon medevacked.

We guzzled water and smoked and watched while the jungle exploded under a new barrage of tactical air terror. There was no reason to believe the jet jockeys would get it right on the second try, but since we had no say in the matter, we concentrated on resting and psyching ourselves for excursion number three. We could only hope that they had expanded on their original bulls-eye. I was soaked with fatigue, but that is what I had spent twenty-one weeks in training to endure, so I did what I could to shake it off. More than anything I wanted to grieve, but I couldn't afford to drift. Not now. I had to stay locked into survival mode. There was unfinished business at hand; everything else would have to wait.

I oiled the .50 and hauled up two more boxes of ammo while the jungle cooled. Others replenished magazines and checked their weapons. No reminders were needed when it came to flak jackets and steel pots. Conversation—what little there was—was limited mainly to taking down the dirty little brown men. For the most part, everyone kept to themselves. This was not a day that would be looked back on in a positive way, no matter how it turned out. I was pretty sure about that.

When the time came, Dickson gave the forward-ho signal and John cranked up the now-baptized ROTTIN "8" NO. III. He aimed it at the treeline and rolled. As we closed on the wall of green, I could feel the anger rising up once again. Maybe it was just a way of masking the fear. It didn't matter. What mattered was that I was consumed with the need to smack them down. If they wanted to take us on again, that would be just dandy. I no longer cared that our tracks had no business there to start with, and I no longer cared that no amount of cached goods or dead bodies could compensate for our losses. I only cared about pulverizing their asses and then stomping on their corpses.

By now, the trail was well blazed, and our progress was quicker, even without elbow room. There were no immediate signs of bomb craters, but the jungle simmered with puffs of smoke and crackling fires, telling me the aerial assault must have had some effect, even if it couldn't be trusted. We came to the bend and stopped long enough to drop the troops.

The ruins of 1-3 welcomed us back to the mouth of the dragon. I kept a hard grip on the .50's handles with thumbs planted firmly on the surface of the butterfly. I had the barrel pointed up-trail and slowly swiveled it back and forth, hoping to cut reaction time. I was steeled and pissed off and lusting to blow bodies open with red-hot machine-gun rounds. My unblinking eyes were locked on the underbrush, desperately searching for the slightest hint of movement. Any excuse to light them up would do.

John eased the track to a stop. 1-3 sat fifty feet to our front. 1-2 and 1-1 tracks inched in behind us. The rest were out of sight to the rear. So far no attack. I expected Littlefield to order a mad minute then and there, if not as a way to get in the first lick then at least as a safeguard. Instead we were told to proceed. John swiveled slightly left and crunched through the brush to squeeze around the husk of 1-3. Still no attack, but I wasn't fooled. I silently dared the bastards to blink. If one of them even picked his nose and I sensed it, that would be the last act of his sorry life.

We came alongside the charred metal box that used to be 3rd Squad's track. Most of the top deck and part of the front had disintegrated. The blackened barrel of Dave's .50 maintained its lopsided upward angle, as if trying to position itself as a grave marker. Smoke drifted in wisps from the seared steel. Whether the RPG had detonated against the turret or impacted him directly, it was likely that Dave never knew what hit him. At some point his mangled body had slipped limply through the gunner's hatch into the fiery steel hold that would become his coffin. Ammo within continued to cook off like lingering kernels of un-popped corn.

The sight of it fed the hate rolling around my insides like a deadly undertow. I wanted to kill something, in spite of the underlying fear. If the NVA wanted to try their luck again, allowing us to get in deeper was the best way. They could isolate 1-4 by cutting loose once we put the destroyed track between us and the rest of the platoon. I didn't give a shit. Let 'em do whatever their rice-sucking bony asses wanted. Because when they did I would administer hellfire upon them until my gun melted in my hands or they were all wasted, whichever came first. I wasn't rational enough to consider that no amount of payback was worth my life.

John remained steady and workman-like, a required trait for drivers. He angled 1-4 back onto the pathway. Still no ambush. Nothing. The other tracks fell in behind. I waited for it, wanting it. The trail widened up and the pace got quicker. The jungle thinned some. Still nothing. No resistance. 1-1 moved alongside and soon other tracks joined the column. I finally had to accept the fact that neither side would get another chance, at least not here.

Gradually, the internal seething slackened, but we were well along before I was able to ease my grip on the gun. When I finally did, that simple act caused the tension to fall away like a dropped rucksack after an all-day hump. There was no relaxing, but the imminent threat had clearly passed. I should have felt relief. Instead I remained obsessed with hunting them down. Once again they had proven that mechanized infantry was always good for a sucker punch when shackled by terrain. We had foolishly allowed them to dictate the terms of engagement. It was as if we had brought a gun to a knife fight and still lost. Even though they had likely sustained greater losses, the psychological edge was theirs.

The jungle continued to thin, and we soon rolled into a shaded clearing concealed on all sides and above by lofty trees. A scattering of structures came into view, and without fanfare we entered the now-vacated base camp and pulled to a halt. It was immediately apparent that there were no dead bodies, no surrendering NVA with their hands in the air, and no imposing stacks of weapons or munitions. The place was deserted. There wasn't a bomb crater to be found. There had been no second line of defense, no last stand, no do-or-die. The compound had warehoused nothing that couldn't be carried off or left without consequence. Their forward guard had held us off long enough for the rest of them to collect their wares and move on, leaving little more than bums would in a hobo camp. A few of the cook fires were still hot with ash-laden coals.

A hasty perimeter was formed while the dismounts ransacked the place for anything worthwhile. Other than scattered trash and other prized bounty such as eating utensils, spilled rice, and a handful loose rifle rounds, the place was bare. It was a sad conclusion to the events of the last four hours. John and I sat atop 1-4 and watched, mostly without conversation. There just wasn't much to talk about.

"We should have given chase," I finally said. John arched his brows but said nothing. I wasn't sure if he disagreed or just considered it wishful thinking. "I mean, we've got mobility now and there's nothing here anyway. We're letting the fuckers get away clean."

"Littlefield's either not interested or he's under orders," John said. He didn't expand on it.

I thought that over for a second. "Either way, it's wrong," I said.

John lifted his heavy glasses and rubbed his eyes, rotating the heels of his palms slowly. Being a practical thinker, he knew what I knew: that higher-up now considered the mission complete and no amount of second-guessing would change that fact. He just let my words hang, probably hoping I would shut up.

So I shut up, lit a cigarette, and leaned back in the turret. I kept an eye on the woodline, even though I knew as sure as I knew my name that there would be no counterattack. The fatigue I'd kept in check moved in to fill the void, and I had to struggle against it. There would be no real rest for hours yet to come. I shifted in the seat and reached for a canteen, needled by the notion that just because we had reached our objective the mission was over. In a war where success was measured in bodies, I had lately learned another aspect of nefarious scorekeeping—that the end was less important than the means. With exit strategies in the forefront, expectations had been lowered to the appearance of making progress through "Vietnamization." Attrition in enemy ranks was relied upon to help move it along. Meanwhile, an imperative for career officers was to get their combat tickets punched while there was still a war available. I resented that the top brass was satisfied with treading water instead of winning. Even the officers who wanted to make a difference weren't given enough field time to do so, and they weren't required to accomplish much. They just had to reach objectives and not fuck up. Colonel Stiles was no doubt hovering in a chopper somewhere, feeling pigeon-chested over conquering this base camp. Not his fault the cowardly enemy had run off. He would report whatever body count Littlefield and Bravo's CO came up with and then figure on adding another ribbon to his collection. Even if we out-killed them ten to one, so what? That wouldn't rock the table at the peace talks and it wouldn't bring Dave or anybody else back.

"Didn't find jack shit," Bucky said as he and Snake climbed topside. "This whole thing's been a big fuckin' waste."

"Roger that," Snake said. "Can I have one of your Kools?"

Bucky reached for his smokes and they both lit up. I said something about reconning for bodies back down trail and that the day was getting on. Bucky agreed and left to go see what he could find out. A few minutes later, he was back.

"Dickson says there won't be a recon for bodies. We're heading back to the laager site and set up for the night."

"Since when they don't care about body count?" I asked.

"Can't say, my man. Maybe tomorrow."

The decision-making all day had been idiotic, but I couldn't see the use in pressing the point. Spencer and the others climbed aboard and we worked our way out of the jungle for the third time. Once we were positioned for the night, I busied myself with the usual chores of wiping down the .50, dusting the top deck of the track, and setting up the RPG screen. I thought I could eat, but the food had no taste and I gave it up. Instead I nursed a canteen of warm water and smoked cigarettes as the sun dipped below the distant treeline.

The despair inside continued to swell, and at dark, when I realized I could no longer share watch with Dave, or anything else, ever again, it bore down. Everything we had ever shared was buried with him in the bottom of 1-3. His death was going to take some serious adjustments, and at the moment I wasn't up to making any.

There was little chat as the night deepened, which was best, given my mood. I smoked and stared at the sky, wrestling to comprehend it all. I stood my watch, then tried to sleep, but I kept waking up to the faint sounds of 1-3's ammo still occasionally popping off, like stubborn embers in a dying fire. Sometime in the wee hours, a heavy rain fell, and it stopped.

Sunrise brought Colonel Stiles, who landed dead center of our perimeter in a Loach and straightaway informed Littlefield that he wanted 1-3 recovered. It was welcome news. What was less welcome was the news that only 1st Platoon tracks would be dispatched to bring it out.

When Sergeant Dickson gave us the word, the reaction was predictable. "What the hell," Ned said. "The place is crawling with NVA."

"The place *was* crawling with NVA," Dickson replied. "The base camp was empty, remember? They've cut out. Gone di-di."

"And that's guaranteed, right?" Ridgeway said it almost absently while rummaging around a carton of C-rations, not expecting an answer.

"Come on, guys. You know I have no leverage as acting lieutenant. For that matter, if Stiles is calling the shots, Littlefield doesn't have any leverage either."

"So three tracks go in," I said, "and if the dinks have figured on just such a stupid move, maybe none of us come out. We can start an APC salvage yard right here."

"Look—"

I raised my hands in surrender, unable to muster real resistance. "Hey, I'm not arguing, I'm just throwing that out to chew on."

"They could send dismounts from the other platoons along for security," Bucky said. "It's not as if they've got someplace to go in the meantime."

"Well, that's the other thing. Not everybody goes. Drivers, gunners, and a few extra hands to help with the hookup."

Bucky's eyes narrowed.

"Check that. I'll be going, too," Dickson said.

We just stared at him. Dickson knew what we were thinking, but since he was in the same kettle there was nothing to be gained with more objections.

"Like I said, guys, it's not my decision. Just be ready to move at 0900."

All this time, Spencer stood idly by, examining his dirty fingernails, apparently without opinion, at least one he cared to share. He had evidently gotten accustomed to Bucky doing the talking. The rest of us went about the business of mounting up. John, who had simply uttered the word *fuck* when the details were laid out, had nothing further to say.

Dickson joined the crew on 1-2. Our group included Gibbs and the newbie Longacre. 1-1 also carried four troops, making the total an even dozen.

Yesterday's fear breezed in strong as the emerald wall of jungle closed in to consume our tracks. While it had been an illusion to think we had safety in numbers yesterday, knowing we had none today made it seem as if a heavy door had shut behind us. Three tracks, lightly manned, would be easy pickings if the NVA had come back to rake the cinders or to maybe catch us doing the same. A couple of Claymores and a few RPGs could cripple us for the kill. There had been plenty of time to mine the trail or even boobytrap the wreckage. We also had to watch our rear as well as our front and flanks, unlike before.

Once again, 1-4 was point, followed by 1-2 and then 1-1. John took it slow, but I couldn't see that it made any difference. We might as well have been convicts lugging balls and chains over the fence in view of the guard towers. Sizing us up was a simple matter, and there were only two logical outcomes: either we completed the mission without incident or a lot of us died, right here, today. We would leave this jungle as duty-bound soldiers following orders, as victors of a slugfest, or in rubber bags. I could envision no alternatives. With that settled, I slowly swung the gun's barrel back and forth, my eyes locked on the now-familiar tangle of greenery as we inched along, accompanied by the churn of the treads.

John negotiated the bend in the trail and gassed it just a bit, causing the track to lurch. It was an effort to throw off the accuracy of any aimed RPGs. Knowing he still had a card or two left to play was no surprise, and it gave my confidence a lift. It rose even more when we pulled up behind 1-3 without being hit.

The other tracks pulled in behind and we waited, fingers on triggers. When this failed to launch an ambush, Dickson decided it was safe for the labor contingent to dismount and get busy hooking up. It seemed unlikely at this point that the NVA were holding back. They could have had us six ways from Sunday by now if they wanted. Even so, I kept my eyes glued to the forest.

1-3 was stone cold. It sat like a used appliance illegally dumped on the roadside. Those on the ground determined that it might still roll, in spite of the heat generated by the fire. This would lower the difficulty factor considerably, and that meant getting out quicker.

I stared at the blackened hulk and thought about Dave's remains, entombed there, melded with ammo boxes, engine parts, and incinerated gear. It was degrading that his final resting place was to be in a military scrap heap in a country as vulgar as Vietnam. The odds of recovering enough for a funeral had to be nil. In a way I thought it would be more dignified to just leave him here, on the battlefield where he died. But Stiles wanted to see the results of his handiwork, and our job to deliver unto him. From where he stood, it didn't run any deeper than that.

With some effort John crushed enough brush to turn the track around, and cables were attached from its back to the front of 1-3, which was then dragged around in the exit direction and pulled far enough forward to maneuver 1-2 behind it. A V-shaped tow bar was then connected between the front of 1-2 and the rear of 1-3 so it could be pushed while we pulled. 1-1 would take point.

Progress proved to be excruciatingly slow. All of 1-3's lubricants had burned away, causing the roadwheels to grind and scrape and turn only grudgingly. Tethered together, we snailed our way toward daylight foot by foot, more vulnerable than ever. I wanted to believe we would get away clean, but held it in check. Until we broke free into the sunshine I had to assume the worst could still happen.

It took half an hour to make the journey. Once afield, something compelled me to twist around and take a lingering look at the curtain of green as it seemed to close with finality behind us. My eyes then shifted to the wreckage we towed, knowing what was sealed within. Tomorrow a Sky Crane would come from Vietnam and unceremoniously deliver it to the garbage pile.

We unhooked inside the perimeter next to the CP. The job was done. The colonel's retrievers had obediently fetched for him, and finally we could breathe again. I took a seat on the ground at the rear of 1-4 and leaned back, trying to keep all that had happened in the last two days from taking over. Sadness and fatigue were prominent players, but an unnamed anger burning like a slow fuse somewhere inside my head got top billing. As the afternoon wore on, I became agitated to the point I felt like a ticking bomb. I managed to respond to idle chit-chat, but couldn't carry a real conversation. I just wanted to isolate myself somewhere and try to ride it out, or better yet destroy something.

By sunset, the muggy air was infested with mosquitoes, further aggravating my state of mind. A Chinook thumped in to drop off supplies and kicked up a good wind, but it gave me no relief. I watched as C-ration boxes, assorted clothes, and a water blivet were off-loaded. Following this, out strolled some rear echelon dude in clean fatigues who was quickly identified as a dispatch from Graves Registration. It should have been no surprise, but it immediately struck me as an affront. What was the point? There was nothing to recover. If they wanted to confirm Dave's death, all they had to do was ask. I watched as he chatted with Littlefield, resentment flaring like a struck match. Two words flashed through my mind: Grave Robber!

He was a mousy-looking fucker with curly black hair and over-size army-issue glasses. I tracked the intruder as he headed for 1-3, where he nonchalantly hoisted his uninvited ass topside, armed with a flashlight and a small bag of some kind. I had to force myself to stay put. The impulse was to throw this stranger back on that chopper after a good ass-kicking. The arrogant bastard apparently thought he could just waltz in here and rummage around elbow-deep in the ashes of someone whose boots he wasn't fit to polish.

Right or wrong, rational or not, I had granted myself spiritual proprietorship over Dave's remains, and when the Graves ghoul violated that sanctity, it triggered an adrenaline flow that pulsed in my temples like sharp needles. I watched him with feral eyes, fighting urges to move on him. I was vaguely aware of someone's voice saying my name, but I tuned them out and they went away. I had to stay focused so that any false moves by Mr. Glasses would not go undetected.

I didn't know how long I could keep the coiled spring inside compressed. It would only take the right trigger. I had no clue what that might be and didn't care. I just knew that if the wire was tripped that something bad would happen. If he hadn't come here, I wouldn't be forced to stand up for what was right. It was entirely his doing and I hated him for that, too.

A quick glance around revealed that others were not alarmed. I couldn't understand it, even though I expected as much. Someone had to be the advocate, and there could be no stronger one than me. It was as if they knew the store was being minded. In reality they were just going about their business, but it seemed to me they were waiting to see what *I* was going to do about it. So be it. It was a situation I was powerless to change.

For some reason, it was important that I not get up. If I did, I believed the world around me might blow. The remaining threads of self-control I still had struggled to hold that threshold. I couldn't tell what Mr. Glasses was actually up to, but with the sky turning slate I could see the beam of his light moving about from time to time as he rooted around. *Mind your Ps and Qs, pal,* I silently warned. *Just mind your fucking Ps and Qs. If you don't, I won't be able to help myself.* I grabbed a rubber canteen and swigged water, never taking my eyes off 1-3. My M16 was cradled in my lap. For the first time, I noticed there was a body bag draped over the rear of the track. *You won't find enough to fill a pocket, dickhead,* I thought, *much less that fucking plastic bag.*

Then I noticed something else. Curiosity seekers from Littlefield's command post had slowly migrated toward 1-3. For a second I couldn't believe it, but there it was. These non-line troop rubber-neckers had decided to pass the evening by moseying over for look-see at the wreckage, maybe even glimpse some body parts. Maybe even climb up for ringside seats to see what Mr. Glasses pulls from the depths. I watched in disbelief as the congregation grew. Those in front kept edging closer, until a ring formed halfway around the track. My stare became a glare aimed at this new, bigger threat. The man inside the track was temporarily forgotten. My eyes stabbed at the gathering, determined to will them back into the shadows from which they had lurked.

One of them chuckled at something another said. I interpreted it to be directed at me personally. They might as well have been pissing on the track. My insides knotted up. Another whispered remark, another chuckle. This time there was no deliberation, no effort to hold back, no thought process whatever. The over-torqued guy-wires holding me down broke with a sharp snap, causing a complete mental disconnect. I sprang to my feet, rifle in hand.

"Motherfuckers!" I screamed.

John was standing nearby and I heard him say, "Oh shit," but he made no move to stop me, nor did anyone else. I took long stiff strides toward the scene of the desecration. All eyes turned my way. A few immediately realized they had crossed somebody's line by sniffing around and quickly moved off. The rest stood their ground.

"You fucking bastards!" I yelled again. "Get the hell away from there! Get out!"

The remaining violators looked at me with puzzled expressions, as if they couldn't imagine what I might be uptight about. Some looked as if they were afraid to move. A couple of them seemed unaffected, figuring they were under no obligation to take orders from a lunatic. Mr. Glasses popped his head out of the track and surveyed the landscape like a groundhog might do, then looked at me questioningly, wondering if he was included in the directive. Otherwise, facing a disturbed person with a gun didn't seem out of the ordinary for him.

My weapon was at waist level, pointed in their direction, safety off. I stopped at about twenty paces to keep them all in my field of fire. "Move it, goddamn you!" I hollered. A few more backed off. "You think this is some kind of freak show? Some kind of fucking circus act?" I could almost see the venom projecting from my eyes like gusts of hot air. They would by God get the message, one way or another. A couple more eased back into the shadows, but the commotion had drawn the attention of half the company, bringing even more onlookers. For the most part, the new bunch had sense enough to keep a distance and not be mistaken for perpetrators.

"Fucking leeches. Get away. Move!"

"What about me?" Mr. Glasses called out. "The light's almost gone and I'd really like to finish this up." He said it in a way that sounded reasonable, and it caught me off guard.

"I don't like you!" I yelled.

He just stood there with an exasperated expression.

"Nobody asked you to come here, goddamnit!"

"Look, he said calmly. "Just let me finish up, okay? Then everybody can go about their business."

Before I could tell him to hurry the fuck up and do it, I saw Littlefield from the corner of my eye. He had eased up on my left flank.

Just try to grab me, fucker, I thought.

I tersely informed Mr. Glasses that he couldn't go back to work until everybody else cleared out. "Did you get that?" I hollered at the on-lookers. By now all but three had left. The die-hards had apparently decided I was bluffing and figured on facing me down.

The next voice I heard was Littlefield's. "Put the weapon down, Ross," he said. His voice was low but firm.

"Not until these cocksuckers move out," I said, my eyes still locked on the rubber-neckers.

"They're afraid you're gonna waste 'em. If you'll just put the weapon down I'm sure they'll comply."

His voice was smooth, sincere. But I wasn't about to be snookered.

"Not until they're gone . . . sir."

Dickson had moved up next to Littlefield. There was a whispered exchange. I sensed trickery and shifted my position slightly to keep both sets of adversaries in my field of vision. The lackey from Graves had disappeared back inside the track, evidently deciding that the drama had reached its climax. I started to call him out, only to realize there was nothing to be gained by pushing it. My demands had been mostly met, leaving me with little left to confront. My grand stand was about to unravel. In the space of a minute, the fire inside had died, giving birth to shame and remorse.

"How about if I order them back to their tracks?" Littlefield finally said. "Will you let them go?"

He was giving me an out. I hesitated long enough to make him think I was deliberating, as if I still had leverage. Then, with as much conviction as I could dredge up I said, "Okay. Tell 'em."

He looked at me, waiting. I slowly lowered my rifle. He turned his attention to the three holdouts. "You men over there move out. Go on back to your tracks."

They looked at the captain, then at me, and slowly started backing away. "Go on, damn you," I said weakly, and turned away. I walked over to face my superiors.

"Now what?" I looked directly at Littlefield. I had no idea what the consequences might be. I supposed he could have me busted or thrown in Long Binh Jail. Looking past them, I could see most of the platoon watching.

Littlefield said calmly, "Now you return to your squad."

I just stared at him, completely deflated. Dickson's face showed surprise, but he said nothing. He looked relieved.

"What about later?" I asked.

"There is no later. This incident is history."

Dickson turned to leave. I just stood there, mystified.

"Get going," he said.

And with that I shuffled back to the track, not understanding why he had let it ride. I realized later that despite his shortcomings, Littlefield was adept at sizing people up and he knew when not to push or overreact. He had shown more confidence in me redeeming myself than I would have.

Shortly thereafter, Mr. Glasses emerged from 1-3, his work now done. He had recovered a few bone fragments, a couple of teeth, and a ring, nothing more. I stood watching with Bucky at the back of 1-4. I felt like a fool for the spectacle I'd made, yet I knew that if the clock were rewound I'd do it all again. Bucky explained to me over a pair of Kools that without getting some positive ID on Dave's remains he would have been listed MIA. "Best to make it official than to leave his family wondering," he said.

This hadn't occurred to me. "Thanks," I said. I stood there with my head hung in shame. I felt completely worthless.

"You cracked, but you didn't break," he said. "That's the important thing." He patted my shoulder and moved on, leaving me with my own thoughts.

I chain-smoked in silence through the first watch, then crashed out and slept like a drunk. At sunrise a Huey came to pick up Mr. Glasses, followed by a Sky Crane that hoisted 1-3 into the air and disappeared. The incident was now a bygone topic, at least on the surface. For that, I was grateful. I now understood that I had undergone a hard-learned lesson, one precipitated by a shaky mental state that could have ended tragically. I was sorry for it and embarrassed by it, but I couldn't un-do it and there was no practical way to atone for it. One thing I was certain of was that regardless of what the future brought I would never cross that line again.

The company broke camp and reconned clearings and hedgerows for the rest of the day. More than once, I caught myself looking where 1-3 should have been, each time reminding myself that I had to somehow push the whole business out of the way and concentrate on the present. Unmet dangers awaited, and I would be no good to myself or anyone else wallowing in a mire of self-pity.

20

The Importance of Fruit Salad

The number of medals on an officer's breast varies in inverse proportion to the square of the distance of his duties from the front line.

—CHARLES EDWARD MONTAGUE

Early June 1970. 25th Infantry Division. The Cambodian jungle in NVA Base Area 707.

Once again, Colonel Stiles choppered in and took command, directing the company into the canopy about an hour before sunset. Somewhere inside the thickness, the tracks were used to crush down enough saplings to expand a small clearing and we set up in a tight perimeter with slim space between us and the undergrowth. The reason for this was known only to Stiles.

Except for emotional numbness, I was back on track. I silently mourned the loss of my friend, but couldn't let myself be consumed by it. The business at hand left no room at the table for things beyond my control, no matter how strong the pull. I had to suck it up and keep doing the best job I could, and that meant staying alert and focused. Failure to do so would come with a price.

After trip flares and Claymores were set, I hunkered down with John and some of the others to scrounge for Cs and bitch about what a dumb fuck Stiles was.

"Can't use Starlight Scopes or the M79s," John lamented.

"There it is," Vernon said. "Kinda like bein' shoved up against a wall. Probably smell their breath before we know they're there."

"You guys complain too much," Bucky said. "At least here they can't mortar us."

"Don't need to," John said. "From this close they can just sling satchel charges."

"Does anybody even know what we're doing here?" Jeff asked. Being a rookie he wisely kept his questions short and simple.

"Negative," Bucky said. "The colonel, me thinks, is looking for trouble, and he's willing to stick our chins out as far as it takes to find it."

"It's bullshit," Ned said.

"The dude needs an attitude check," Snake said. He worked a P-38 around a can of peaches. "He's seen too many war movies. This is stupid."

That seemed to cover it, and the business of eating took over.

Spencer finally spoke up. "Let's get a watch list set. It's almost dark."

When it was done conversation fizzled. The consensus was that Stiles was playing loose with our lives once again. We would just have to deal with it the best we could.

I was on watch around midnight, snugged in behind the .50, concentrating on sounds. It was impossible to see anything. If they managed to get by the trip flares, our only chance would be to hear them before they were on top of us. I flinched when squelch broke unexpectedly on the radio. I picked up the handset and pressed it to my ear. A voice from the CP, presumably the colonel's, quietly announced that in exactly one minute from when he signed off we were to blow our Claymores and then commence a mad minute.

Blow the Claymores? Was he serious? He wanted us to destroy our first line of defense on the off chance somebody was nosing around? Mad minutes were done with fire directed beyond the Claymores and trip flares. This was completely nuts. I made a spot decision not to comply and had to believe that others would do the same. When the firing commenced I jumped in with a blaze of .50-caliber slugs. From what I could tell, none of the Claymores went off, leaving the security of the perimeter uncompromised.

I fully expected a company-wide ass-chewing to commence as soon as the guns fell silent, but it didn't happen. Either the colonel didn't know the difference or he had realized the stupidity of the order and wanted it quickly forgotten. Either way, I was already fed up with Stiles and his ignorance. In the morning Ridgeway was the first to bring it up.

"What the fuck is wrong with that dude, man?" He didn't expect an answer. He just wanted to get it out there.

"Cambodia's bad enough," John said. "Now we got this guy driving the bus." I was seated inside the track with John, Ridgeway, Vernon and Jeff. Somehow I managed to capture cans of both peaches and pound cake, and the prospect of having a cake-with-fruit breakfast gave me a lift. I was too hungry to get involved in the conversation, and anything I added would be redundant anyway. The others batted it around. I munched while they bitched. It was generally agreed that Stiles was a menace, and that some of his stunts were crazy even by Littlefield's standards. The captain, it was noted, had been conspicuously quiet, suggesting he'd been muzzled by the colonel. Lucky for us, Stiles skied up after the company returned to the wide open spaces, allowing nerves to settle and the risk meter to dip below redline, at least for now.

With no explanation why we had spent the night in the hangman's noose, we resumed normal operations. Another two days of patrolling brought rain, bug madness, and bad dispositions, but no action beyond blasting treelines here and there to see what they might hide and a few instances of sniper fire.

We had set up in an open area outside the jungle not far from the site of the Memorial Day brawl. It was hot and the ground was wet from an afternoon downpour. Grimy fatigues had started to smell like mildew. With the bugs added in, the evening bull session suffered a shortage of energy. It finally got going with a story that Stiles had pulled another boner while imposing his version of mechanized warfare on Bravo Company.

"Dude orders out an AP at dusk," Bucky reported. "Not good."

"Sounds familiar," I said.

"This can't have a good ending," Gibbs said. He sat on his steel pot, scraping his dirt-caked nails with the tip of his bayonet.

"Six guys. First he sends them a half-klick across the open, then puts 'em on a trail into the jungle for a couple hundred more yards. By now it's dark."

"On a trail, no less," Mike said.

"Shoulda told him to fuck off," Ned said. There was no anger in his voice. It was just a flat statement. I noticed he was sweating a lot. He looked pale.

"Next thing you know a dozen NVA squatting around a pot of rice hears them coming and commences to light 'em up with AKs and grenades. The whole thing lasts less than a minute. The story goes that they never got off a shot."

At this point he had our full attention.

"The CP couldn't raise anybody on the radio, but Stiles wouldn't let the captain order out a reactionary force. His reckoning was that they either got their radio shot up or that it was a trap of some kind."

John shook his head. "Jesus, Joseph, and Mary," he said.

At this point, Ned got up and left. I couldn't tell if he was more feverish or just more disgusted.

"The colonel was of the opinion that the patrol had retreated to a defensive position and would either return intact or send a runner at first light. In the meantime, the two survivors—count 'em, two—were slowly bleeding to death. One of them, who was shot through the neck, managed to drag his gut-shot buddy into the brush and hide while waiting for help to arrive."

"The help that never came," I said.

"Ten-four. He was still waiting at sunrise, barely alive, propped up against the body of his now-dead buddy."

A sense of gloom hung in the air like sour mist, making me wonder how things had turned so depressing so fast. I knew that such stories were often exaggerated or even completely made up, but with this battalion commander, anything seemed possible. I could only imagine what his next trick might be. The combined antics of Stiles and Littlefield had placed an extra burden on our ability to stay healthy. Like most career officers, the hunt for fruit salad was always on, though in the case of Littlefield, time had gotten short. Word had recently circulated that he was due to rotate out in a matter of days. As we were about to bear witness, the downside to this happy news would be suffering through his severe affliction of short-timers syndrome.

It was no secret that the decorations on Littlefield's dress greens already scratched at his jaw, so he could afford to lay low. The colonel, on the other hand, had just come on board and needed beaucoup combat actions in order to get the awards necessary to assure future promotions. The best we could hope for was that he would hang out anywhere but here, or better yet haul it back to Cu Chi to poke pins in maps and do his communicating long distance.

I noticed Dickson walking toward the CP with Doc Johnson and wondered what was up. A few minutes later, Doc came back and pulled a litter out of his track. Then Bucky informed us that a medevac was on the way. "Ned's sick as a dog," he said. "Doc thinks he has malaria."

This raised some brows. The only way to get malaria was by not taking your malaria pills. Everybody forgot occasionally, but few actually stopped taking them. Those who did saw it as a clever way to terminate their combat duties. I wanted to give Ned the benefit of the doubt, but suspected that he may have found his way out. It was no skin off my nose. I was just glad it wasn't me.

"We'll need to revise the watch list," Bucky said. And with that Ned Shelton became a memory.

———·———

The company gradually worked its way back to the vicinity of Krek. The rains became more frequent, bringing momentary cool-downs but elevating the bug population. At least there was less dust to swallow. There had been no sightings of Stiles since Bravo's ambush patrol got wasted, meaning there was a good chance he had returned to his air-conditioned office.

"Makes sense," Dewayne said. "The man's got a career to think about. He's gotta make sure the reports have the story straight."

"Not to mention the awards clerk will need help with the citations," Vernon said. "Gotta make sure the action is described just right, you know."

"Don't get your hopes up," John said. "He could show up in the next five minutes and drag us back into the jungle."

"There it is," Mike added. "Littlefield would freak out."

The captain's behavior had gotten more precautionary almost by the hour. We had set up early on a bald knoll within spitting distance of the paved road. A small rubber plantation faced us on the other side of the blacktop. Otherwise the countryside was a patchwork of cultivated paddies tended to by ordinary farmers. It was as peaceful a setting as I'd seen since crossing the Rach Cai Bach River so many days before.

1-4 track was positioned at about two o'clock in relationship to the blacktop. The small plantation fronted the highway directly across the road, its right edge ending at about one o'clock in relation to the track, where it gave way to the rice fields. I spent my watch slapping mosquitoes and eyeballing the patch of rubber trees, the only possible point of attack. It should have had me chewing my nails, but I couldn't get wired over it. The vibes here were good. I slept well.

The sun had barely bobbed to the surface when I crawled from my nest inside the track to take a leak. Men were milling about the perimeter, sipping coffee and shooting the breeze. Invisible Willie climbed down from the last watch and I prepared to assume the position while I had a bit of breakfast. There was a light breeze and the air temperature was tolerable. There had been no orders to mount up and rush off somewhere, so I lingered for a moment, surveying the misty fields while cranking open a can of fruit cocktail. There were no scooters or foot traffic on the road, but it was early.

With Littlefield now essentially in hiding, I began to think we might have an easy go of it until the change of command. Hopefully, the new CO would be a respectable improvement. He could always be worse, but I was willing to take my chances. I finished off a smoke and drug a spoonful of the chunky fruit from the can, wishing I had some pound cake to go with it when the first mortar whammed into the earth like a massive bolt of lightning, shaking the tracks and stinging eardrums. My canned breakfast went flying and screams of "INCOMING!" went up. Surprised men hit the ground under tossed canteen cups and C-rat cans, followed by a mad scramble for fighting positions. I jumped inside the track, head spinning but fully aware of what had just happened. Dirt and debris billowed up near the edge of the road, about fifty yards from 1-4.

I vaulted into the .50 turret and cut loose on the rubber trees, knowing only that it had been either a mortar, rocket, or recoilless rifle round. It didn't much matter. I just knew that it had to be stopped. I got off about thirty rounds when another one slammed the ground, this time a few yards closer in. I winced but didn't let up. There were only about five tracks in a decent position to engage in counter-fire, but 1-2, to my left at about one o'clock, and 1-4 had the best angle on what seemed to be the most likely avenue of attack. The company's mortar track got busy lobbing rounds into the plantation, but had no fix on the enemy and the effort was haphazard. There was no other incoming. It was straight-out bombardment, apparently from a single tube.

I pumped a line of crimson tracers into the rows of heavily leafed trees, slowly swinging back and forth, moving from just left of the plantation's corner to about halfway down the right side, which extended away from the road a couple hundred yards before disappearing over a rise. Hopefully, their aim was pure guesswork, but if they had actual line of sight, it would be easy enough to adjust for accuracy and cause real havoc if we didn't move.

Round three smashed the ground twenty-five yards out, jabbing my ears painfully and spraying dirt fragments across the track's deck like slung marbles. It should have caused me to flee. Instead it made me mad. "Fuck you!" I yelled through the noise. "Fuck you!"

The rubber trees gave up no muzzle flashes, making me think they had a forward observer relaying adjustments to the hidden gun position. How any forward element could survive the machine gun fire raking the plantation I had no idea. If nothing else, it should have kept their heads down.

The next shell was a step closer, and the pain in my ears was so sharp it felt like they had been hit with shavings of seared steel. I knew then that it was bigger than a mortar, whatever it was. The shower of debris momentarily blocked my view, but I didn't let up. When the smoke cleared I discovered that I was the only machine gun still firing. The others had jumped ship. A direct hit was a real possibility, but I wasn't quitting. For no logical reason I believed that I could silence them.

I heard a voice yelling for me to get down. Except for our own mortar-men, it was just me. In my thinking, dueling mortars wasn't going to cut it, but as crazy as it seemed, Littlefield apparently had no intention of sending a contingent of tracks across the road to put them out of business.

I started running low on rounds but there was no time to get more. I heard more yelling. It was Bucky's voice, hollering for me to get off the track. "They're walkin' 'em in," he yelled. "Get off there, Ross!"

I pretended not to hear. Yep, they were walking them in and I still had no clue where they were, but I couldn't have been pried out with a crowbar. It was as if I had grabbed a live wire and couldn't let go. I believed that if I just stuck with it a little longer I would have them. I had bailed before, on Highway 1, but not this time. Fuck them.

"Get down from there!"

It sounded like Spencer, not that it mattered. I kept my grip on the .50, slowly working my way down the outside edge of the plantation. Round five, in perfect alignment with number four but a few steps closer, rocked the track. The deafening crack drove ice picks through my tender eardrums and I recoiled from the pain. More dirt showered over me, and I struggled to keep my senses. The next round could take me out, even if it wasn't a direct hit. What intellect I still had told me to get out of the way, that it was idiotic to give up my life over a one-sided game of chicken. Everyone else understood this, yet I remained locked in place by some instinct telling me I would prevail. I was cuffed to the .50. I could not wrench my hands from the gun's grip.

There was nothing left to shoot at except for the point where the plantation disappeared over the distant rise, a good three hundred meters away. I directed a heavy stream of burning lead into that faraway patch of trees without moving the barrel so much as an inch. It was my final chance. The last of my ammo was about to hop out of the can and twitch its way through the gun. The hunting trip was over. Fifteen seconds later the last slug spun from the gun and it fell silent. There was no time to reload. I had to get off the track, like it or not. I grabbed my M16 and dropped through the turret hatch to exit via the lowered rear ramp. As I ran toward the inner perimeter, I noticed that the next incoming round hadn't made the trip. By the time I joined the others, it was apparent that there would not be another one. It was over.

Maybe, like me, they had run out of rounds. Maybe I had finally taken them down. It didn't matter. I had stood my ground, no matter how stupid it was. Everybody was staring at me.

The truth would never be known, because Littlefield ordered no recon. We had suffered no casualties or damages, so no harm done, at least in his mind. My ears were now ringing twice as loud as before, but it was my own doing. No Purple Heart there. Bucky approached and for a few seconds just stood there, looking at me like I was an escapee from the madhouse. Then he grinned and offered me a Kool. "Crazy bastard," he said. Once again, I had made a spectacle of myself, but at least my actions had been directed at the real enemy this time.

It was possible I had saved a track, but that was about it. Bucky insisted I had acted above and beyond, so I allowed him to think that. It felt good to be noticed in a positive way, even for dumb behavior. It was possible I had taken a small, if awkward, step toward redemption. More than anything I wished I had that can of fruit cocktail back.

No rounds had found their way inside the perimeter, but the incident sent Littlefield's growing sense of paranoia into outer space. He was on deck for his last night in the field, and his sanity had taken the early bus to the rear. All day we roamed essentially tame terrain, stopping to unload on every hedgerow we came across, no matter how thin. It was an expensive day for the taxpayers. Mikey, who was down to around thirty days, thought it was right on.

"We should do this every day, man!" he said. We had circled the wagons for a lunch break.

Ridgeway, near the same place on the calendar as Abbott, was in full agreement.

"There it is!" he said. "We're like a rolling firestorm, man. Nothin' survives this shit."

John was less than impressed. "We're lucky somebody hasn't been hit by a ricochet or shot themselves," he said.

"C'mon, old man, be happy," Mike said. "No way we'll get ambushed doin' this shit."

I could see John's eyes narrow behind his glasses and the cigarette perched in the corner of his mouth twitch. I fully expected him to lunge from his seat on the driver's hatch, but he relaxed instead.

"You're lucky I'm tired today, asswipe. Otherwise I'd make you pay."

Mike let it ride. He just held a big smile on his face and chewed his food. I busied myself oiling the .50 and hauling up more rounds, figuring the afternoon would bring more of the same. I could only hope there wasn't a stray farmer or two out there full of holes.

"What's the word on Littlefield's replacement?" Gibbs asked. "Anybody know?"

"Don't know shit, man," Ridgeway said. "It's kinda like Christmas. What's in the package might be something really cool, like a Panasonic reel-to-reel, or it could be a pair of Bermuda shorts."

"A GTO would be better," Vernon said.

Invisible Willie spoke up then. "Cars, man, that's where it's at," he said. "I'm savin' every dime, and figure I'll have just enough for a new rod when I get home. I'm thinkin' Four-Four-Two or Superbee."

"I'll have to get a job," Ridgeway said. "Most of my money's been spent on pussy, beer, and R& R."

Willie chuckled at this and shook his head.

"You're lucky you don't have the black syph," Mike said.

"I'm not stupid, Mikey. I don't screw Vietnamese whores. These were Thai chicks in Bangkok."

Gibbs laughed so hard at this he spit food all over his knees.

"What about that bitch McDonald snuck into LZ Devin that time?" Mike reminded him.

"Oh yeah, I forgot. Okay, one then. And if she had the black syph I'd know it by now. So would half the platoon."

The conversation ended with the order to mount up. Speculation about the new captain was forgotten. The company laagered for the night well before sunset in a clearing big enough to hold a pair of aircraft carriers. There was no jungle in sight, only weak stands of brush and trees in the distance. The afternoon had been a repeat of the morning. Our accomplishments included burning up thousands of rounds and starting a few brush fires.

The resupply chopper brought mail, sodas, and Ranger, who rejoined the squad. It was shaping up to be a night when the war got put on the back burner in favor of sipping sugary beverages and reading letters from home.

I filled Ranger in on current events, then we joined a platoon briefing, where Sergeant Dickson timidly broke the news.

"The CO's sending out six APs," he said. "He wants them positioned so we can have .50 cal mad minutes every two hours."

For long seconds not a word was said. I stood next to Ridgeway, who started grinding his teeth. Bucky was leaning against the track, arms folded, chewing hard on a piece of gum. It was Ranger, fresh from the Rear, who broke the silence.

"Has he lost his fucking mind?"

Dickson didn't immediately answer.

Gibbs took it from there. "What does he think, that we're gonna dig in, and then synchronize watches so we know when to duck?"

"Lemme get this straight," Mike said, his voice dead serious. "He wants to fill the spaces between the APs with machine gun fire? For real?"

"That's affirmative," Bill answered.

Bucky, clearly agitated, finally spoke up. "Best to go back and tell Littlefield he can have mad minutes or APs, but not both." He looked Dickson dead in the eyes when he said it.

Ridgeway followed up. "If that doesn't work, I'll tell him myself. I'm too short to give a shit."

"Take it easy," Dickson said.

"Nobody's blaming you," Mike said. "Why not check with the other platoon leaders and see what they say?"

"All right. Everybody stand by. I'll be back." With that he shuffled off.

Tomorrow couldn't come soon enough. Littlefield was pushing it, and the mood was getting hostile. My recent behavior had taught me to choose my battles, so I kept my mouth closed. Being a .50 gunner, I was not in the mix for APs anyway. I was expected to do my part during mad minutes if I happened to be on watch, but in this case I would simply not comply. I expected no one else would either. As crazy as it all sounded, I couldn't get out of joint over it. Littlefield was about to find out that he could no longer impose his will.

Feeling melancholy, I climbed topside of 1-4 and re-read a couple of letters while Dickson consulted with the junior officer corps. The tug of homesickness was always there, but spiked with each batch of new mail.

Even so, I was grateful that I had no wife or kids to worry over me or to think about. The married guys suffered longings I could only imagine. I had no idea how most of them ended up in Vietnam. Their lives had been jerked off track, mine had never gotten on track. Even now, I didn't know what I would do if I made it home. I supposed I would get a job that paid enough to buy a car and maybe use the GI Bill to finish school. I couldn't plan beyond that. None of it had any importance until I was on that freedom bird anyway.

I climbed down when Dickson reconvened the meeting. The sun had set, which meant this had to get settled quick. Evidently somebody had reeled Littlefield in from the stratosphere and he realized he was inviting mutiny with his insane orders. "Everything's copacetic," Bill said. "There won't be any APs, but the mad minutes are still a go."

"He actually backed down?" Ranger said. "I'd a bet he went batshit."

"There's still time," I said, not sure if I was joking or not.

"All right, guys," Bill said. "Hopefully there won't be any more meetings tonight." He then turned to leave.

"Hey, Bill," Bucky said. "You make a good LT. Thanks, brother."

Dickson responded with a sheepish smile and went on his way.

———

The new CO was Captain Jim Schroeder—barrel-chested, red hair in a short flattop, fair-skinned, and freckled. Rapport was instant. He introduced himself to every man in the company with a hearty handshake and a genuine smile, asking each of us where we were from and what our complaints were. He was a second tour officer and wanted it known that he was accessible to anybody at any time. We had hit the jackpot. Littlefield beat it out of there without so much as a goodbye, good luck, or eat shit.

Activity in our neck of the woods had slowed, though we did take custody of a surrendering NVA along an Ambush Alley tributary southwest of Krek and found a small arms and food cache several miles east of there on the same day. With little action, the company covered a lot of ground, and after several more days of ransacking the countryside without contact we were ordered back to Vietnam on June 15.

Alpha's tracks crossed the border amidst whoops and hollers and swirling colors from tossed smoke grenades. It was weird to think of returning to Vietnam as cause for celebration, but that's how it felt. After more than a month in Cambodia, getting back to a familiar area of operations better suited for mechanized infantry was welcome. Crossing the border brought a sense of relief and expectations of some down-time as a reward for what had been a tough mission. We were not disappointed.

At day's end, we rolled into the recently vacated Fire Support Base Rawlins near Tay Ninh. Rawlins sat on a level plain, with the nearest hedgerow a thousand yards away. Outside the wire, bare ground littered with discarded barrels and other junk gave way to low ground cover a few hundred feet out. In the distance stood Nui Ba Dinh, the Black Virgin Mountain, which rose from the flatland as a geologic anomaly, not unlike a lone oak in the middle of a prairie.

The rest of the battalion had already returned to Cu Chi. We heard that they had been welcomed by the division band and a squadron of Donut Dollies. Good for them. An official reception would've been nice, but what I most cared about was a bunk, hot food, a shower, and cold beer, in whatever order I could get them. They were giving us a week to rest, perform maintenance, and enjoy whatever goodies they could wangle from Cu Chi via the daily Chinook. The first load was already on-station, and it was a bonanza—ice, sundry packs, mail, clean clothes, hot chow, and beer—limit of three per day. Our only assigned duty beyond guard would be escorting an occasional convoy around the mountain. For the first time in over five weeks I could afford to breathe easy. It felt like the weight of a truck had slid off my back.

Later, lying on a worn wooden bunk in a dusty bunker, I marveled at the fact that Cambodia was finally done. They had been hard days. Our ranks were thinner, and those who had endured were beaten down from the strain. I couldn't even guess what the rest of my tour would bring, but I wanted very much to believe that the worst was behind me.

21

Same Question, Different Answer

Even a paranoid can have enemies.

—HENRY A. KISSINGER

Nighttime. Mid-June 1970.
25th Infantry Division. LZ Rawlins.

I was on watch. Beyond Rawlins, toward the mountain, I heard the eerie echo of artillery, and I flashed back to a night only days after Dave's death. The company had been laagered on the high ground then, elevated above a long shallow valley surrounded by double-canopy. The sky was clear, the moon high and haloed. The circle of bulky APCs were silent silhouettes against the moonlit nightscape, under scrutiny giving themselves away. I had glimpsed a faraway battle while on guard then, too, evidenced by faint sounds and the barely discernible glow of distant flares. My mood was dark, and I was bone tired, the kind that soaks to the marrow. I couldn't hear the crack of AKs or the answering pop of M16s, but I knew the dance, and I couldn't look away. In spite of my fatigue, I felt a momentary adrenaline surge, followed by a mix of anxious thoughts pulling this way and that. Above the canopy, I saw a few rapid flashes, telling me that a Cobra was on-station, delivering a torrent of meat-grinding hell that would quickly assume dominion over the real estate below. Shortly, the last of the illumination blinked out, like stage lights at the end of the final act, and it was over. The curtain had dropped. The End.

Thinking back on that night as I stared blankly in the direction of Nui Ba Dinh reminded me of how repetitious and mostly vain our efforts were. The artillery barrage that had stoked the mental fire was done. The dark landscape before me was silent once again. It got so quiet that only muted squelch from the radio and the whine of mosquitoes verified that I hadn't gone deaf. Stars filling the heavens continued to wink indifferently. Tomorrow, those who survived the scuffle that had ended with a salvo of artillery would move on, setting the ravaged earth free to regenerate. As with every other violent encounter, within days the scorched brush, broken tree limbs and stripped saplings would sprout new foliage. Insects would reclaim their territory, the animals their lairs. Even the puddles of blood would seep deeply into the soil and vanish without a trace. In time, there would be not the slightest hint that anything unnatural had occurred there.

I was seasoned enough to know the downside of solitude, of being occupied with nothing but my own thoughts. But such knowledge wasn't enough to stop a wave of sadness from washing through like angry surf. I couldn't even define it; it was just there, sloshing around, trying to drown what little faith I had left. Back in the World occasional episodes of despair only lasted until my fortunes changed, usually a matter of days. It didn't work that way here. I fought back the tears that come from emotional beatings by rubbing my temples and forcing my mind to go blank. It wasn't much, but it would have to do.

———•———

Day two at Rawlins brought more hot chow, more beer, and no duty except perimeter guard. When I assumed the position for watch in the wee hours that night, I should have been well rested and mellowed out, but instead I was hyper and consumed with a sense of vulnerability, and that led to a state of quick-trigger paranoia. With the base being inactive, the only protection beyond what we had in the field was a droopy wire fence. With no moon, the scrubby flatness beyond the wire was completely blacked out, and the Starlight scope was useless. Before long, my nervous mind conjured up unseen bad guys creeping around the darkness like cockroaches. I strained to see past the berm, but it was as if some evil-doer had enameled the backs of my eyeballs.

It's never this dark in the World, I thought. *It's blacker out there than the inside of a damn coffin. Or a . . . body bag.* I shook my head and rubbed my eyes, determined to see where it was impossible to see, at the same time realizing that I needed to change the subject.

I heard something and stiffened. It had sounded like muffled scraping. I leaned forward, head cocked, and listened hard. A faint click that sounded like it was outside the wire further aroused my fear. *The bastards are coming,* I thought. I couldn't see much past the end of my nose and they knew it. A moonless night, a supposedly safe LZ, and a bunch of GIs who think they're on R&R. It was perfect. A lump blossomed in my throat.

I grabbed the Starlight scope and scanned the foreground, but all I got was an eyeful of eerie green sparkles. The horizon couldn't be distinguished. If there were Cong moving around out there, they had little fear of discovery unless they tripped a wire. If they got past the flares it would be easy going. They could even . . . *turn the Claymores around.* That thought struck me like a snake bite, causing my stomach muscles to jerk. I visualized a Claymore mine's bold lettering stamped onto its plastic case: FRONT TOWARD ENEMY.

My first night in the field I had been jumpy and paranoid because I didn't know what to expect. Now I was jumpy and paranoid because I knew exactly what to expect. I reminded myself that hearing a little noise didn't mean a damn thing. *Keep cool,* I thought. *You're too experienced to react like a newbie.* The area had been without activity for quite a while, or so we were told. Still, the notion that the Claymores could now be pointed at me refused to go way. Blowing them at this point was out of the question, no matter what.

I tried to shore up my anxiety and think rationally. Time passed. I began to relax. Then a tiny *pop* to my front and the unraveling began in earnest. There was definitely something out there, something I couldn't see, something coming. My mind ran wild. *I might as well be blind,* I thought—as blind as Audrey Hepburn's character in *Wait until Dark.* I had no idea where *that* came from, but it chilled my insides, and I couldn't shake it. Just like in the movie, my stalkers were methodical, slowing closing in, knowing I couldn't see them. The Claymores were out of play, and the slinking VC were now too close for the M79. I quietly lifted my rifle from where it was slung on the gun turret and flipped the selector to full auto. I pricked my ears and waited.

A minute passed. I swept aside an unwanted image of a smelly VC, knife in hand, slithering toward me, inch by inch. I had never forgotten the story of the sapper attack on Cu Chi Base Camp they told us during our in-country orientation, when thirteen sappers breached the wire and straightaway slit the throats of that many berm guards. They then proceeded to wreak havoc by blowing up a half-dozen Chinook helicopters and terrorizing the rear echelon before they were finally taken down by security forces. The last one was caught just short of depositing a satchel charge in the commanding general's hootch.

I winced at a new noise. A light metallic *tink* this time. A splash of fear broke against the walls of my stomach like shattered glass. At this point, there was no reason to believe the dirty little shits hadn't already bellycrawled around to the back of the APC. It was even possible that one of them had spidered his way topside and was behind me now, blade in hand. Pulse pounding, I stiffened at the thought of a filthy palm slapping my forehead and the bee sting of razor-edged steel—

Poof!

An exploding trip flare flashed in blinding white light, splitting the blackness. I felt my eyes bug and my bowels fill with lead. In reflex I emptied my M16 in a single burst and dropped it to the track's deck. I grabbed the .50 with both hands and jammed my thumbs down hard. The detonations of the jumbo shells sent a staccato of glowing red lead through the light of the flare. Seconds later a voice from the radio's handset screamed, "CEASE FIRE! CEASE FIRE!"

Fuck that! I thought. *The fuckers are COMING, man!*

"HOLD YOUR FIRE!" another voice blared. This one came from behind me. I realized nobody else had reacted to the attack, so after a dozen more rounds I forced myself to let up. "Bring it on, you sons a bitches!" I said. Now that a punch had been thrown and I could see my immediate surroundings, the fear was gone. A couple of parachute flares whooshed up, popped, and loomed overhead, their yellow light exposing nothing but the weedy parched earth below. As I looked around, I could see that a lot of troops were up and about. Shirtless men stood in the shadowy light searching for the source of the trouble, some holding rifles, others with hands on hips. I turned back to the ground before me and closely scanned the terrain, but the drifting flarelight revealed no enemy sappers. It did confirm that the Claymores had not been tampered with. The spotty brush was not substantial enough to hide enemy soldiers, even sappers.

I slumped back, aware that I had overreacted, again. I knew that the danger in my mind's eye had been more than walking distance from reality, but in the end, I still preferred being safe instead of sorry. I was also aware that it might be a while before I could suppress the impulse to light up other phantom targets. But so what? Early in my tour, I would have felt like a complete idiot to pull such a rookie move. Now I figured I'd earned the privilege. I could apologize for my lack of restraint, but decided not to. Fuck 'em. If Captain Schroeder or anybody else wanted to chew on my ass, fine by me. I pulled out a smoke and watched the fizzling flares rock their way to earth, pulling the curtain of blackness with them. Show over.

A brief sunrise search outside the wire turned up one bullet-mangled Vietnamese dog. Nothing more came of the incident, though Spencer couldn't resist reminding me of the on-watch protocol, which was to use only the M79 in response to trip flares. I listened but said nothing. Fuck him, too.

I spent a lot of time atop 1-4, thinking things over and staring in the direction of Nui Ba Dinh and Cambodia. The Black Virgin Mountain rose freakishly out of the flat ground to dominate the landscape. As a strategic landmark, we owned it, but becoming king of that hill some years before had been a bloody conquest, and even with an entrenched U.S. base now perched on its peak, its jungled slopes were infected with Viet Cong whose job was to make misery a way of life at the summit. They also used the mountainside to lob explosive projectiles at convoys passing by below. The only access to the LZ was by air.

Beyond the mountain lay Cambodia, a nation of gentle people sucked into the quagmire of war though no wish of their own. I had no trouble vividly recalling every kill zone and every despairing moment there. I saw

Dave over and over. Dave clowning on a bicycle in a deserted Cambodian hamlet. Dave and I posing for a photo in front of a pagoda. Dave smiling. Dave burning. Reliable as a rock Dave, who was at war with no one but performed his job admirably. The whole movie was queued for replay at the blink of an eye. No admission charge, no time limit. In fact, I was certain it would be the premier feature in town for a long while to come.

I wanted to make sense of it all, but it was obvious that a week of staring at that mountain wouldn't get it done. I had to accept the fact that the optimism I'd carried with me back in the World had been permanently disfigured. Cynicism now looked like the better way to go. After all, hopes that don't exist can't be snuffed. Without expectations there are no disappointments. It was a strategy that basically added up to shifting from player to spectator, but it would make my surroundings more tolerable and slow the wear and tear on my wounded mind.

Toward the end of our week at Rawlins, I was promoted to Specialist E-4. It came as a surprise given my time in-country. What made it more odd was that it happened in spite of my recent outburst involving Mr. Glasses, not to mention the matter of the murdered dog. Then Dickson told me that it had been Lieutenant Yearout's doing, and it started to make sense. He had put me in for Spec-4 in Cambodia. It was hard to figure how it got by Littlefield, but once Captain Schroeder did the honors at the evening formation I was officially no longer a private.

One of the company clerks, Lenny Sanders, was there for some reason or other, and that evening he ended up in a small group session I was in, sipping beer. In the morning, out of the blue, he approached me and asked if I would be interested in replacing him when he left in a few weeks. I wasn't sure what to make of it. We barely knew each other. Rear jobs were coveted and usually went to short-timers. It wasn't even his call to make, yet he acted as if the gift were his to bestow.

For a time, I didn't answer. I was thinking of the day I was dropped off at Battalion HQ upon arrival at the 25th from Long Binh and had been thrown a curve-ball question by the Battalion XO, a question I'd answered in a way he'd had trouble understanding. He sent me on my way, and it wasn't long before I seriously questioned the decision I'd made.

Only four months had passed since then, but it felt like another era deep in my past. Several of us newbies had sat on folding chairs against the wall in Triple Deuce's orderly room that day, twiddling our thumbs while waiting assignment to a line company. All of my thinking had been framed around straight-leg infantry, and I was still trying to get my head around the idea of being in a mechanized unit. After a long wait a major marched out of his office and confronted us. "Any of you men know how to type?" he asked.

We looked at each other but nobody spoke up. I'd had typing classes in school, but I hesitated to own up to it, having learned early to never volunteer for anything.

"Nobody, huh?" he said, looking disappointed. He just stood there, and I wondered if an interrogation was about to follow. The longer he eyeballed us the more uncomfortable I got, and I finally lifted my hand, figuring it best to not withhold the information in case he had some way of finding out.

"I can type, sir."

His eyes brightened and he took a step closer. I stood up at attention. "How well? Better than two fingers?"

"Um, well, sir, I had typing classes in school and—"

"Follow me," he ordered and turned toward his office.

The others stared at me wide-eyed. I just shrugged and followed. He didn't bother to close the door.

The major sat on the edge of his cluttered desk and folded his arms across his chest. He was a big man, with curly blond hair and thick, gray-rimmed Army-issue glasses.

"You've had typewriter training. Have you had any clerical experience?"

"Well, sir, I had a summer job as a file clerk for the department of public safety. Mostly I—"

He waved me off and stood up. "I think you'll do."

"Sir?"

"We need a clerk here at Battalion. Specialist Tucker leaves in two weeks. That should be enough time to get you trained. Are you interested?"

I had no idea what to say. Every moment I'd spent in the army was geared toward combat. I had trained for it, expected it, and spent months revving myself up for it. Psychologically, I had my war face on. Just the diversion to mechanized infantry had thrown me off-center. Now I was being offered a chance to forget the whole business and live the rear echelon life of relative comfort and safety. I could understand a continual shortage of grunts in Vietnam, but clerks? And if they were pulling from the infantry, why not somebody who had already paid their dues? I couldn't be the only typist with a combat MOS.

A quick reality check told me that only a fool would turn it down, never mind why it was offered. Why risk death in combat if I didn't have to? I had nothing to prove.

But I knew that wasn't true. The idea of ducking combat caused the trained warrior inside to reach out and slap me like a scorned woman. Any effort to make me change directions now would be met with resistance, no matter how sweet the carrot. It wasn't me. Deep down, I did have something to prove. I couldn't deny it. As tempting as it was, I knew I would hate myself later if I chickened out now.

"Well?" he said.

Being in the presence of a field-grade officer had me suitably intimidated and reluctant to say anything he didn't want to hear, but I knew I had no choice. "Sir, I really appreciate the offer. I was just wondering if I could have a few minutes to think it over?" I clamped my jaw shut and hoped for the best, having no idea what he might say. I fully expected he would turn me every way but loose.

He leaned in a little, eyes narrowed, looking at me like he couldn't imagine what there was to think over. "You want to think it over." It wasn't a question.

"Yes, sir. If that's okay." Once again, I braced myself.

He held his stare for a minute, then slowly straightened up. "Take a seat in the orderly room while I assign the other replacements."

"Yes, sir." And with that, I hastily retreated from his office to fidget and wrestle with a decision unlike any I'd ever faced. I estimated I would have about five minutes if lucky. I was twenty years old. I tried to understand the forces compelling me toward the frying pan in the face of a perfectly legitimate alternative. I hadn't gone looking for an out. It wasn't my fault.

But that was the thing. Even though I hadn't finagled for it, I also hadn't been ordered to stay behind. If I stayed, it was because I chose to. Likewise, if I chose to go to the field, I alone would be responsible for the consequences. Minutes passed. My initial reluctance held fast against every rationale I could come up with. At last, I knew I couldn't do it. Come what may, I would do what I had been shipped over here to do. Maybe I would regret it. Probably I would regret it.

The major appeared shortly, hands on hips, looking down at me. I immediately stood up, cap in hand.

"Have you thought it over?" He stared at me intently.

"Yes, sir. And well, sir, with all due respect, I really think I belong in the field with the other men. Sir."

There. It was out.

For a few seconds, he studied me, as if looking at someone with no idea their gun was pointed at their own head.

"Are you aware of what you're passing up, soldier?"

I suspected that I did, but I knew I had to find out for myself.

"Yes, sir, and I really appreciate the offer, but—"

His expression changed to exasperation, then acceptance. "Okay. We'll get you on your way, then." With that, he turned and strode back into his office. The resident clerk, Tucker I presumed, looked at me in disbelief. He was still shaking his head when he handed me my freshly mimeographed orders. In minutes, I was on my way to Alpha Company's orderly room.

I never mentioned the incident to anyone.

———•———

"Why me?" I looked at Sanders with narrowed eyes.

"What difference does it make?" he asked.

"It makes a difference to me," I said.

He looked perplexed. "I just happen to think you would be a good choice, that's all."

"Why would they take your word for that?"

"Well, between you and me, your name already came up," he said.

I had to roll that one around. Then it hit me. Lieutenant Yearout was now the company executive officer. He had been responsible for my promotion. He knew I'd had some college. I liked and respected him. Maybe he had noticed.

"It's making more sense now," I said. "Okay. Yeah, I'm interested."

"I head back to Cu Chi today," he said. "We'll see what happens."

———•———

There were no brass bands or Donut Dollies to welcome us home a couple of days later when the company rolled through Cu Chi Base Camp's Ann Margaret Gate. After cleaning equipment and weapons and checking our rifles into the armory, they gave us three additional days without duty, making up for the stand-down jerked out from under us six weeks before. I spent my time at the PX, the EM Club, and sleeping. First Sergeant Kelso arranged for a steaks-and-beer cookout our second night back, and morale was on the upswing when it was time to mount up for another foray into our old hunting grounds near the Filhol Plantation. We took with us Lieutenant Tony Maxwell, Joe Yearout's replacement. The new LT was short, athletic, educated, and blond. He was a pleasant fellow but over-schooled and uninitiated in the ways of non-textbook procedures. Being fresh out of West Point, he didn't know any other way. The first night he moved from track to track to help us establish proper fields of fire using geometric figures on paper. Most of the platoon played along, knowing he would learn soon enough to forget all that nonsense in favor of practical reality.

It was to be my final outing as an Alpha Company line troop. The deal to convert me into a paper shuffler had been struck during the interlude at Cu Chi. Once before, I had said no. I would not say no again. I would accept the job without regret and without guilt. While at Rawlins, I realized that I was one of only three in the entire platoon who had stuck out Cambodia from start to finish. All the rest had made either a temporary or permanent exit at some point for some reason. I'd seen enough. I now knew that the push I'd felt to constantly be in the thick of things was rooted in a compulsion to take down the bully. Few others shared that calling. The reality was that loyalty to each other outside the boundaries of a firefight was thin at best. The same men who formed bonds with each other still had their own futures and families to consider above all. Men came and went. Not everyone got along. Over time, I learned that with few exceptions any opportunity to leave the field was readily taken.

The missions would go on, with or without me, and the outcomes would not be changed either way. If I had been foolish enough to think differently once, I sure as hell wasn't now.

We beat a dusty trail back into the heart of the Filhol, badgered by the sun and otherwise plagued with monotony. The Cong were low on bullets and grub due to our foray across the border, but that didn't mean we had the luxury of limiting our worries to boobytraps and bugs. What it did mean was that contacts would likely be fewer. Mikey finished his tour with a shit-eating grin on his face and bugged out on June 30th, a day John had sworn countless times he would never see if he continued to yap about it.

A week later, I rounded up my personal belongings, gave that beastly .50-caliber machine gun a final rubdown, said adios to my buddies, and hopped the daily supply chopper to Cu Chi. I sensed that my good fortune grated on a few of the troops, but I would just have to live with it. I no longer had any compunction about tasting the gravy while it was on the table. There was no such thing as job security here anyway; I would serve at the pleasure of those in the rear and could be back in the bush on a moment's notice.

As if scripted, my last night in the field as a 25th Division line troop had been spent in a rutted, greasy-smelling sector of the Filhol no different than the rutted, smelly slab of ground where I had spent my first night. During my watch I contemplated the context of coming full circle, thinking about patrols that may have passed here in 1966 and about patrols that might come along years from now. The fact that we were still here proved that little had changed. I reckoned that at some point we would simply walk away and leave the whole smelly wasteland of the Filhol to its own fate. I couldn't imagine another outcome.

On the far horizon, a skirmish broke out, evidenced by the hazy glow of flarelight. After a few minutes, what looked like flashes of heat lighting told me artillery rounds were attempting to douse the fire. Fascinated, as I always was, I watched in wonder, knowing the savagery of it, and knowing I was going to miss it.

22

REMF

*No event in American history is more misunderstood than the
Vietnam War. It was misreported then, and it is misremembered now.*
—RICHARD M. NIXON

July 1970. 25th Infantry Division.
Cu Chi Base Camp.

On a night in mid-July, a brawl broke out at one of the enlisted men's clubs
at Cu Chi, leaving one dead. One week later, a Red Cross Donut Dolly was
raped and stabbed to death in her hootch at the 12th Evac Hospital compound. Nobody heard or saw a thing and the perp left no clues. Soon after,
a jilted private shot his former Vietnamese girlfriend through the head as
she waited tables in the only Asian restaurant on base. Anti-war sentiments
and drug use were both strong among staffers at 12th Evac Hospital, and
an increasing number of militant blacks regularly refused orders to the
field. The army handled all this turmoil by dispatching convicted offenders
to Long Binh Jail, also known as LBJ, where they served dead time, meaning none of it came off their enlistment obligation.

Even with so much to police, the MPs found time to hang around the
entrance to the PX and refuse entry to any soldier who happened to have a
pocket unbuttoned or a shirttail out. Because grunts were regularly shot at
and generally lived like wild animals, some of them had difficulty respecting

rear echelon jerk-off cops who somehow believed such things mattered. Provoking these men was apparently an MP sport, and it often was met with belligerent refusals to comply. On some occasions fists flew and batons swished, leaving bloodstains all over the sidewalk there.

All these things helped keep life interesting at Cu Chi, which otherwise was a yawner. The Alpha Company orderly room workday was from 7:00 A.M. until the 5:00 P.M. formation, six and a half days a week. Sunday afternoons were free. Larry Wilkins, a sturdy six-foot Alabama boy as gentle as a Teddy Bear, was the other clerk. First Sergeant Kelso managed the work flow and helped us keep an eye on Benny Stoops, the awards clerk, a shrimpy and excitable Texan whose signature answer to anything he disagreed with was "Bullshit mountain!" Stoops was neither a lender nor a borrower, and was not apt to grant favors without compensation, although it was common knowledge that he had been in cahoots with Littlefield on numerous citations for alleged bravery. Lieutenant Yearout helped maintain harmony and served as rear liaison to Captain Schroeder. Larry and I shared a small, partitioned-off sleeping space sandwiched between the orderly room and the open-bay barracks to its rear, which was mostly empty when the company was in the field.

The work was busy but not challenging. We prepared daily, weekly, and monthly reports, typed stencils for the mimeograph machine, processed men coming and going, maintained the company roster, answered the phone, amended manuals, scheduled R&R leave, and regularly prepared for IG inspections that never took place. I developed a routine of going to the EM club after evening chow and loading up on cold Schlitz to slurp while parked on a bench at the brigade's small outdoor movie theater, where they screened such epics as *Yellow Submarine* and *Patton*. While I didn't miss the bugs or the risks that came with being in the field, I missed the action and the adrenaline flow it provided even more than I thought I would.

Cu Chi was about as secure as a base could get, but my affliction of hypervigilance still flared at times, and almost always paid a visit during CQ duty after hours. Being alone in a brightly-lit room all night was enough to send the fear factor on a joy ride. Every unusual sound had the potential to be sappers about to burst through the door. Sitting under the fluorescents armed only with the LT's measly .45 gave anyone a prime opportunity to draw down on me through one of the screened-in windows. Even slipping outside to the latrine made me feel ripe for attack; after all, what better place for assailants to hide? Never mind that none of this squared with the fact that other nights I slept peacefully ten feet away behind a thin plywood wall while someone else guarded the place. It was a demon I couldn't banish.

On a busy morning in August, the lieutenant handed me the phone after speaking with a caller at some length. Puzzled, I pressed it to my ear and listened as a captain from Battalion informed me that my paternal grandmother had died and after being contacted by the Red Cross, they had authorized emergency leave for me to attend her funeral.

I hung up the phone and looked at the lieutenant, shocked as much by the prospect of going home, today, as I was by grandma's passing. The LT asked me what I wanted to do, and, once again, I hesitated, feeling the familiar tug that reminded me not to shirk my duty. I got no help from the lieutenant. He knew it was a personal decision. I hadn't seen grandma for a few years, but had spent a lot of time with her as a child and loved her like my own mother. Finally, I said, "I think I'd better go."

——•——

Getting out of Vietnam proved to be a risky proposition, one I couldn't have handled more recklessly. I called the flight controller at the airstrip and was informed they had nothing going to Long Binh that day or the next. I wasn't sure what to do. My orders would get me on the first available flight once I got to Long Binh, but that was where the privileged character status began and ended. Battalion had no trucks going that way either. I had to get there today if I hoped to make the funeral. Finally, I hitched a ride in a jeep to the main gate to see if any other traffic might be going that direction. I hung around for an hour before accepting the fact that it was hopeless. Without giving much thought to what I was about to do, I exercised the only option I had left. I presented my leave orders to the gate guard and started walking. It was either that or give it up. For whatever reason, he didn't ask how I planned to get to Long Binh. I had no weapon, just a duffle bag and a piece of paper.

The road was active with commerce and I soon encountered locals on bicycles and a few on motorbikes. I knew this was a bad idea. I also knew I couldn't walk the thirty miles to Long Binh, but at this point I was committed. I stepped lively for about a mile, trying to blend in with the rickshaws and scooters and bicycles that busied the highway. Occasionally, beat-up French automobiles left over from the previous war muscled their way through, horns honking. I was nervous about how far I'd distanced myself from the safety of the base camp, but all I could do now is keep my thumb out. This was a supposedly friendly population center dependent on the base for jobs and economic viability, but I knew that in truth there was no such thing as a secure area in Vietnam once you were outside the wire. Tet of 1968 proved that. In the blink of an eye, I could be shot or kidnapped and never heard from again. The fact that I was afflicted with knee-jerk paranoia didn't help.

I struggled to suppress these thoughts, but was sinking deeper into the whirlpool of fear. I had gone another quarter mile when a car came alongside me and slowed. When I turned to look I was met with the smiling face of a middle-aged Vietnamese man in a rickety jalopy the likes of which I'd never seen. In a heavy accent, he said, "Where go, GI?" He wore a soiled gray button-up shirt and filthy straw hat and had a toothy grin with gums blackened from years of chewing betel nut. His face hadn't seen a razor in days. Based on his appearance and demeanor, I had strong doubts that he was an agent of the VC out cruising for unarmed GIs stupid enough to be hitchhiking alone.

I pointed in the direction he was headed. "Long Binh," I answered.

"Okay, Long Binh," he said and motioned me to get in.

I reached for the door handle, scanning the car's interior to make sure there were no obvious surprises waiting for me, and hopped in after tossing my bag in the back. The Vietnamese pressed the accelerator and off we went, dodging our way through an obstacle course of moving objects that consumed a roadway with no rules of engagement. There was little chit-chat between us, just periodic smiles and nods.

Roughly an hour later, he pulled over at the access road to the base's gate and simply said, "Long Binh," with the same toothy grin. I had spent much of the ride scolding myself for pulling such a dangerous stunt and sweating out whether it would end in disaster. I also wondered how I was going to get on base once we arrived. Now I was about to find out. I gave the Vietnamese five dollars MPC and sent him on his way. He seemed delighted with that and waved heartily as he pulled back onto the roadway.

I stared after him as he drove off, wondering what had motivated him to ferry me all this way with no promise of a reward. I could only assume that it hadn't taken him much out of his way and that he had figured to get something out of it. Whatever the reason, I had been one lucky bastard.

When he was gone, I started hoofing my way toward the gate, with no plan other than to wing it when stopped by the guards there. Sure enough, the first MP that saw me coming leaned forward and shaded his eyes, locking in on me. When I got closer he held out a hand in the STOP gesture, as if he had decided I might be an imposter.

"Hold it right there," he said. I was about ten feet away. He was a standard-issue spit-and-polish army cop, with a burr head and square face that showed no wear from the act of smiling. He looked me up and down, then gestured with his finger for me to come closer.

"What's your unit and why aren't you with them?" he demanded to know.

I thought it might simplify matters if I handed him my orders, which he took and proceeded to scrutinize with great suspicion. "I'm headed home for emergency leave," I said. "I couldn't get a lift here from Cu Chi, so I hitchhiked."

He looked up at that. "Say again?"

"I said I hitchhiked."

Orders or not, his expression said he wasn't buying any of it, and I worried that he would bust me for breaking some vague military law or even refuse me entry. Instead, he asked me to produce identification, then grilled me as to precisely where I'd come from, when I had left, exactly how I got here, and why I had violated procedure by not taking military transport. The personal risk I'd taken was apparently irrelevant.

I was about to suggest he contact my unit when he handed me back my orders and said, "Okay, get going." I had the feeling he wasn't satisfied but could think of nothing specific to bust me for. Before he could change his mind, I quick-stepped it out of there without looking back. A short distance along, a staff sergeant in a jeep gave me a lift to the replacement company and soon after I was on a bus to Bien Hoa Airbase.

———•———

After we gently lowered grandma into the soft Florida earth next to grandpa, I hung around for a few days with the extended family, doing my best to keep the conversation off the war. I had worn my dress greens to the funeral, and while only one remark was muttered behind my back, it was no secret that several of the cousins were antiwar. The last thing I wanted was to leave a stain on the memory of grandma's passing, so I stuck close to those who believed I was doing the honorable thing. My brother had quit school and wandered off to Denver with his doper pals, so there would be no crossing paths. Any discussions with him about the war would have to wait, which was just as well.

Emergency leaves were set at thirty days, so I returned to Oklahoma and proceeded to lounge away what was left. After napping away most of my first day back home, I sat on a friend's well-worn couch in front of the TV sipping Coors and munching chips. When the news came on, the screen was suddenly filled with color footage from Vietnam while Walter Cronkite recited the day's casualties and highlighted significant actions. It was the first newscast I'd seen, and I found myself watching intently, struck by the juxtaposition. Just days ago I was inside that TV. Now I was outside looking in, as if through a window to another world. The strangeness of it was unsettling.

I tried to avoid it after that, but with only some success, and sometimes when the war snarled out through the screen in mixed company the conspicuous silence from others in the room radiated like poison gas. It made me self-conscious, as if maybe they held me responsible for the latest bloodletting. It didn't help that the reporting was slanted in a way that nourished such thinking. A few episodes of this and I knew how completely misunderstood we were. I had been living it; everyone here in the World was getting abbreviated, superficial snapshots, mostly out of context and focused on the war's underbelly. And yet I couldn't have begun to describe to them the reality. It was bewildering, but there it was. So I kept my mouth shut. Not once did anyone bother to ask my take on it. For that matter, I wasn't asked much of anything by anyone.

There was never a question about going back, but I dreaded it more and more as the days rolled by. I had been abruptly pulled from the fire and given just enough rope to reacquaint myself with such luxuries as a real bed and air conditioning. Being reeled in would not come easy. A lot could have happened while I was gone, and none of it good. I had to tell myself that with luck I would simply pick up where I'd left off and in another few months I'd be done.

———•———

The only thing that had changed was that an E-5 sergeant's slot had opened up and Lieutenant Yearout told me it was mine if I wanted it. For once, it was a decision I didn't have to wrestle with. Accepting Buck Sergeant rank meant an automatic return to the field as a squad leader. Among other incidents, I learned that while I was gone all, five members of a 2nd Platoon ambush patrol had been shredded by a booby trap. Had I planned to be a lifer, it might have been a tough call, but I wasn't about to massage my ego at the possible expense of my life, so I said thanks but no thanks. Being a non-lifer himself, he understood.

With that settled, I put in for R&R but wasn't able to take it until October. A week in Sydney was refreshing, and unlike my return from the states in September, I was in good spirits when the plane screeched onto the runway at Bien Hoa Airbase. This time, though, things at Cu Chi had changed, and in a dramatic way.

As soon as the orderly room's screen door slammed behind me, Larry stood up. "Man, it's good to see you back. I guess you heard the news."

"What news?"

His brows went up. "You don't know?"

I immediately felt worried and extended my arms, palms up, in a pleading gesture. "Do I look like I know? What?"

"We're leaving." He sat down again and began furiously shuffling through a file drawer.

I knew I had heard him right, but it made no sense. "Say again?"

"We're outta here in about three weeks."

"Outta here where? The battalion's relocating? We're going OPCON? What the hell are you trying to say, man?"

He finally stopped moving and looked up at me. "I'm talking about the whole division. We're gone, dude!"

No words would come. I wasn't even sure I understood what it really meant.

"There's a lot of work to do in the meantime. Everything has to be evaluated and either destroyed or packed and labeled. There's transfer orders to cut, R & R orders to cancel, hell, I don't even know what all."

I glanced at Stoops. He was hunkered down at his desk, worrying over a stack of award citations. He hadn't even bothered to look up.

"Going where?" I finally said. It seemed to be the one glaring omission, at least from where I stood.

"Hawaii, the 25th's home base. Where else?"

"We're leaving the *country?*"

"Ten-four, my man."

There had to be a catch. He had already mentioned transfer orders.

"Who exactly gets to go?" I said it and waited, knowing it would be bingo or bust.

"Huh? Oh yeah. Not everybody goes. The magic number is having ninety days or less as of November 25."

My exit date was February 25. That sounded like ninety days dead-on. My mind raced, thinking, *Thirty days hath September; April, June, and November . . . shit!* December and January both had thirty-one days. I snatched the calendar off the wall and threw myself into the chair behind my desk. I started with November 25 and added them up until I landed on February 25. The total was ninety-three days. I let out a groan.

Larry looked my way. "You're short enough, right?"

"Three days, Larry. Three. Fucking. Days."

His expression changed to one of surprise. "Oh hell."

There was nothing more to say. For several minutes, I just sat there, trying to accept the fact that I would soon be in another division somewhere humping a rucksack through the jungle. It was back to square one, and there wasn't a damn thing to be done about it. Sin Loi, GI. Luck of the draw. Bust this time. Maybe bingo next time. Should have taken that sergeant's slot.

After a while, I did the only thing I could—I got back to work. We had less than thirty days to shut everything down, and that didn't leave a lot of time to dwell on it. It also didn't leave me a lot of time to get my mind right.

I'd just have to wing it.

23

We Gotta Get Out of This Place

I found myself back in the sepulchral city resenting the sight of people hurrying through the streets to filch a little money from each other, to devour their infamous cookery. . . . They were intruders whose knowledge of life was to me an irritating pretence, because I felt so sure they could not possibly know the things I know.

—JOSEPH CONRAD, *HEART OF DARKNESS*

Fast Forward: January 1971. 1st Cavalry Division. Somewhere in the mountain jungle southeast of Song Be.

My rucksack had lightened considerably after eating and drinking my way toward resupply, and on the morning of January 9, we had only to hike down the hill we had camped on and follow a trail through a partly wooded valley to rendezvous with the chopper. The goods we took on today would replace the lost weight, so relief was temporary, but that was the life we lived. Healy advised that there would be no water on board, so we used a nearby stream to replenish canteens. It now took twelve quarts to see me through, which aggravated my aching back, but the last thing I wanted was to run out of go-juice in a place where none could be had.

I was sprawled on the ground, propped up against my ruck along with Ranger, Denny, and Steve when Sergeant Ralston came toward us at a run.

"You're going in, Ross," he huffed.

I sat up straight. "What?"

"That's right. DEROS orders. The crew chief gave me your name. You've got about thirty seconds to get on that chopper."

"Must be a mistake," I said. "I've still got—"

"Don't question it, just get going, man!"

"There it is," Denny said.

Steve leaned forward and flicked a bug off his boot, then turned toward me. "You ain't left yet?"

I looked at Ranger. His jaw was slack. He was, after all, two days shorter than me.

I still wasn't buying it. "They don't give forty-eight day drops," I insisted.

Ralston looked exasperated. "Don't fight it, man. Just go."

I turned to Ranger, who didn't say a word. He just gawked in disbelief.

"I'm gone," I said, and hopped up.

Just before I reached the Huey, I heard a pleading voice call out, "Hey, what about *ME*!?"

There wasn't time to bother with goodbyes. Besides, I knew I would be back. Things like this didn't happen. On the ride back to Dragonhead, I refused to get my hopes up. Instead, I speculated about how long it would take to discover the screw-up. The last thing I wanted was for this to be real at the expense of not getting a five-month early-out from the army upon my return to the states. The timing had to be right. Assuming I got the customary twenty day drop from Nam, I would be two days shy of having five months of remaining active duty. If I went home now, I would face reassignment until July, which I wanted to avoid at all costs. In any event, if I got a few days in the rear out of it, I couldn't complain.

I talked to the logistics officer and shepherd of transient troops at Dragonhead, Lieutenant Jeffries, and he had no explanation. The orders had come from Brigade, so I took the afternoon Chinook to Song Be. After checking my weapon at the armory, I spent the night in the company's transient quarters. First thing in the morning, I marched into Alpha's orderly room. There, I made the acquaintance of the company clerk, a Spec-5 with a butch haircut and army-issue glasses who couldn't have weighed more than one-twenty-five soaking wet. His reaction to my story told me he wasn't born to be a problem solver. He knew only that my name and corresponding service number were on the DEROS list that originated at Division and came from Brigade, and as far as he was concerned, it was stamped in stone.

I thanked him for nothing, knowing I would have to continue on until I solved the mystery or hit a complete dead-end. As far as the clerk was concerned, I would have to take it up with Division at Bien Hoa's out-processing center. I knew it was a waste, but on the slim chance that I didn't come back, I left my gear with the supply sergeant, signed out of the company, and retrieved my duffle bag from the storage Conex. The flight schedule showed a Caribou out first thing in the morning.

It didn't take long at Division HQ in Bien Hoa to get the issue resolved. I was right. They were wrong. A young, barely tanned paper-weight warrior behind a tidy desk broke the news about five minutes after I insisted that he double-check the numbers.

"You're on here, all right," he said. "When did you say you arrived in-country?"

"February 25."

"Hmmm. Well, since the orders have been cut, you can process out if you want. Of course, if you take this drop, you won't be eligible for early separation."

I knew it! That was the inevitable catch. Even so, I felt my stomach roll over with disappointment. Whether it was a mistake or some kind of swindle, it came down to the army offering to relieve me of a final four weeks in Nam in return for almost six months of stateside duty. There was no question that I would stick it out. With luck, I would be out of the field and at the relative safety of Dragonhead in a week or two anyway.

I didn't bother to ask him why this was not explained before I signed out of the company and started believing it wasn't a cruel joke. If it was intentional, the answer was simple. Some guys back in the Triple Deuce had taken the bait on the six-year re-up. I had heard that Ned became one of them once he got out of the hospital. No more defying death, no more misery, no more homesickness. Why risk your life, son? Sign here. You'll be back in the World in three days with a small fortune in your pocket. This ploy, if that's what it was, held no more interest for me than that one had.

"If I stay, will I still get the regular twenty-day drop?"

"Sure," he said. "If that's what you want."

"Okay, I'm stayin'. Now if you'll just help me get back to my unit."

I returned to Song Be that afternoon, where it was determined that I no longer existed. The clerk, Bettis, wouldn't let me sign back in. I had been proclaimed gone forever and, like the dead, incapable of returning. "It's impossible," he declared. "You have no orders assigning you here." He paused and leaned forward in his chair. "Your date of eligibility for return from overseas has passed. In other words, you DEROSed. There's nothing I can do. You should return to Bien Hoa."

It took some effort to steady my nerves, time I used to consider how to make him see things my way. He had settled into his chair once again and was absently swiveling back and forth, as if the room were empty and day-dreams were calling.

Finally, he noticed I was still there. "Is there anything else?"

Either he had no clue how to deal with the situation or he simply didn't want to be bothered. The anger had started to churn down low, but I knew I had to stifle it if I hoped to turn this thing around. I put both hands on the front edge of his desk and chose my words carefully. "See, I used to be a clerk, too," I said slowly. "So I understand your problem."

I saw the hint of a smirk on his face.

"I also know how to fix it."

He frowned at this and straightened up, possibly catching a whiff of hostility or suspecting that whatever I had in mind would likely break a whole list of rules. But his expression told me he wanted to find out.

"Is that so?" he said.

"That's so," I answered.

"How?" Curiosity had won out. The game was on.

"Easy," I said, "you simply adjust the paperwork so that my name will show back up on Alpha's tote sheet, the same as if I never showed up here yesterday. No one will be the wiser."

He immediately shook his head at this, but I ignored it.

"Then you call Battalion and tell them there was a mistake with the orders, and that it will be—"

"Can't do it," he declared, still shaking his head. "Your DEROS orders have already been distributed to Battalion, Brigade, Individual Concerned—that's you—Enlisted Personnel Branch, MACV, Division CSM, Chief of Staff, and USARV." He drew a breath. "Trying to change all that would require a task force. It's too late." He sat back tight lipped in assumed authority.

I attempted to explain through slightly clenched teeth that as a result of my visit to out-processing at Bien Hoa, all of that would be rescinded and new orders cut when the time came. But he wasn't about to take my word for it and didn't feel obligated to spend time verifying what I'd told him. He defended his right to disavow my resurrection per procedure. We bantered. We argued. He wouldn't budge. He sat there stubbornly with his arms folded across his chest.

I could have asked to see the first sergeant or the XO, neither of whom were on hand, but I didn't think I should have to go beyond Bettis just because he refused to do his job. I was too seasoned and too short to put up with clowns like him. Finally, white-knuckled and just shy of my flash point, I leaned on the edge of his desk and with heated but measured words informed him that the only real problem he faced was the beating he was about to experience if he didn't immediately proceed to breathe new life into my corpse. His reaction to this was a look that expressed fear, surprise, and indignation all rolled together, but he held fast.

I picked up his pencil and slammed it on the desk hard enough to make him jump. "You have thirty seconds," I said, and I wasn't bluffing. I was on the verge of lunging across the desk.

His eyes widened and he pulled back a bit, staring at the pencil.

I looked at my watch. "Twenty seconds, fucker."

That snapped him out of it. He looked at me again and then caved. "All right," he said. "Just cool it. Cool it, for God's sake."

He hastily scribbled some notes and amended the company roster. When he was done he stood up. "There's gonna be hell to pay when the first sergeant gets back," he mumbled. "Hell to pay, I'm sayin'."

"He'll know where to find me. Now call the armorer and the supply sergeant and tell them I'm coming for my stuff." I waited impatiently until he was off the phone, then pointed at my duffle bag. He grabbed a key ring and took me to the storage Conex. "Okay, it's done," he said, snapping the lock shut. "But it isn't over."

"As far as I'm concerned it is," I said, and left. I collected my weapon and gear and headed to the air strip, where I took the afternoon Chinook to Dragonhead. I suspected that rather than whine about me to the 1st Sergeant, the little weasel would choose to save face and do whatever he could to get the paperwork right. Either way, I was too aggravated by the whole business to care. What could they do, send me to Vietnam?

Back at the LZ, I tracked down Lieutenant Jeffries and explained the situation. He promised to follow-up and make sure I wasn't listed as missing. We ended up having a pleasant chat, and it so happened that he had just been authorized to fill a resupply slot. He offered to put me to work then and there loading out-going choppers. We shook on it, and I went to find a place to hang my hat for the night, believing that this was one instance where things happened for a reason. I spent the evening sipping beer with the crazies in the mortar platoon, marveling at the twist of fate that had retired my rucksack. Dragonhead wasn't exactly the rear, but it was a major step back from trolling jungle trails for trouble. I vowed to be the most proficient stock boy the LT'd ever had.

———

Assuming the twenty-day drop materialized, I was down to twenty-five days. I took over a recently vacated steel culvert-half layered with sandbags and claimed it as my home. It was about twelve feet long and perched on top of a mostly below-ground Signal Corps bunker between a three-man shower stall and the mess tent. I lived there like a rat in a rat hole, with just enough space to crawl inside for sleeping. Even so, it was a sight better than the soggy jungle floor. I could stock all of the beer and soda I could pay for, and I only worked about five hours a day. The rest of my time was spent reading, letter-writing, and counting days. I was rapidly becoming the shortest man on the LZ.

The work was routine, but the place got festive when the line companies rotated and the Donut Dollies showed up from Bien Hoa, round-eyed and ponytailed. I knew their hearts were in the right place, but mostly they just stirred up hormones better left alone with their sweet smiles and miniskirts that barely covered their Gardens of Eden. I supposed it might be argued that they helped renew the will to live in the most beaten down among us. More likely, they only reinforced resentment toward the officers fucking them back in the land of hangars and flush toilets.

Alpha Company choppered in from the bush on January 17, giving me a chance to trade addresses and hang out with my Mob 1 buddies during their five days at Dragonhead. Ranger was left behind when they rotated out, whereupon he assumed the enviable position of shortest man on post. When he left on January 27 for out-processing, Lieutenant Jeffries cut me loose so I could pack my gear and prepare to follow. No more jungle, no more bugs, no more guard duty, no more C-rations or burning shit or dodging booby traps or ambushes or sleep deprivation or ducking bullets. I was going home. *Alive.*

That is, I was going home if the LZ wasn't overrun or my sleeping position wasn't disintegrated by a freak rocket or my chopper didn't get shot down or my freedom bird didn't crash or I didn't drop dead from a blood clot in the brain first. There was no sure way to head off such disasters, but I was just superstitious enough to know I had to do something. I decided to grow a mustache.

———·—·———

On the morning of January 29, I crawled out of my rat hole, stood up, and yelled, "SHORRRRRT!" as loud as I could. That afternoon, knowing it couldn't be avoided, I boarded the Chinook that I knew was marked for destruction and spent the entire trip to Song Be staring through the floor's open lift hatch, watching for green tracers to rush up and knock out a rotor or rupture a fuel tank. Amazingly, we landed without incident, and as soon as my boots hit the tarmac I headed for Alpha's armory and turned in my M-16 for the last time. I then went to the orderly room to sign out and get my duffle bag. Specialist Hell-to-Pay Bettis took my orders and then looked at me, frowning slightly upon recognition. He retrieved my duffle bag and then handed me a clipboard for my signature. So far, not a word had been said. I scrawled my name, transferred my worldly goods to the duffle bag, and then dropped my rucksack and steel pot on the floor in front of his desk. "You never know when you might need this shit," I said, and then I was out the door.

I made it back to the airstrip in time to catch the last Caribou to Bien Hoa, knowing it was going to crash but unable to stand the suspense until the next day.

Not one to be suckered by decoys, I wasn't fooled when the transport landed safety. If anything, I was getting more paranoid. It's being saved for the big one, I reasoned. Just when I think I've got it made that freedom bird's gonna have a mid-air collision on its final approach to Oakland with a Cessna driven by a transplanted Vietnamese struggling to understand tower instructions. "TWO HUNDRED TROOPS SLAIN BY LONE VIETNAMESE," the headlines will scream.

"Nonsense," Ranger said. "Stop worrying. The real danger is where we just came from." We were in a Vietnamese restaurant at the division compound, waiting on orders of pseudo cheeseburgers and what would have to pass for fries.

"I'll believe it when I walk through the front door of my house," I said.

———•———

It took a couple of days of standing in lines to get past the jitters, but my irrational fear was ultimately replaced with impatience. Even though we enjoyed the comforts of the rear, transients were locked out of the barracks at six in the morning each day and forced to loiter until the rest of the base opened for business two hours later. We couldn't even get breakfast until seven. Clearing finance would be the last hurdle, and I saw myself skying up the day after that. I mentioned this to Ranger as we sat on a bench outside the barracks at six-thirty, woefully tired from late-night drinking at the EM club.

"Don't forget Long Bien," he said with a yawn. I'm headed there later today.

"Long Bien?" Then I remembered. A lifetime ago, I had swept floors there. Of course I would have to go through Long Bien, only now I saw it as just another delay rather than the triumphant return I had once imagined it would be.

"Yeah, Long Bien," he repeated. "You didn't think they would make it easy and just send us across post to the airfield, did you?"

"How long will that take?" The thought of cooling my heels for who knew how much longer got my agitation meter moving again.

"Couple of days, maybe. Not sure."

I went into a minor funk and stayed there until I got Pabst relief after the clerks closed up shop that afternoon. Then I remembered that I needed the extra days to keep the five-month early-out. With Long Bien factored in, that would get me out of here on February 5, which broke the five-month threshold and was dead on with the twenty-day drop. I decided to just relax and enjoy it.

On the shuttle ride to Long Bien, I recollected my time there almost a year ago. I wondered if I would encounter newbies and whether they would look at me with awe and envy. The thought didn't make me smile. Instead, it brought sadness. I could only hope their tours would be short, that some kind of conclusion would be reached, and that they would not one day face other newcomers or die or be maimed before they got that chance. I also wondered whether grunts who had left here in 1966 may have had the same thoughts.

Unlike Bien Hoa, there were no lines to stand in. A group of us were briefed in the same room I had swept out, or one like it, though this time there were no new arrivals doing busy work. We were told to expect a two-day wait for a flight. In the meantime, we would exchange currency, leave a forwarding address, turn in whatever army-issue goods we chose to leave behind, get a haircut, and have our possessions screened for contraband. There would be no formations and no work details.

Ranger was gone. Good for him. Likely, I had missed him by hours. Newcomers were about, but in fewer numbers, or so it seemed. I couldn't understand why divisions were pulling out and still replacements came in, men whose lives were put on the line so President Nixon could achieve "peace with honor" in our withdrawal from a politically bankrupt South Vietnam. Had I spent any time with them, words of encouragement would have been hard to come by. I thought it best to keep to myself. One of the EM clubs there was open twenty-four hours with continuous stage acts, so I had no trouble killing time.

When my name showed up on the flight manifest, the final bit of business was a luggage check conducted by a master sergeant and two

underlings in a room with tables along all the walls and several large barrels in the middle.

"Listen up, gentlemen," he said, his hands clasped behind his back.
"I'm sure that everyone in this room wants to go home, so I'm going to put
this in the simplest terms I can, and I'm only going to say it once. In a
minute, I'm going to walk out that door and lock it behind me. You will
then have exactly three minutes to remove any and all illegal contraband
from your luggage and place it in the barrels for disposal, no questions
asked. I repeat, no questions asked. Upon my return, your luggage will be
inspected. It will then be too late to get rid of your stash, unauthorized
weapon, explosives, et cetera. If you have any doubt about whether an item
is contraband or not, get rid of it. If you think you can slip one by, it is at
your own peril. You will go to the stockade, you will not DEROS, you will
not leave the country, and you will not be given a second chance. This is
your last stop, gentlemen. Don't blow it. Use the barrels."

With that, he and his cadre left the room, locking the door behind
them. I heard a few items clunking into the barrels, but I was busy with my
own bag and didn't pay attention. I spent the time pulling out virtually
every military article I had. I had donned khakis for the flight and kept
only my dress greens and the few civilian clothes I had. My bayonet had
gone to a new guy before I left Dragonhead. The rest of it I piled on the
table—fatigues, field jacket, boots, poncho liner, all of it. I had lived with it
so long that never seeing it again would be too soon.

When the search took place minutes later, nobody ended up in cuffs. It
was now time to board the bus for the shuttle back to Bien Hoa. It was
time to go. It was time to GO! Nothing on the planet had value compared
to that.

At the terminal, I joined more than a hundred others, some in khakis
and some in greens, milling about anxiously. Laughter regularly punctuated
conversations. My insides crackled with excitement. All thoughts of crashing
planes and other calamities were gone. I was consumed with a sense of eupho-
ria that went beyond anything I had ever felt. The real celebrating would happen once I was home, but the internal celebration was well underway.

The Boeing 727 that would take us out of Vietnam was already on the
tarmac, refueling. We were advised by ground personnel to stay clear of the

exit doors until arriving passengers made their way into the hangar. I watched as they shuffled in, clones of ourselves from a year ago, wearing non-faded fatigues and expressions of curious apprehension, their foreheads already beaded with sweat. I felt no particular emotion. I empathized with them, but I could do nothing for them. Even if I could stay in their place, I wouldn't. I had done my time, they would have to do theirs. Their destinies were far beyond my reach, and at the moment I had no available space for worries over my replacement. It was time to go. Today. Now.

Once on board, the level of chatter escalated to the point that cabin announcements could barely be heard. This all stopped when the plane began to taxi. It seemed that all breaths were held, either in reverence or anticipation. Minutes later that silence was replaced with cheers when the wheels broke free of the runway and physically separated us from the country of South Vietnam. I had a window seat on the port side, and my heart raced as I stared down absently while the jet climbed at a tilt, still trying to grasp the fact that it was really over.

I had no idea which direction the plane was pointed, but we were over jungle now, and below I could see a bald spot in the sea of green that I recognized as a firebase. Seconds later, it registered like a sharp slap. It was Dragonhead! I twisted in my seat for a better look. There was no mistaking it, having flown in and out of it on choppers as much as I had. Men I knew were on that base, some of them no doubt pointing and waving at the freedom bird passing over, as I had once done. I kept my face pasted to the glass until the LZ faded into the ocean of green and disappeared, knowing it was a moment I would always remember. It was sobering, like a sad good-bye, and as I settled back in the seat I felt as if a small part of me had just slipped out that window.

———•———

It was dark outside. The cabin was dim and quiet. At Bien Hoa's PX, I had picked up a copy of Kesey's *One Flew over the Cuckoo's Nest* (a title I could identify with), but I was too keyed up to read and put it down after a few pages. I kept thinking about passing over Dragonhead and how I'd just happened to have a window seat on that side of the plane. It was a strange coincidence, but there it was. I tried to sleep, but without luck. Every time I closed my eyes, the projector wired to the optic nerve started clicking, reminding me that I would be living with a lot of memories for a long time.

Lost in thought, I was startled by a soft *bong*, followed by announcements as power was cut and we descended into Tokyo to top off the tanks and change crews for the long stretch across the Pacific. Once on the ground, I got up, stretched, walked the aisles, and tried again to read. But the book was soon in my lap as I found myself visualizing San Francisco. I had crisp recollections of my time there a year ago, especially at Oakland Army Base, the way-station, where men go away from and a lesser number return to. It was a place I had hated. Now I couldn't wait to get back there.

Somewhere in the middle of the Pacific we flew over a thunderstorm. Lightning flashed below in a tremendous light show. Above, the night sky sparkled. At some point the sun came up again. I still had not slept. While food was being served, the voice on the intercom promised to advise us when the coast was in sight. I doubted that we would need any help.

Some hoots and hollers went up at the first glimpse of land on the horizon. The descent had begun, and it was getting tough to control a piece of window. Things settled a bit when the seatbelt announcement was made, and I had a good view of the landscape beyond the airport during our final approach. The elation I felt was electric, but at the same time something seemed out of place, something that made me slightly uneasy. This was momentarily forgotten when the rubber met the runway and deafening cheers drowned out everything. During the long taxi to the gate, I soaked up the scenery, still troubled by something that didn't look right, causing a vague feeling that I couldn't put my finger on. Vulnerability? Then it dawned on me. The base merged gracefully with its outer surroundings. There was no berm, no bunkers, no wire—just a barely discernible fence. No wire! I was awed by this in a way that I knew I shouldn't be. Yet for the life of me, I couldn't understand how they expected to defend themselves without such things.

EPILOGUE

I feel your dark wind
and jerk the shutters closed.
But the storm of your memory
pries loose the groaning hinges
Weakened
from the corrosion of tears.

—J. R., "INTRUSION"

Family members and friends listened politely but asked few questions. More than once those first weeks home, I found myself rambling on, like Captain Queeg, as if explaining everything to myself as much as to my audience. Virtually nothing had changed in my absence. My friends were mostly in the same situations with the same head. There had been no time passing and no meaningful events for them. It was like I had never left. Some of them were not aware that I had.

I found out quickly that I didn't know how to spend time. Generally speaking, the word *Vietnam* made people act like they wished they were someplace else, and I soon shut up about it. I buried the turmoil, went to work for a construction crew, and returned to school. By 1976, I had finally finished a degree program—in psychology of all things. By then, I was on my second marriage. Still I kept shut.

In 1982, I made the pilgrimage to Washington, DC, for the dedication of the Vietnam Memorial. I was joined by a hometown pal and my old dog-handler buddy, Jerry, from our days in the meat grinder at Fort Polk. With my emotional shield firmly in place, I absorbed it all like shrapnel

hitting a sandbag. The parades, parties, and performances made for a grat-
ifying experience, but it was the bulletin boards in the building that served
as the central gathering point that left the most indelible memory. They
were cluttered with notes from buddies and loved ones seeking information: "Looking for anyone who knew my son, please call. His name was . . ."
or "If you knew my father" or "If you were with Tommy when he died . . ."

The shield cracked soon after, and I started reading the books, dozens
of them. I also started writing, getting temporary relief from externaliz-
ing the dark brew fermenting inside. It wasn't much, but better than
nothing.

———•———

In 1985, I made a final hands-on encounter with my war experience
when I developed a nagging urge to go back to Fort Polk, to revisit the
place that had prepared me for the most significant event of my life. Jerry
and I had kept in touch, and when he moved from North Carolina to
Baton Rouge, I knew where our next meeting would be. From Oklahoma,
it was only a day's drive, and when I entered the town of Leesville on a
divided four-lane, I quickly learned that years of progress had made the
place over. Fast-food joints and chain motels lined both sides of the alien
boulevard, and traffic signals flashed at every corner. Everything, it seemed,
centered on this bustling thoroughfare that had either consumed or concealed familiar landmarks.

I motored through, then turned about, figuring some of the original
township had to be there somewhere. Halfway along, I turned east onto a
side street, and a couple of blocks along intersected the old strip, where one
look served up the Leesville I remembered, standing almost exactly as it
had. Along one side of the street, glass and wood-frame storefronts, mostly
taverns and secondhand shops, lined the road as it sloped downhill. On the
other, the old courthouse stood stately amid drooping shade trees. Here
and there, I could see myself mirrored in the faces of young soldiers meandering up and down the grainy sidewalks.

I made the turn and cruised it both directions a couple of times, then
headed for my rendezvous with Jerry. We checked into a motel and spent

the evening rehashing our grueling eight weeks in Tigerland over prime rib and a parade of premium beer. In the morning we downed a quick Mc-breakfast before heading to the main gate turnoff. A sign near the entrance informed us that Fort Polk was now home to the 5th Infantry Division (Mechanized).

At the same gate where I had once stood duty, a polished PFC, uncon-cerned that we could be vandals or spies, waved us through with a gesture. Beyond, nothing looked familiar. Many of the buildings appeared vacant, and I was struck by the quietness, even for a Saturday morning. The Provost Marshall's office seemed a good bet for directions, so we pulled in on our second pass. The MP on duty, a young sergeant, offered little help.

"We trained here back in 1969," I said. "It's our first time back and we're a little disoriented. Can you tell us how to find Tigerland?"

"Tigerland? Nothing here by that name, fellas," he said. "Not that I know of."

I glanced at Jerry in surprise, then focused again on the MP.

"Sure there is," I explained. "Tigerland, at North Fort. Where they trained for Vietnam. It's famous. Everybody knows about it."

"Sorry, guys, but . . ."

Jerry, the cooler head, took over. "Can you just tell us how to get to North Fort? Draw us a diagram or something? We'd appreciate it."

"No problem there," he said. He went to his desk and retrieved a printed brochure. "Just head straight out Mississippi Avenue and follow this map."

Jerry motioned me toward the door before I could reopen the discussion.

"Can you believe it?" I said, once we were in the car. I couldn't fathom that Tigerland had been forgotten. "How can a legend die that quick, espe-cially in the place it was born?"

Jerry seemed unaffected. "Maybe it was only legendary in the minds of those who lived it," he said.

I wanted to argue, but just looked at him instead, contemplating the unwanted truth he'd just dropped in my lap.

"Don't be surprised by what we may find up there," he went on. "They may have bulldozed it all down for all we know.'

As the first buildings came into view, it looked as though not only Tigerland, but all of North Fort had been forgotten. Sagging roofs, peeling paint, and un-mowed grass were the rule. We passed a sprawling motor pool on Avenue K where dozens of abandoned APCs sat silently rusting. Only a fraction of the buildings were in use; nearly all of the rest were in a state of decay. There was no traffic and few signs of life. We had entered a ghost town.

"My, my," Jerry said. "Not like the days of old, is it?"

"At least it's still here," I said. I turned onto a road that I knew led to my basic training company. I spotted the PT field first and pulled over. We walked around. The eroded run-dodge-and-jump pits and corroded horizontal ladders were not far from being reclaimed by the earth. Scraggly grass grew tall around the cracked and broken oval track. Across the way, one of the barracks had new siding, but the others, as well as the mess hall and armory, were badly weathered. Even the blacktopped assembly area where I had stood at attention dozens of times to answer the call of my name or joyfully accept mail was fragmented and pocked with weeds.

The buildings were locked, but we were able to peer through windows. My old barracks had been partitioned into dormitory rooms, and the mess hall was stuffed with dusty furniture and surplus equipment. The latch and lever on the armory's great sliding door was glazed with rust.

Signs warned that the field training areas were restricted, but a drive in that direction led us as far as the old tear gas building, isolated in some trees along the roadside. It was padlocked and rotting, but the fallen sign had been propped up against the wall, identifying the structure's former use as the MASK CONFIDENCE EXERCISE. We took photos, and then drove back to the main road, where we turned down the hill toward the Advanced Infantry Training compound at Tigerland. Some of the company areas had been scraped clean, but the old swimming pool, now a depository for falling leaves, was easy to spot. It had been right next to our former home at Delta-3-3.

Like the rest of North Fort, the old company compound had seriously decomposed, but the buildings still stood. We parked, and for a few minutes just stared, feeling the emotion brought on by the influence this place had exerted on our lives. When we walked through, it was a slow and reverent journey. The door to our barracks was nailed shut, but through dirt-glazed windows we could see part of the first floor, the latrine, and the staircase leading up to our bay. The roof was wavy, and the once sparkling strip of gravel surrounding the building had been devoured by weed-infested sand. All that remained of the walkways were hunks of crumbly blacktop peeking up through the soil, and the horizontal ladder that had once been our appetizer to every meal stood weakly in front of the dilapidated chow hall, its members bent and tarnished. We took more pictures and then just sat down for awhile in the shade of the trees, pointing to this and that and reminiscing.

In only sixteen years, Tigerland had morphed from a place where thousands of young men became spirited warriors into an array of empty, meaningless buildings. I should have been able to shrug it off, having known since early in my Vietnam tour that nothing would ever again be the same, but this was like visiting the grave of a worthy soul that had been left unmarked and untended. I couldn't help but feel disillusioned and somehow shortchanged.

Before leaving, we stopped to visit the small chapel where we had gone to church some Sundays, agreeing that it had been the one soft spot in an otherwise harsh environment. On the way out, we searched and searched for the once prominent billboards announcing Tigerland's domain, but like our hurried youth, they had vanished without a trace.

GENERAL GLOSSARY

AFVN: Armed Forces Vietnam Network—a Saigon-based a military operated radio station that broadcast to U.S. and allied forces all over Vietnam.

ANN MARGARET GATE: A gate at Cu Chi Base Camp named in honor of the actress for her United Service Organization appearances in support of the troops.

AO: Area of Operations.

ARC-LIGHT: Nickname for a U.S. B-52 bomber strike, the attack most feared by Viet Cong and NVA forces.

ARVN: Army of the Republic of Vietnam—commonly used as a noun describing South Vietnamese soldiers.

AWOL: Absent Without Leave.

BEAUCOUP: French, meaning "many."

BOOM-BOOM GIRL: Prostitute.

C-4: Brick-shaped plastic explosive used extensively by allied forces.

CARIBOU: A prop-driven transport plane.

Cs, C-rats, C-rations: Combat Rations.

CQ: Charge of Quarters—the person on duty in a unit's orderly room after hours.

CHINOOK: CH-47 helicopter, used to transport troops and supplies.

CIB: Combat Infantry Badge—an insignia awarded to infantry soldiers once they have been under enemy fire.

CONCERTINA WIRE: Razor wire manufactured in large coils that can be stretched out and staked in place to form a defensive barrier.

CONUS: Continental United States.

CSM: Command Sergeant Major—the highest rank among noncommissioned officers.

DEROS: Date Eligible to Return from Overseas.

DI-DI MAU: Pronounced *did-ee mau*—"leave," "go away."

DRAG: Bringing up the rear; last in line.

DUSTOFF: Same as Medevac, or Medical Evacuation Helicopter.

DX: Direct Exchange, a term used when a piece of equipment was beyond repair and had to be replaced.

E-4/SPEC-4: Enlisted rank of E-4, the equivalent of corporal and one pay grade below sergeant.

F-4 PHANTOM JET: Air Force fighter jet armed with bombs that flew in support of infantry units.

FIELD-GRADE OFFICER: All officers above the rank of captain.

FIFTY: .50-caliber machine gun.

FO: Forward Observer, an artilleryman assigned to an infantry unit for the purpose of coordinating artillery support.

FRAG: Short for fragmentation grenade.

FRUIT SALAD: Slang for the collection of colorful ribbons worn on dress uniforms representing medals and citations.

FUCK-YOU LIZARD: A small, indigenous lizard whose nickname was derived from its call—a loud, distinctive "Fuck" followed by a drawn out "Youuu."

GOOK: Derogatory name for Viet Cong and NVA.

HAM & MOTHERFUCKERS: Ham and Lima Beans, the most rejected among C-ration meals.

HASH MARKS: Diagonal stripes displayed on a dress uniform's sleeve, each of which represents three years of service.

HUMP/HUMPING/HUMPED: To march or carry a rucksack on foot patrol.

KIA: Killed in Action.

KLICK: One kilometer (1,000 meters), which is equivalent to 3,281 feet or .62 miles.

LAAGER: A word of German origin defined as a defensive camp characterized by encircled armored vehicles.

LIFER: Career soldier.

LINE TROOP/PLATOON/COMPANY: Those on the front line or forming the first line of defense in an infantry unit.

LT: Short for lieutenant.

LZ / FSB: Landing zone/fire support base. Fire support bases housed artillery units in support of infantry. An LZ could simply be a suitable place to land or a drop-off/pick-up point, though FSBs were referred to as LZs.

MACV: Military Assistance Command, Vietnam.

MAMA-SAN: Married or mature Vietnamese woman.

MEDEVAC: Medical evacuation helicopter.

MPC: Military Payment Certificate—issued by the military as currency in place of U.S. greenbacks.

MOS: Military Occupational Specialty.

NCO: Noncommissioned Officer, such as a corporal or sergeant.

NCO SCHOOL: A twelve-week training course whose graduates are promoted from Private to Sergeant E-5.

NUMBER TEN: The worst, as opposed to Number One, the best.

NVA: North Vietnamese Army.

OCS: Officer Candidate School, a six-month training program whose graduates were promoted to second lieutenant.

OD GREEN: Olive-drab green, the standard color of U.S. Army fatigues.

OPCON: To be placed under the "operational control" of another unit.

PIASTER: Vietnamese currency.

PISS TUBE: An open-ended shell canister or pipe driven into the ground at an angle and used as a urinal at fire support bases.

POINT: The lead man or vehicle on a patrol.

PT: Physical Training.

PX: Post Exchange, the equivalent of a civilian department store.

RANGERS (U.S. ARMY): Elite, highly trained special operations soldiers that typically operated in teams, often as small as three men. Rangers were often deployed behind enemy lines to collect intelligence or to carry out surgical attacks.

REMF: Rear Echelon Motherfucker, derogatory name for rear support personnel.

R&R: Rest and Recreation.

ROCK APE: A mythical, upright walking apelike creature said to inhabit the deep jungle and sometimes attack humans, though most likely it was one of the larger primates common to Vietnam.

ROCK 'N' ROLL: Slang for a weapon set on full automatic.

RTO: Radio-telephone operator.

RUCKSACK (OR RUCK): Name for backpacks carried by infantry soldiers.

SAPPER: Highly trained enemy infiltrators, usually armed with explosives.

SATCHEL CHARGE: Explosive charges carried by the Viet Cong and NVA in canvas satchels.

SHAKE 'N' BAKE: Nickname for E-5 sergeants and second lieutenants who attained their rank from attending NCO School or Officer Candidate School (OCS) rather than being promoted through the ranks over time.

SHAPED CHARGE: A directional explosive.

SIN LOI: Vietnamese for "sorry," "too bad."

SIXTY: M-60 machine gun.

SLICK: Nickname for a Huey helicopter.

SMOKEYS: Nickname for drill instructors who wear Smokey the Bear–style hats.

THE WORLD: Slang term for the U.S.

TI-TI: Pronounced *tee-tee*—"little" or "few."

TOE-POPPER: A small, improvised explosive device, typically a .50-caliber shell casing filled with gunpowder and scraps of metal that fired when stepped on. Modern versions are slightly larger, made of plastic, and mass produced.

USARV: United States Army, Vietnam.

WILLIE PETER: White Phosphorus.

COMMON WEAPONS
EMPLOYED IN VIETNAM

.50-CALIBER MACHINE GUN: Officially the M2, the .50 cal is the largest and most powerful of machine guns used by U.S. forces. It can be used as an antipersonnel or antiaircraft weapon with a rate of fire of 550 rounds per minute and the ability to penetrate one-inch-thick steel at 1,000 meters. Its effective range extends to 2,000 meters, with a maximum range of four miles.

.51-CALIBER MACHINE GUN: The communist counterpart to the U.S. .50-caliber machine gun.

90mm RECOILLESS RIFLE: Officially the M67, the 90mm recoilless rifle is a large, crew-served, shoulder-fired or fixed-position antitank weapon used in Vietnam primarily against ground assaults and enemy fortifications. Because the "recoilless" backblast issued from the back of its tube was a hazard, the M67 saw limited use by most infantry units.

AK-47: Russian made 7.62mm assault rifle that was standard issue for NVA and Viet Cong soldiers.

BOOBY TRAP (EXPLOSIVE): Any number of devices concealed and usually triggered by the victim. Booby traps in Vietnam ranged from 750-pound bombs to small tin cans filled with glass, nails, and other objects.

CHICOM CLAYMORE MINE: Same type of weapon as the U.S. Claymore, except the Chinese Communist Claymore was round in shape and deployed in sizes up to several times larger than its U.S. counterpart.

CLAYMORE MINE: Officially the M18A1, the Claymore is an above-ground antipersonnel mine containing 700 ball bearings propelled by 1.5 pounds of C-4 explosive and is used primarily as a line of defense by the U.S. Army and other services. Concave in shape, it expends fragments in a sixty-degree, fan-shaped pattern and has an effective kill zone up to fifty meters in distance.

COBRA HELICOPER GUNSHIP: The most prevalent of assault helicopters in Vietnam. It was highly maneuverable and had a narrow profile, being only three feet wide. It was armed with two rocket pods, a 40mm grenade launcher, and a minigun.

FLECHETTE ROUND: An artillery or shoulder-fired projectile containing thousands of tiny, fin-stabilized steel darts used to repel ground attacks. Also known as "beehive" round.

FOUGASSE: A highly flammable fuel gel contained in fifty-five-gallon drums with a detonator that was used to repel ground assaults on fire support bases.

FOUR-DEUCE MORTAR: Refers to the 4.2-inch mortar round, the largest used by U.S. forces in Vietnam.

HOWITZERS: Artillery guns that range in size and effectiveness. In Vietnam, most common was the 155mm mobile howitzer, which fired a projectile weighing ninety-seven pounds with a range of about eleven miles. Others in use in Vietnam were the 105mm, the 175mm, and the 8-inch. Shells commonly used included high-explosive fragmentation, white phosphorus, illumination, chemicals, and Flechette.

LAND MINES: Explosive devices planted in the ground detonated by a pressure-release device when stepped on or by electrical current via a handheld detonator, also referred to as "command det."

M16: Officially the M16A1 during the Vietnam era, it is an American made, standard-issue 5.56mm assault rifle with a muzzle velocity of 3,100 feet per second and a rate of fire on full automatic of over 700 rounds per minute.

M60 MACHINE GUN: The M60 is the workhorse of American military machine guns. In use since 1957, it weighs twenty-three pounds, has an effective range of 1,000 meters, fires up to 750 rounds per minute, and can be either mounted or carried.

M79 GRENADE LAUNCHER: The M79 is a lightweight, shoulder-fired weapon that launches a 40mm grenade round through a rifled barrel with an effective range of 350 meters. At twenty-nine inches in length and weighing just six pounds, it was widely deployed during the Vietnam War.

MINIGUN: Officially the M134, the minigun is a Gatling-style machine gun with six barrels that can fire up to 6,000 rounds of 7.62mm ammunition per minute. In Vietnam, it was used primarily by helicopter and fixed-wing gunships, riverboats, and some armored vehicles.

MORTAR: Fin-stabilized, muzzle-loaded projectiles launched from stand-mounted tubes at a high angle. In Vietnam, these included the U.S. 81mm and 4.2-inch mortars. Communist counterparts included the 60mm and 82mm.

NAPALM: A highly flammable jellied mix of chemicals and jet fuel that when detonated sticks to its targets and burns at temperatures up to 5,000 degrees Fahrenheit. Deployed in bombs of various sizes, napalm was used extensively in Vietnam as an antipersonnel weapon and to clear vegetation.

PUNJI PIT: A concealed hole in the ground into which sharpened stakes were placed by Viet Cong for the purpose of killing or seriously injuring American and allied soldiers.

RPG: Rocket-Propelled Grenade—a shoulder-fired weapon containing an explosive warhead pushed by a solid fuel rocket that could burn through armor. Used extensively by Viet Cong and NVA forces as both an antitank and antipersonnel weapon.

TYPICAL U.S. ARMY UNIT STRUCTURE

SQUAD: Smallest unit, usually consisting of seven to ten soldiers and led by a sergeant.

PLATOON: Three or four squads, usually commanded by a first or second lieutenant.

COMPANY: Three or four platoons and a command post, usually commanded by a captain.

BATTALION: Several companies as well as support units, usually commanded by a lieutenant colonel.

BRIGADE: Several battalions and other supporting units such as aviation, artillery, supply, intelligence, administrative, etc., usually commanded by a colonel.

DIVISION: Currently the largest operational military unit, comprised of several brigades and usually commanded by a brigadier or major general.